ADVANCED RACING TACTICS

ADVANCED

RACING

TACTICS

By

STUART H. WALKER, M.D.

Illustrations by THOMAS PRICE

W · W · NORTON & COMPANY · INC · *New York*

Library of Congress Cataloging in Publication Data

Walker; Stuart H
  Advanced racing tactics.

  Includes index.
  1. Sailboat racing.   I. Title.
GV826.5.W28   1976   797.1′4   75–37583
ISBN 0–393–03184–5

Printed in the United States of America

To my girls—Light Brigade, Shenandoah, Lee, Susan, Frances, and Alice—each of whom has made a unique contribution to this book.

Contents

V. *Reaching*

VI. *Running*

VII. *Finishing*

Foreword

In the past decade far more sailors than ever before have reached a superior level of competitive ability, and racing is conducted far more often on properly established, large triangles in open water. The skills necessary to success continue to evolve. A level of ability that could provide a reasonable rate of success a year ago is insufficient today. The few individuals who remain at the head of competitive classes year after year must constantly improve their skills. Even a superior background must be enhanced by continuous competition. To pass up the big regattas for a year is to be left out.

My own experiences reflect this general trend. When I wrote *The Tactics of Small Boat Racing* ten years ago, my racing had been done chiefly in the International 14, usually in small fleets with but a few highly qualified competitors, and often in confined waters. In the past decade, I have raced largely in boats of the Soling class (as well as 5.5-meters and International 14's), in large fleets, in open waters, and against dozens of highly qualified competitors simultaneously. My experiences in the Olympics, in World, North American, European, and various national championship races, and in Olympic trials, CORK, and SPORT, are representative of racing at today's high standards; many of these experiences are described in this book.

The principles set forth herein are primarily applicable to racing in major regattas, in big fleets, against top competition. They embody understanding gained on Olympic and Gold Cup courses in open water. The same principles may be appropriate to racing in smaller fleets in confined waters, but in these circumstances other matters may be of greater significance. Race-committee behavior, shoreline effects, "local knowledge," aberrant starting lines were discussed in *The Tactics of Small Boat Racing*. The present volume presumes a thorough knowledge of the racing rules and of boat-handling skills. It deals neither with the determinants of boat speed (for a complete analysis see *Performance Advances in Small Boat Racing*) nor with the variations in surface air flow that determine strategy (see *Wind and Strategy*). What is considered is the most advantageous means of starting, beating, reaching, running, and finishing in the close proximity of large numbers of highly competent competitors.

I have kept a complete record of the factors that determined the outcome of every race in which I have competed for the past eight years. My recommendations are based upon the analysis of these races—the mistakes and the successes. I have tried to present what mattered, what consistently provided an advantage. I have ignored tactical flourishes that worked occasionally, but risked greater loss or disqualification. Consistency is what provides series success. It is better always to do the "right" thing—even though it turns out to be wrong 20 percent of the time—than to experiment and risk being wrong 50 percent of the time. And there are basic principles of starting, beating, reaching, mark rounding that are "right," that should be practiced every time. Forget about boat speed (once you've got it), forget about the grand strategy (once you've understood its determinants)—and sail the boat.

My good friend Robert Bearer commented after observing a group of sailors racing in the Bahamas that what they seemed to want was not to learn to race better, but rather to be moved up five places by a beneficent god. This book will provide no such magic. It will, however, stimulate the reader to analyze for himself the determinants of tactical success. He must look around, examine his own mistakes and successes, record them, review them, remember them. When he recognizes from his own experience the validity of the principles presented here, they will become useful to him. When he has incorporated them into his regular racing patterns, he will have made a five- or ten-year leap forward. However, only continuous participation at the top level will maintain him at that level and permit him to keep pace with the competition.

ADVANCED RACING TACTICS

I. *General*

1. Series Strategy

Success in series racing depends upon success in individual races—in every individual race of a series. The basic requirements are a competent skipper and crew, boat speed comparable to that of the upper 20 percent of the fleet, and a clear understanding of the overriding strategic and tactical principles. Experience must provide the ability to start with clear air, take advantage of wind and current variations to windward, round marks effectively, achieve top speed on the reaches, and use wind shifts appropriately on the runs. Among crews with these abilities, all capable of winning individual races, series success depends upon consistency, and consistency—the avoidance of mistakes—depends primarily upon psychological factors. Confidence provides the determination to prepare properly, to sail effectively, to avoid major errors, to place well repeatedly. Confidence coupled with mental toughness prevents distraction by immediate tactical problems and permits concentration upon the outcome of the race and the series.

Series victory requires more than adaptation to differing conditions, more than boat speed in both light and heavy air, more than windward and reaching ability, more than a combination of tactical and strategic skills. Such skills, both individually and in combinations, are possessed by many; their regular application, leg after leg, race after race, is possible for only a few. Only a few are able to free themselves sufficiently from preoccupation with the minutiae of tactical situations and boat-speed problems to concentrate on the predominant elements of strategy. Losers are unable to follow a plan—because they do not establish one, because they make one inconsistent with their abilities, or because they become so preoccupied that they neglect it. They shift rapidly from one concern to another: Is the mainsail set right? Will the spinnaker go up cleanly? Will the boat on the lee bow force them about? Being so busy, they miss the things that matter and so lose and, being so busy, hardly notice that they are losing—until it is too late. In contrast, the single-minded determination of the series winner is as recognizable as is his past record. He is consistent because he is not bogged down in a mire of doubt, indecision, and distraction. He does well in *every* race, in part because his attention is constantly upon the things that matter, in part because almost no one else's attention is.

Those who do not have this self-contained, non-distractable personality can acquire it. Practice and experience, which provide skill and understanding, eventually also provide confidence. With confidence, the minute-by-minute management of the boat can be ignored and attention focused upon the determinants of victory. The overriding factor in each portion of the race is recognized; the most likely major error is understood. The probability of success is greatly increased; the risk of disaster is greatly reduced. Consistency is the result.

The fastest boat is often (perhaps even usually) not the winner, and I am often amazed at how little the winner understands the behavior of the wind in which he operates so effectively. Boat speed in excess of the competition's, awareness of strategic factors unknown to the majority, dramatic maneuvering skills, are unnecessary advantages, crutches for the diffident. Although they should be acquired and treasured, they must be ignored once the race is under way. To become preoccupied with them is to admit that if they were not available, if they were to be acquired by others, the series would be lost.

Major series are sometimes won by specialists. Their ability to do dramatically well in a particular condition or on a particular leg of the course provides the assurance of success that permits them to concentrate upon essentials. More often the series winner has all-round capabilities, perfected with the support of innate confidence and determination. Paul Elvstrom seems daring to the uninitiated; he is so certain of his strategic understanding that he tacks directly to the new lay line when he suspects a persistent shift. He starts in a congested mass at the port end of the line and emerges on port tack, having missed a starboard tacker's bow by six inches. His books reveal the attitudes which determine his success: belief in his own abilities, fanatic determination to be the best in every respect, disregard—sometimes scorn—for his competitors. Hans Fogh, a student of Elvstrom, has many of his master's characteristics, including an impressive certitude of ultimate triumph (despite any and all setbacks). In light air, I once watched him tack out of a progressive lift to salvage tenth, while the rest of the fleet, vainly hoping for a shift back, continued on starboard— right down the drain! Bruce Goldsmith, though less assertive, is probably no less determined. He too has the ability to ignore the immediate adversity and get on with the things that matter. At St. Petersburg, I once watched him sail half a mile in the backwind of a boat ahead so as to escape an unfavorable current. Buddy Melges may be the most determined of them all. At the 1972 Soling trials he put together a new mast after breaking one and failing to finish the third race, then went on to win the Olympic berth with two firsts and two seconds. He sails *all* out, *all* the time, never letting up whether ahead or astern.

The series winner differs from the loser not only in his resistance to preoccupation but in his awareness of the proper focus of his attention. He recognizes that the keys to victory are an avoidance of major mistakes on the first three legs of the course and an all-out drive to win on the last three. Before the start he considers the possible factors which could alter the distance to be sailed or the speed of boats in different locations on the course, and he establishes a plan. At the start he concentrates upon obtaining clear air, knowing that a competitor's initially better position may easily be overcome by proper utilization of subsequent differences in available air. After the start he checks to see that the considerations which determined his plan remain valid. He continues his initial tack or makes a first (or second) tack in accordance with his plan. He recognizes that the primary requirement for the first leg is to reach the weather mark among the leaders, that it is essential not to have a disastrous first leg (which almost always means a disastrous race). The start and the beat need not be the best, as long as they are not *bad*. Successful reaching should result in little or no loss to the top competitors ahead, separation from the boats astern, and the passing of several of the less competent. The leaders need not be overtaken, as long as they are not allowed to get away.

The first three legs serve to narrow the race to four or five leaders; the goal of the prospective winner is merely to be among them. The final three legs select the best from among the leaders. During the first three legs, the essentials are to avoid major risks, accept temporary disadvantages, concentrate upon ultimate goals. It is on these legs that series are lost, that mistakes become disasters. Here is where confidence provides the freedom to analyze and to act without the interference of doubt and indecision. The final three legs require maximum attention to boat performance, to strategy, and to tactics. Here is where inches and seconds count, risks must be taken and daring exercised. Here, relentless determination despite apparently insurmountable deficits brings victory.

In a series, the early races should be sailed conservatively, so that one can establish a firm base while sizing up the competition. The first step is to eliminate the also-rans, those who will have a chance only if others are stopped by disaster, those who will undoubtedly have disasters themselves. Early in the series the strategy depends upon ignoring the competition as individuals, seeking safety first and position second. After the third or fourth race, the competition becomes obvious and should be recognized.

Over a series of five, six, or seven races the conservative approach, the avoidance of disasters, will, in competent hands, provide a standing among the leaders. Acquisition of the lead means that the top competitors have made major mistakes. If they have not dropped far back in points, the pressure will be on them to catch up. They will take greater risks then the leader and can be expected to make greater mistakes. The leader neither looks back with concern nor increases his risk-taking to maintain his lead; he allows his competitors to make the mistakes. Again, confidence pays. Even if one is behind by as much as ten points midway in the series, the game plan should be followed: conservatism on the first three legs, daring confined to the last three—after potential disasters have been avoided. If one is behind by more than ten points, a less conservative approach becomes necessary. Disasters must be risked. The lead must be acquired early in the race, through a dramatic start or a tack all the way to the advantageous lay line. Again, determination pays. Pressure must be maintained until the last yards of the last race; the leader may still make that major mistake—through neglect or preoccupation or fear—that throws the series to the more determined, more attentive, more confident competitor astern.

The diffident and the timid seem to avoid recognizing their close competitors, to avoid looking at the score sheets at the end of the day, and to avoid analyzing their own positions vis-à-vis those of their competitors. Persons who hide from the recognition of one-to-one conflicts ashore may be expected to hide in the same way afloat. But to act as if the closest competitor is not on the course is to give him the opportunity to escape, an opportunity that he will be delighted to accept. The confident and aggressive maintain full awareness of their standing and the standing of their competitors. Before the later races they record graphically their own scores and the scores of their close competitors, together with an indication of the gains needed or the losses that may be tolerated. This acknowledgment of the facts is not only more rational than avoidance but is an indication of the confidence that is essential to victory.

As the series grinds onward and one competitor after another is struck by disaster, few remain in contention—and a new phase begins. Consistency, the avoidance of mistakes, is no longer the determinant of victory. Now the watchword becomes, Beat the boats that have to be beaten. Where previously it was essential to ignore one's competitors, it now becomes essential to watch them constantly. The good start and the sensible first leg are as important as ever, but now what is good and what is sensible become relative—relative to the boat or boats in contention. Fifteenth at the weather mark may be quite acceptable if the contender is twentieth; fourth, of little value if the contender is first.

Careful preparation before the race, concentration and the avoidance of distraction during it, are as important, more important, then ever. The overriding requirement is to know what is advantageous, so as to obtain a little more of that advantage than the competition. Unless only one boat is in contention, and all others may be disregarded, the proper start is the same as in the previous races: one which insures clear air and freedom to tack. The ideal start at the upwind end of the line is fraught with potential disaster and may terminate the contest on the line. It should not be risked in a large fleet unless it is uncontested. Once on the beat, the contender or contenders must be carefully watched. They must not be allowed to continue farther than oneself to the advantageous side of the course. On the other hand, one should not continue a tack significantly beyond them. If two or more are in contention, one should stay with the boat on the most advantageous course, leaving it to the others to make the mistakes. On each leg, the course presumed better should be selected but only pursued to a degree slightly in excess of the contenders. If one is ahead, it is only necessary—by adhering to basic strategic principles—to avoid mistakes and win. If astern, the same adherence to basic principles should provide ultimate victory, and the certainty of that victory should be assumed, at least until the final legs. Doing the obviously wrong thing never pays—or, at least, pays insufficiently often ever to warrant doing it. For two good reasons it is better to continue dead astern, if necessary, to the bitter end rather than to assume a major risk of loss: one keeps the pressure on the leader, who may consequently do something stupid, and one remains in the proper position to be in contention if something unforeseen occurs. The leader may have been over the line early, may have a breakdown, may be disqualified because of a prior incident. The *only* way to win is to continue to do the *right* thing until the finish line is crossed; and doing that, one must confidently assume, will be enough.

If only one other boat is in contention—with the others so far behind in points that they haven't a chance—then, and only then, specific action against the contender may be justified. (If more than one is in contention, the third will be delighted at the advantage gained from any conflict between the other two.) If superior ability in the conditions can be taken for granted, the game plan should be unchanged: get a good start, do the right thing, get on top, and cover. But if superiority is questionable or if the conditions are subject to major flukes—light air with the imminence of unpredictable persistent shifts—the lone contender should be attacked. In these circumstances, match-racing tactics are appropriate. Obviously, such tactics are as suitable to the contender behind in the scoring as to the contender ahead—to one's opponent as to oneself. The intention of applying match-racing tactics against a contender must thus be coupled with an expectation that he will apply them as well, at the same time and in the same manner.

When only two boats are in contention, the scoring system becomes significant. (When more than two boats are in contention, direct involvement of one boat with another is usually disastrous; the only effective approach is to sail well, ignoring the score.) If a throw-out is available, the boat with the best score in the preceding races may throw out the finale, using it to force the contender into a worse position. A minimal lead can best be protected down in the fleet, where in order to win, the contending boat must acquire and maintain a weak competitor between her and her opponent. In the 1969 International 14 National Championship series (using a straight-line scoring system), we had such a lead going into the final race, with but one boat in contention. By controlling her from astern we forced her into a late start well down in the fleet and subsequently kept a small strategic advantage leg after leg to finish fifth (and win), with the contender tenth. At the 1973 Great Lakes Soling Championship series with a six-point lead and an Olympic scoring system, we correctly assumed that only Hans Fogh would be a major contender in the final race, in heavy air. We made a good start, sailed a better first leg, and sat on him until halfway up the final beat, when there was no longer any possibility of his catching the leaders or finishing six points ahead of us. When more than one contender has a mathematical chance of victory, it is sometimes possible as it was in this race, to determine in advance that only one boat will threaten, thereby justifying match-race tactics.

Match-race tactics are intimidating to some helmsmen. Their use in pre-start maneuvering may so threaten such opponents that they surrender (unconsciously) in advance. Although a series victory by gift is unlikely in high-caliber competition the possibility must be recognized in any appraisal of oneself. The winner must not only be able to sail consistently mistake-free early legs, and press on to a top position in the later legs of all the early races of a series, but must also hold up under the pressure of the final race. There will almost always be at least one other boat in contention in that final race whose capabilities are equivalent to one's own. Victory will be attained by the helmsman who in head-to-head confrontation is the toughest, the most determined, and the most confident of achieving his expected goal.

Series victory thus depends upon the following:

1. Acquisition of basic performance capability in advance of the series, so that boat-speed determinants and maneuvering techniques can be ignored during it

2. Confidence, determination, and mental toughness which prevent distraction

3. Constant awareness of the determinants of victory (concentration upon the avoidance of major mistakes)

4. A conservative start and first round in each of the early races

5. An aggressive drive to win after the first round in all races.

6. If ahead in the standings, conservatism maintained in the later races, in the expectation that the contenders will make the mistakes

7. If significantly behind, aggressiveness increased and applied earlier in the later races

8. Alertness to the score, and the application of appropriate match-racing tactics when only one contender threatens in the final race.

2. Major Mistakes

Most races are not won; they are lost by all those who do not finish first. In the best competition there may be six or eight—rarely more—who do not throw away a race by making a major mistake. In poorer competition even the winner makes one or more. Hence, avoiding major mistakes is the first requirement for winning. In good fleets, doing this will result in placement among the first six or eight; in weaker fleets, it will result in victory. The primary competition is not among boats of varying speed, nor among seamen of varying talents, but among helmsmen of varying awareness and attentiveness. Most reasonably competent helmsmen are able to recognize their errors after the race—as they are usually obvious. The need is to recognize them in advance, and the problem is to recognize them in the heat of battle when so much else is distracting. It is fortunate that sailboats move so slowly; our limited minds have so much difficulty keeping up with them as it is.

It is unreasonable (and dangerous) to assume that mistakes will not occur. The very fact that most helmsmen lose races regularly because of them indicates that they must be expected. No race is ever sailed perfectly. The great helmsmen are those who are able to recognize the imminence of a major mistake and to act so that it is either avoided or prevented from reaching major proportions. Because they expect to make minor mistakes, and to come periodically to the brink of major ones, they are prepared for them and at ease with them. The less competent, being less prepared, are not only more likely (almost certain) to commit mistakes, but taken by surprise, become preoccupied by them. They spend the remainder of the leg, and sometimes the race, worrying the memory; distracted by the past mistake, they succumb readily to the next. The great helmsmen are characterized by an ability to disregard what has been—what cannot be undone—and by an ability to get on with the race. Even when, occasionally, they make a major mistake, they surge back by doing the right things, and pass their preoccupied competitors as *they* commit additional mistake after mistake.

Certain mistakes result in the loss of hundreds of yards in a brief period of time. Because these critical errors are common to most sailors, they can be listed and remembered. The most useful exercise for helmsmen, the procedure which will advance their competitive standings most rapidly, is recording their mistakes after each day's racing. No one should expect that a mistake will not be repeated once it has been recognized and recorded. But a critical mistake which is detected again and again will eventually be faced, expected, and avoided. The situation in which the mistake arises will be recognized. Underlying the large number of major mistakes that have been recorded, just a few basic errors will be found. When these are recognized, an organized approach to avoiding them can be undertaken.

The most serious mistakes occur early in a race, when boats are still close together and a small loss in distance leads to a large loss in boats. A loss of a hundred yards shortly after the start may result in a loss of twenty boats; a similar loss on the final beat may result in the loss of one boat. Furthermore, a loss of twenty boats early in the race means not merely a loss of twenty points, but also the introduction of obstacles to recovering a position at the head of the fleet. Each of the twenty boats ahead is thereafter disturbing the wind and water, reducing your speed, and each of the twenty is thereafter forcing you from your desired course. For the remainder of the race you will sail more slowly than the boats in the lead, and you will be forced to sail a course longer than that of the boats in the lead. And to the extent that you become preoccupied with the boats ahead, you become more susceptible to making additional strategic errors. After a major disaster on the first round, the only hope of recovery is in the expectation that the boats ahead will commit major mistakes. But even if these do occur, they may not help enough, for on the later legs major mistakes usually result in only minor losses.

A disaster resulting from a decision made after weighing the risks of its occurrence may be acceptable. A disaster resulting from a failure to recognize its imminence is completely unacceptable. A system must be developed to assure that each possible disaster is considered in advance. Before the race the "disaster list" should be reviewed, and during the race, at the appropriate times, the possibility that particular disasters may occur should be reviewed again. The following list of major mistakes includes all the likely disasters.

Preparation

1. Failing to understand the instructions

2. Failing to check the wind direction with the compass for an adequate length of time

3. Failing to check the current

Starting

4. Failing to attain clear air (if the starting tack is to be continued)

5. Failing to attain freedom to tack (if an early tack is required)

Beating and Running

6. Failing to recognize the presence or imminence of a persistent shift

7. Failing to recognize major differences in wind strength or current in different areas of the course

8. Failing to find the weather mark (long before the lay line is reached)

9. Failing to avoid other boats with right of way

10. Failing to plan the best approach to, and departure from, each mark and the best approach to the finish line

11. Failing to keep the boat moving in light air; tacking too often and not jibing often enough

12. Failing to steer properly because of preoccupation with the crew, the boat, the competition, the immediate crisis, or the past disaster

These twelve errors of omission underlie almost all the significant mistakes which are made on the course. (It is, of course, possible to lose a race because of lack of adequate advance preparation—failing to replace the fraying sheet, failing to train the crew, failing to bring the stopwatch, and so on. However, the helmsman able to develop an organized approach which will forestall disasters afloat is hardly likely to fail in such obvious matters as these.) The list should be reorganized as a duty list, to assign responsibility for avoidance of each possible disaster. The helmsman is clearly in charge of starting (4 and 5) and race management (mark rounding, light-air maneuvers, and steering—10, 11, and 12). As far as possible, he should be relieved of the primary responsibility for the data collection required for the other items, and he should be assisted, through reminders from the crew, in the avoidance of failures for which he is primarily responsible. On every boat except a single-hander, someone other than the helmsman should be in charge of navigation, with responsibility for avoiding potential disasters in this area. The helmsman can then concentrate on steering, with the assurance that the necessary data will be collected and interpreted even if he is preoccupied. The third member of the crew (if he exists) should have boat speed as his chief concern, but may, in addition, be assigned primary responsibility for the avoidance of one or more disasters. The essential element of disaster avoidance is organization, and organization requires a precise delegation of responsibility.

In the formation of his plans, the skipper must think through the possibilities of disaster. Working with the navigator he prevents strategic disaster by analyzing the strategic determinants of the race. But he must also remember, perhaps through the development of an appropriate acronym or the presence of a set of labels on the deck, that he has specific responsibilities as a helmsman. To prevent first-leg disasters, he must manage the start in a way that guarantees reaching the advantageous side of the course in safety and in clear air. Hence, he must frequently forgo a start at the upwind end of the line, or one that permits crossing the line with the gun, in order to be certain that he will have clear air (if he intends to continue the starting tack) or freedom to tack (if tacking is necessary). The skipper as helmsman is also responsible for managing the rounding of marks in the same organized fashion—safely, in clear air, and so as to reach the preferred side of the subsequent leg. The mark rounding should be planned as carefully as the start, with the full participation of the crew members responsible for navigation and for the preservation of boat speed. The navigator may be required to remind the helmsman to consider his plan, at some appropriate distance from the mark. In light air the helmsman must think speed, avoid situations which require frequent tacking, sail the boat well off the wind when beating and high on the wind when running (tacking downwind). The crew member who manages boat speed may be assigned the responsibility of reminding the helmsman, before and during a light-air race, of this overriding need. Steering is always the job of the helmsman; he must be allowed to exercise this responsibility without interference or suggestions.

While beating, one member of the crew must be responsible for finding the weather mark and for announcing the imminence of starboard-tack boats (8 and 9). The navigator must thoroughly understand the instructions (1). He must attend the skippers' meeting and read the race circular with such care that no mistake regarding the instructions is possible. He must insist that despite the skipper's distractions before the start, he spend sufficient time checking the wind direction. The navigator must also see to it that the strategic factors are considered and that reference data are recorded (2, 3). Is the wind oscillating, dying, or likely to develop a persistent shift? Is there a significant current and does it vary in different parts of the course (6, 7)? Although the skipper should assume leadership in data collection, he must not be relied upon to conduct it himself.

The greatest mistake of all is failing to recognize a mistake in progress. The organized approach described here should prevent most mistakes, but some are bound to occur. If observation of other boats indicates an unexpected strategic advantage on the opposite side of the course, an immediate tack is essential. Continuing in the wrong direction converts a mistake into a disaster. If a start is poor, clear air must be obtained first and strategic advantage second. If a foul is imminent, collision must be avoided. Alertness and flexibility must accompany planning and organization. Avoiding mistakes is only the first step toward success. The confidence engendered by freedom from mistakes supports the courage necessary to take appropriate risks.

3. Race Management

Major mistakes, the determinants of the outcome of most races, are predictable and preventable. As we have seen, the greatest mistakes are of omission: failing to understand the course missing a persistent shift, failing to check the current—failing to plan. Such failures are chiefly due to preoccupation with lesser matters, which are continuing distractions both before and during the race. A planning system which provides for the consideration of all pertinent factors, which prevents their being overlooked, whatever the distractions, is essential. Since the skipper cannot expect to remember everything, he must delegate much of the responsibility for planning to his crew. The crew should be responsible for data collection, the skipper for making decisions relative to the collected data. To be effective, the system must include a means for recording the data upon which major decisions are based. This practice is desirable for two reasons: first, the necessity of recording the data is a reminder to collect it; second, once recorded, the data remains available for future reference.

Prior to the race, information pertinent to the expected weather (from weather maps and forecasts), the effects of local geography (from local racing experts), and the current (from current tables and charts) should be obtained and preferably recorded. Records of previous experience in the area at the same time of year should be checked. Before the boat leaves the dock, the existing wind, cloud cover, and temperature (of air, water, and land surface) should be evaluated. This information combined with the data already collected will indicate which sails should be taken aboard and which should be set initially. It is not possible to arrive on the race course too soon. Collection of the necessary data will require at least thirty minutes in the racing area. While en route to the start, and in its vicinity, one should repeatedly test the wind direction and the close-hauled course on each tack. This testing will reveal a progressive persistent shift, which should be correlated with the changes in wind velocity, the time of day, and the proximity of the shore. Additional testing on the course should be utilized to detect the presence and range of oscillating shifts. With this data (preferably recorded on a race plan), an estimate of the wind to be expected during the race can be made. Before the warning signal, the current at a starting mark (and, if there is time, elsewhere on the course) should be checked by ascertaining the rate and direction of movement of a current stick.

In addition to recording the collected data and the consequent predictions on a permanent form, I note the important elements in grease pencil on labeled segments of the main traveler thwart. I use an acronym—ODSSSIC—derived from the major strategic factors to be considered, as a reminder to determine (1) whether the air flow is unstable and Oscillating; (2) whether there will be a persistent shift, due to a change in wind strength (Dying), or to one of the three S's (Sea breeze, Squall, or Shoreline), or to the breakthrough of an Inversion; and (3) whether a significant Current is present. I record under "Alert" any of these factors which I feel may affect the outcome of the race. Next I record, under the appropriate labels, the median wind direction and the compass directions for each leg of the course (these can be calculated if the direction to the weather mark is known). In addition to the direction of the run, I record the dead-downwind direction and, for each possible jibe, a direction 20° to either side of dead downwind. The latter provide a guide to the headed jibe, the jibe best aligned with the course at an appropriate sailing angle for the conditions. I record the range of compass headings for each tack (preferably obtained over an ob-

servation period of at least thirty minutes) and, if the wind is
oscillating, the median heading for each tack.

With this data the race plan can be completed. All of the
ODSSSIC factors are considered in determining the advantageous
side of each leg. The significance of precisely predictable factors,
such as the current, is weighed against the significance of impre-
cisely predictable factors, such as persistent shifts. The likelihood
that an inversion will break through and cause the wind to die and
back is weighed against the likelihood that a sea breeze will appear
immediately thereafter and cause the wind to increase and veer. The
preferred tack for crossing the starting line, and the end of the starting line which is farther to windward, are ascertained, and this information is correlated with the direction which must be sailed to
reach the preferred side of the first beat. The caliber and size of the
fleet determine whether an ideal start at the favored end on the
favored tack will be feasible or whether a compromise to assure
the far more important attainment of clear air will be necessary. If
the wind is oscillating, a start must be planned which will permit
being on, or tacking to, the lifted tack immediately after crossing
the line. An awareness of the oscillations up to the moment of the
start is necessary to predict which tack will be lifted as the gun
fires. The final element of a good start which must be arranged in
advance is a technique of ascertaining when the boat is on the line.
If at all possible, the starting marks should be aligned with a distinctive feature on the shore or on an anchored boat (the port-end
line observer, for instance) so that the crew will know when the
boat is on the line.

Planning the race and the start is, of course, only the first step.
Once out on the beat, the recorded data should be frequently con-
sulted both to assure that the race is being managed according to
the plan and to assure that the observed conditions correspond to
those anticipated when the plan was developed. Unexpected
changes in conditions must be detected immediately, for pursuit of
a plan based on error does not court disaster—it assures disaster. The
recording of data permits the immediate recognition of an unexpected shift, an alteration in wind velocity or a change in current,
and an immediate revision of the plan.

The management of the race in accordance with the plan and in
the certainty that major errors will be avoided requires that each
member of the crew assume specific duties. A duty list should be
provided, or at least discussed, in advance of the race, so that each un-

derstands precisely what his responsibilities are and are not. To the extent that a crew member does someone else's job, he is neglecting his own. In two- and three-man boats in hotly contested races, each person usually has more to do than he can optimally handle. The skipper must be involved at every moment in considerations of strategy and tactics. He should be required to do as little as possible in the handling of the boat. As he must steel himself to avoid the distractions emanating continuously from the race itself, he should not in addition be distracted by the crew. The skipper must not be preoccupied with data collection, and his attention must not be absorbed by inappropriate or unnecessary reports from the crew. The crew member responsible for boat speed has little time for anything but sail trim. Since the apparent wind changes continuously, sail trim can never be correct. When he is not directly occupied adjusting sail trim or fulfilling other assigned duties, he should be observing the performance of other boats as an indicator of the appropriateness of the sail trim at that time. His reports to the skipper must be confined to data regarding boat speed. The third member of the crew (if he exists) should be responsible for the observations required for strategic and tactical decisions. He should call the compass on windward and downwind legs and keep a record (on a plastic-covered form mounted on his leg or on the deck) of the extreme headings or calculated wind directions on each leg. He must be constantly alert to possible changes in wind direction or velocity elsewhere on the course and report these changes to the skipper. He must be aware of the position of other boats and predict their relationships at marks and in overtaking and crossing situations. He must confine his reporting to these matters; additional and extraneous data can only be distracting.

Races are won by efficient crews who do their jobs of boat handling and of data collecting and synthesizing in an organized, purposeful manner, undistracted by immediate problems. When they allow themselves to become emotionally concerned with temporary setbacks, minor errors, or the minutiae of immediate tactical situations they fail in their primary responsibilities. Useless observations —"we're not going," "we're on the wrong side of the shift," "you can come up"—evident to all, are distracting, and they indicate that the speaker is not functioning in his assigned role. The crew's job is to supply information, not conclusions and not solutions (unless assigned such responsibility). The skipper's job is to synthesize the data and make choices. Everyone must assist in freeing the skipper from preoccupation with unnecessary information and from doubts concerning his ability to reach appropriate decisions.

Planning requires anticipation. The plan for the weather leg, and thus for the start, is based on the expected major strategic determinants of the weather leg—the ODSSSIC factors. The same factors largely determine the plan for the reaches, run, and subsequent weather legs. An original plan based upon the expectation of a backing wind may require the use of a small, flat spinnaker on the first reach. If data collected on the preceding beat indicate that the wind has veered instead, a different spinnaker and a different tactical plan may be needed, for managing a broad rather than a close reach. The plan for each leg must be made in advance and then reevaluated in the light of data collected on the preceding leg. Anticipation is required continuously, but particularly at the crucial times of the race—the start, the mark roundings, and the finish. To the same extent that the start is planned—with an awareness that its exact character will depend on the strategy of the subsequent leg, the positions of other boats, the maintenance of clear air—each mark rounding should be planned. The course desired for the reach as well as the position of the neighboring boats at the commencement of the reach should be anticipated. The approach to the finish line requires the same analysis; the relative positions of all boats in contention must be recognized. The score is kept at the finish; nothing can be left to chance.

The crew should complement the skipper. One of the reasons that wives make such good crews is that they understand the limitations of their skipper husbands. The good crew notices if the skipper becomes preoccupied, and recalls his attention to the things that matter. The good crew is aware of the aspects of the race that the skipper neglects, and insures that they are not overlooked. The good crew recognizes when the skipper is so involved in steering that he is unable to plan the management of the leg ahead. As the skipper threads his way through the boats converging on the weather mark, the good crew is analyzing the reach to come. Foresight by the crew is as essential as foresight by the skipper. One must complement the other.

Winning requires that the race be managed. Whatever can be anticipated must be anticipated. If there are moments when a member of the crew is not fully occupied in handling an immediate problem, he must apply himself to aiding the skipper in preparing for a problem to come. The crew must act and report in a manner which directs the skipper's attention to valid data and actual problems and which supports his confidence in ultimate success. The skipper must occupy himself with continual reevaluation and modification of the plan; he must not allow himself to become distracted by the crew, the boat, or his competitors.

PRE-RACE CHECK LIST

1. *Data Collection*
   (*to be recorded*)
   Wind strength
   Wind direction
   Close-hauled headings
   Current—strength and
      direction
   Reach and run directions
   Downwind jibing angles

2. *Race Plan*
   ODSSSIC factors
   Preferred side—beats
             1st reach
             2nd reach
             run
   Starting plan—preferred
             side 1st
             beat
             upwind end

3. *Mistake Control*
   Crew responsibilities (1–12)

4. *Sail Trim*
   Check trim chart
   Mainsail—mast bend
             outhaul and
             cunningham
             tension

vang tension
leech tension
boom position
Jib—lead position
   luff tension
   leech tension
Spinnaker
   selection—1st reach
             2nd reach
             run

5. *Equipment Check*
   Shroud position and tension
   Spinnaker—sheet selection
             lines attached
             pole hoisted

6. *Performance Modifications*
   Primary modification if
      performance defective:
      speed
      pointing
      leeway
   Gust control—traveler?
             mainsheet?
             backstay?
             vang?
   Tacking
      technique—traveler?
             backstay?
             vang?

CREW RESPONSIBILITIES ON A THREE-MAN BOAT

FOREDECK MAN

Sail Trim: Manages boat speed
                      Controls jib and main (jibstay sag, mast bend,
                          leech tension, and the like)
                      Trims spinnaker

Mistake Control: Detects right-of-way boats (9) *
                      Finds windward mark (8)

MIDDLE MAN

Strategy: Calls compass headings (records extremes) (2)
                      Checks the current (3)
                      Presents data summaries (prior to each mark,
                          after each mark, and after recognized
                          changes) concerning
                              wind velocity
                              shift
                              current

Mistake Control: Understands course and instructions (1)
                      Watches boats on the weather quarter (detects
                          persistent shifts, current changes) (6, 7)
                      Detects downwind end of the finish line (10)

HELMSMAN

Sail Trim: Trims mainsheet and traveler

Strategy: Looks around

Mistake Control: Starts in clear air and/or with freedom to
                          tack (4, 5)
                      Rounds marks properly (10)
                      Steers, and keeps boat moving in light air
                          (11, 12)

---

* Numbers refer to the major mistakes to be avoided. (See Chapter 2, "Major Mistakes.")

4. How the Specialists Win

Syd Dakin is a light-air specialist. Syd has been amazing Soling sailors with his light-air wizardry since his remarkable showing in the 1971 World Championship. He rounded the first leeward mark twenty-ninth in one race of a recent North American Championship and not only won the race but dragged his six closest followers into the top places along with him. In the dying air of a race at CORK, 1973, I tacked for the shore and the thunderclouds inland (Figure 1). Close to the lead, I tacked to cross the fleet, while Syd continued to the starboard-tack lay line. As the wind disintegrated further, Syd had all that remained. He went on to win by nearly a leg of the course. He shows an uncanny knack for recognizing where the dying wind will persist the longest and where the new wind will appear the earliest. And he couples this perceptivity with the courage to go all the way to the lay line in pursuit of the expected advantage.

Since light air is characterized by variation in wind velocity (resulting in enormous differences in boat speed), ability, such as Syd's, to find the wind is the greatest possible asset to a light-air sailor. When Syd is right he wins, and wins big—not by a few feet

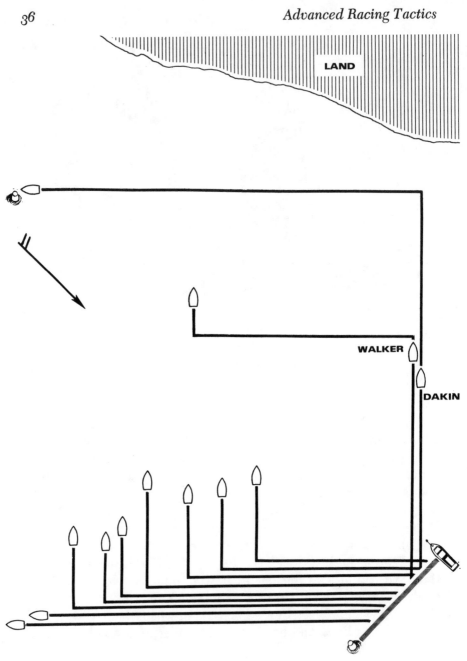

FIGURE 1

in a seesaw battle to the line, but by hundreds of yards, with a victory predictable for minutes and sometimes hours before the finish. In moderate air, boat speed is most useful, but even then the fast boat can be beaten by superior tactics. Bruce Goldsmith, who is a specialist in moderate-air windward work, claims that he has never relied upon boat speed. His ability to calculate the risks and do the right thing to windward wins regattas. He rarely finishes down in the fleet; if disaster threatens, he relies upon his ability to come back on subsequent windward legs. Sam Merrick is a downwind specialist; he takes the right jibe regularly and dares to take it even when the entire fleet has assumed the other. In heavy air, boat handling is what counts. Buddy Melges does everything well, but his specialty is boat handling in a big breeze. He knows that he can make up the needed places on the reaches and that if he is ahead at the weather mark he will have an insurmountable lead at the leeward.

All of these individuals are good all-round sailors. In addition, however, they are specialists, superior to almost any potential competitor in *their* conditions—on *their* leg. Each uses his special competence to win races and ultimately to win series. Peter Warren has made the point that in big regattas with Olympic scoring, the chance of a win is worth any risk. The advantage of having a first is greater than the disadvantage of having a thirtieth (particularly with a throwout!). In almost every series, the specialist is able to find one (or more) races which he can reasonably expect to win. He knows that his race is coming and his leg is coming.

John Illingworth, in his excellent little book about 12-meter match racing, says, "One of the real lessons to be learnt was the need as a skipper to be able to switch to passive sailing at will; to concentrate on getting to the next mark as quickly as possible regardless of one's opponent ahead; relying on one's prowess downwind or on some other advantage to come." Confidence in the victory to come makes possible this passive sailing, this willingness to concentrate on doing the right thing—the safe, sensible thing— until opportunity knocks. The specialists have this confidence; they not only win when their turn comes, but make few mistakes while waiting.

Many sailors become bogged down after a major mistake, so preoccupied with analyzing it, justifying it, punishing themselves with its remembrance, that they fail to concentrate on the business at hand. When they fall behind they forget their race plans, the strategic necessities, the things that count. Maneuvering becomes reactive: a tack away to obtain clear air, a jibe opposite to that sought by the majority, a course well above or below the rhumb line on the reach. The specialist, confident that his time is coming, concentrates on staying close. He remains in the dirty air of the boat in front if he is heading out of an adverse current; he sails to leeward on the reach if doing so will give him an inside overlap at the jibe mark; he ignores the boat that charges past to windward, assuming that she has a different wind. He has no need to panic, his time is coming.

Not everyone can possess the talents of a Dakin or a Melges; in their absence, one would be wise to concentrate on a particular aspect of racing performance so as to become a specialist. With the confidence arising from the acquisition of a special ability would come a general improvement in performance. And whether or not such an ability is attainable, the desirable attitudes that go with it should be within reach. None of us needs to throw away advantages once attained or to be so burdened by setbacks that we are subsequently unable to make rational decisions. We don't need to, but we will—unless we see the lesson of the specialists. Every race demonstrates that confidence wins and that we must assume ultimate success if we are to be alert to the task at hand.

5. Flexibility

Planning is essential to racing success. But planning must be dynamic, both expectant of change and susceptible to change. Planning is based on the data collected, and is only as good as the accuracy and the timing of the data collection. An oscillating shift, which need be recognized only as it occurs, can be predicted within a few minutes of its occurrence. A persistent shift, however, must be recognized before it occurs, and although its occurring can be anticipated hours in advance, the time of its appearance can only be estimated within a range of hours. For an oscillating shift there is only one response: to tack when headed beyond the median wind. For a persistent shift an almost infinite variety of response is possible, with the choice dependent upon its magnitude and rate of development. The effects of current may vary through time and space and be modified by wind and season and depth of water. Planning for the presence or absence of strategic modifiers is not enough; their time of appearance and the rate of their progression or retrogression must be calculated as well. Data collection must continue not merely up to the moment of the start but throughout the race. Not only must the plan be predicated upon progressive change in the expected determinants, it must provide for the appearance of the unexpected as well.

The plan may be wrong. It may be based upon an inaccurate analysis—a faulty assessment of the relative significance of various factors, on a mistaken estimate of the time of their appearance. It may be based upon data from which a significant determinant has been omitted. The plan must include a complete analysis of the race instructions and must also accommodate the possibility that the race committee will fail to produce a race in accordance with the instructions. The navigator, as well as the skipper, must be constantly alert to indications that the plan is in error or that previously unrecognized factors are affecting it. The best means of detecting the unforeseen is by observing other boats, particularly those at the extremities of the course. It is unwise to conclude that their unexpected behavior is inappropriate (or stupid) until a reasonable explanation for it has been considered. "They" may know something you don't.

I recognize more and more often that flexibility is a mark of the winning sailor. It is easy to excuse a poor finish by blaming the race committee, the weather report, or the intrusion of a cruising boat. I often deny the significance of a race in which the wind blows less than 15 knots and there is no thirty-minute buck dead to windward to start things off. If I build my boat for certain conditions and they are never provided, I can always justify a defeat. Seeping through my insistence on rigid requirements, however, is a growing awareness that others are willing to race in the conditions existing and are able to win despite them.

During the 1967 Prince of Wales Cup racing at Cowes, I didn't win the practice race because the committee boat wasn't on station, the race for the Lowestoft Bowl because the "windward" leg was actually to a mark on a beam reach from my mid-leg position, the race for the Humstanton Town Plate because the weather mark was set in a fluky wind zone a hundred yards from the beach, the Prince of Wales Cup because the 3-knot weather-going tide condensed the mile-long beats to about ten minutes each (and because of the intrusion of the *Queen Mary!*), and the race for the Weymouth Town Trophy because of the sudden appearance of a 45° header after I had made the perfect start. Now eighty-eight other boats in each of these races probably had other excuses (though I heard several using mine) but in each instance the ninetieth had no excuse. She won.

Before the start of the race for the Lowestoft Bowl, I asked a member of the committee in a rescue boat where the weather mark lay. He, quite improperly, pointed it out—on a close reach from the starboard end of the line. As this was completely outside the range of my expectations of what a race should be, I took off from the port end and with two-thirds of the fleet sailed at least a mile off course. I later learned that Robin Webb had asked the same man the same question, and unhampered by a rigid psyche, had sailed straight to the mark indicated, to finish second. If in some subsequent race I were to ask that man again, I wonder if I would believe him?

There was very little wind at the start of the race for the Weymouth Town Trophy, and to the starboard side of the beat there was considerably more weather-going current (Figure 2). I planned to take off from the starboard end of the line and tack out into the stronger current immediately. Since the fleet was gun-shy in the weather-going current, I was able to break away with the gun, almost alone, right at the mark. To my surprise, I found that I was laying the mark, so there was no indication to tack. The boats astern in my backwind did so, however. But they could be no threat, I reasoned, as I would gain on them in a header and they were already overstanding. I was in the lead, fat, dumb, and happy, when suddenly the boats far to leeward tacked to port at an angle which would take them across my bow—and they had a breeze! They had more and more breeze, and lifted higher and higher on port. But I was still laying the mark. One never tacks away when one is on the lay line, or even close to it—never. (I must have written an article on *that*.) By the time the new wind reached me, ten boats had crossed my bow on port, and, when I finally tacked, another ten which had tacked out into the current behind me swept by on starboard. It just wasn't fair—and besides it completely contradicted all the basic rules of racing to windward!

And then there was the *Queen Mary*. Would you believe that I never saw her until she appeared a hundred yards ahead, crossing behind the first five boats on the third leg of the Prince of Wales Cup race? By the time I was aware of her presence a dozen of my closest competitors, including Stewart Morris, had luffed far to weather to cut across her stern, and I had dropped from sixth to twentieth.

Now you are not likely to look up from your preoccupation with the spinnaker luff or the mast bend during your next race for the

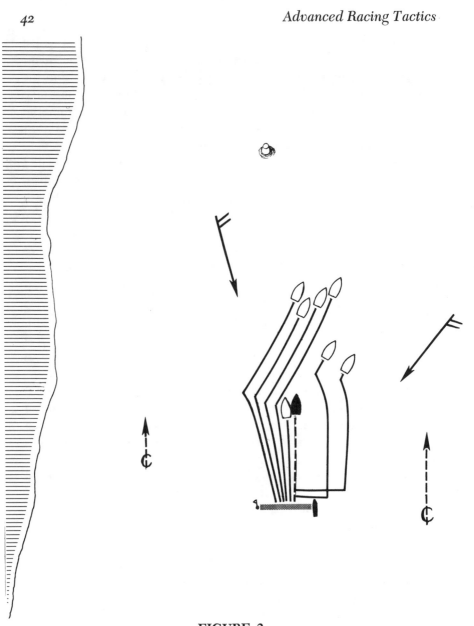

FIGURE 2

club championship to see the *Queen Mary* gliding across your bow —but something equally catastrophic will undoubtedly occur. And if your psyche prepares you no better than mine for such derangements of your race plan, you will have no more chance of picking up the silver at the Annual Awards Dinner than I did of winning the P.O.W.

Although Stewart Morris didn't win any races in P.O.W. Week either, he did accept what the fates presented with considerably more equanimity and flexibility than I (or at least he gave me that impression). I strongly suspect, in my aging wisdom, that this flexibility is one of the secrets of his greatness. Perhaps the English are better trained for this; the individual who has raced in Chichester harbor (or any of those tiny channels that the English seem to thrive on) should be prepared for anything. I've always claimed that the plan's the thing and that you should stick to it. Stewart Morris has demonstrated again and again that it may have to be discarded.

Few among those I race with regularly will believe me when I say I'm going to be more flexible in the future. However, I am going to be alert to the new wind (from the direction opposite to my predictions), aware of the current eddy flowing against the predicted stream, prepared for the unexplainable difference in wave patterns along the shore, ready for anything—even the *Queen Mary* crossing my bow.

6. The Obviously Wrong Tack

"If several of your adversaries are faster to windward than you are, then of course your chance of winning is small and the only thing to do is to take out a line of your own; it is useless to do the same as the other boats do, so you must stand off on the opposite tack to them even if it is obviously the wrong one and crosses a lee tide, or has some other decided disadvantage attached to it, but it is your only chance so you should take it." *

Few can accept this recommendation—but many behave as though they do. It is clearly irrational. Doing what is obviously wrong cannot possibly be right. Indeed, one of the most distinguishing characteristics of the great sailors in our midst is their clear rejection of this thesis, their ability to hang in there, awaiting their chance. Yet the tack to the opposite lay line, far from the mass of the fleet, is often practiced and often defended. It takes a certain admirable idiocy, I suppose, to believe that one is right and everyone else is wrong, but it is a very ineffective way to win races. And the "wrong" choice is not necessarily a dramatic one; it may merely

* Written in 1882 and quoted by Richard Ewart-Smith in a recent issue of *Gossip,* the British 14 newsletter.

be a tack away from a single boat close on the lee bow that is going in the "right" direction. The wrongness of the choice is clearly evident later, but so often obscured at the time. This going off in the wrong direction is practiced at all levels; it is not limited to neophytes. And it is not tried just once and then discarded. Rational experience does not interfere with irrational behavior.

Since doing the wrong thing contributes nothing to winning, it must have other benefits. For the many who seem to apply this technique deliberately, its function is to avert the acknowledgment of defeat. The sailor who leaves the fleet to take a flyer beats himself and thus avoids being beaten by his competitors. He is able to believe that he could have won had he not taken the wrong tack, and at the bar after the race he is able glibly to make this claim. A disqualification often has the same genesis. Many seem to need such an excuse. If they realistically expected to win they would spend more time developing their boat speed and learning from their racing experiences instead of repeatedly avoiding the issue. However, each time they go out, inadequately prepared, they find themselves behind, and seeking to escape recognition of their inadequacies, take their flyer and perpetuate their problem.

The positive approach is, of course, to stay with the fleet and beat the competition at their own game. This approach provides (1) the possibility of winning, (2) the probability of learning for the future, and (3) a psychological lift which will carry over into future races. Winning depends upon being close at the crucial points on the course, and particularly at the weather mark. Once the fleet takes off on the reach, the leaders, in clear air, break away; the mass of the fleet sets up a barrier of backwind, blanket, and wake; and the tailenders are blocked from ever catching up. It is essential to stay close on the beat, but once behind, only those with the confidence that they will ultimately prevail have the determination to stay close. It is not easy to hold a tack in dirty air or in a position where other boats close ahead have a seemingly insurmountable advantage. But when the other tack is "obviously the wrong one," this is the route to victory.

Pressed by the competition to ideal trim, the leading boat of a group always sails faster than one which sails alone. Thus even if the obviously "wrong" tack is no worse than the one favored by the fleet, the boat sailing alone upon it will find herself astern at the mark. And regardless of whether staying close leads to success in a particular race, it provides the opportunity to learn for the future.

The best means of acquiring information about boat-speed determinants is to sail competitively, alongside another boat. This is a far more accurate method than tank testing or evaluation by any available speedometer. The development of boat speed depends upon repeated evaluations of performance, and the ideal opportunities occur during racing. To develop the habit of winning, one must regard each race as a testing ground for future races. Ultimately, the use of data accumulated in previous races makes it possible to trim the boat properly right off the starting line in every conceivable condition. Of course, close racing provides learning experience in sailing techniques and tactical maneuvering as well—experience which is completely missed by the helmsman who takes the obviously "wrong" tack, and separates from all his competitors.

There may be an even more significant advantage. The irrational response that is expressed by the tack away does not prevent the eventual recognition of failure. And repeated failure erodes confidence, the confidence which is so essential to an attitude of continued striving, to an unwillingness to quit, to hanging in until the finish line is crossed, to victory at last. John Illingworth, in describing the need for "passive sailing" by the boat astern, indicates that the psychological consequences of a bad defeat consequent to taking a flyer may adversely effect performance in subsequent races. He recommends that when there is no hope of catching the boat ahead during a particular leg, the boat astern should follow in his competitor's wake, staying close enough to be able to profit from a subsequent opportunity. Staying close, losing no more or possibly gaining a little, helps to maintain optimistic future expectations. Losing by a huge margin merely substantiates all the anxiety-ridden feelings of inadequacy which determined the irrational response in the first place. Thus the pattern is confirmed: I am unable to win; I fear the demonstration of my inability; I must do the obviously "wrong" thing once again.

The establishment of the "pecking order" so characteristic of most of our fleets owes much to this phenomenon. Irrational behavior is typically repetitive. The same people tend to be last surprisingly often; their irrational responses lead them to the wrong choices again and again. Recognizing irrationality can be useful. A tremendous possibility of gain is available to those who have been unwilling to test their talents openly; they may learn much and arrive at the real likelihood of winning.

7. Greed

Greed, a little of which goes a long way, must be rigidly restricted. Bob Mosbacher reminded me of the need for constant alertness to this danger after the fifth race of a recent Soling series in Bermuda. He had been in second, a quarter mile astern of us, spinnaker-reaching along the Somerset shore, when he spotted a likely-looking patch of better air nearer the beach and went for it. By the time he reached the area the wind was gone, and he was trapped under the blanket of the Somerset hills while the whole fleet closed in. After the race Bob admitted that it was greed that had taken him off the course; he was going for first, unwilling to settle for second (which he eventually reacquired). When I thought over the race, I realized that (for a change) I had won (with a lead of half a leg) by restraining my own greed.

I had opted for a late start at the weather (starboard) end to insure that I could be first off on port toward the better wind to starboard. Ten seconds before the gun, a six-foot slot appeared between the boat ahead and to leeward and the weather-end flag. It was *so* tempting, but I restrained myself—and waited until the leeward boat was across the line (having ultimately passed within three feet of that flag!). Subsequently, I tacked with each minor shift, toward each better patch of wind, and was soon in the van. Several times I was tempted to split away from the majority of the fleet toward what looked like better air. But each time, I came back to cover first the boats on one extremity of the fleet, then those on the other. I was moving faster than the others, and two-thirds of the way up the leg, obtained the lead. I had not been greedy but had settled for one small gain at a time, nibbling away at the leads of those ahead—and won the race by half a mile.

I have emphasized my restraint because I have such difficulty displaying it, because I savor the remembrance, and because it contrasts so markedly with my management of some of the other races in the same regatta. I had won the first two races of the preliminary three-race series and had a 3.5-point lead going into the final race. All I had to do was stay within two boats of Sam Merrick, and that's just where I was rounding the leeward mark. But did I follow him on port to the Somerset shore? No—I was greedy. I took off on starboard looking for the channeled shift to the south, which never appeared until it was too late. Seeking to win the race, I lost the series.

Now you may say that my conduct was foolish rather than greedy. But greed does enter into many situations, often more subtly than here, seeming even more reasonable. In the second race of the major series, we had gradually worked through the fleet to take the lead at the second weather mark, and then lost it on the run. The wind was light, spotty, and unstable. As we rounded the final leeward mark, Bill Abbott and Buddy Melges were in the lead, with Bob Mosbacher close astern. Both took the headed port tack, and we elected the starboard-tack lift. They tacked to cover, but it was too late. Three hundred yards from the weather mark we crossed them, and thereafter we maintained a tight cover, gradually pulling farther ahead. Two-thirds of the way to the finish we were on port slightly ahead and fifty yards to weather of the second boat which (with the next four) was also on port, well under control (Figure 3). We seemed to have it made until we noticed Kirk Cooper, who had rounded the leeward mark and continued far out on starboard. Kirk was returning on port almost on the lay line in a big lift with a wind of his own.

If a shift is likely to be persistent and another boat on the same tack is lifted by it, the proper maneuver is to tack. Tacking takes one toward the shift (the essential maneuver) and covers the threat

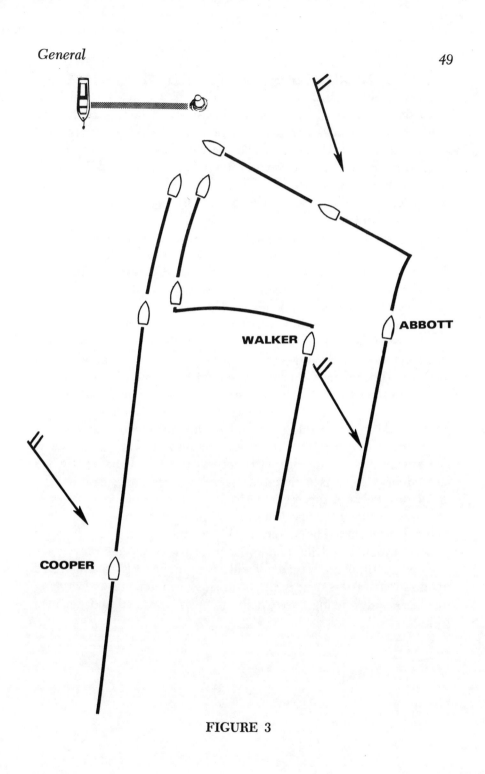

FIGURE 3

when the lifted boat is astern and to weather. There would be no persistent shift in this wind, however. Kirk was roaring up in a transient oscillation of the light northwesterly. A tack to cover him would be a tack away from the next shift. A tack to cover him would release Bill Abbott to reach the next header in front and to leeward of us. A tack to cover him might not be successful. A tack to cover him might cause us to lose Kirk *and* Bill. Enter greed. A tack to cover might permit us to catch Kirk and return on his lee bow before Bill escaped. We tacked.

We didn't quite catch Kirk, and after a series of tacks he beat us across the line by a few feet. Bill continued in the lift, tacked in the next header, and in a good breeze roared across the line fifty yards ahead of us both. Greed obscures an accurate assessment of the risks and blocks a rational choice. We had traded a certain second and a near-certain first for a probable (and actual) third.

Where is the line drawn between an appropriate desire to win— an expectation of winning—and inappropriate greed? The intention to win, the belief in winning, is essential to competitive success. It stimulates the effort that is indispensable before and during the contest. Victory cannot be achieved without the confidence which permits taking reasonable risks, but confidence alone does not win races. It must be based on a realistic appraisal of what is necessary, and a willingness to do all that is necessary, in the belief that when all is done victory is obtainable. Greed is unrealistic, irrational, a belief that because success is desired it is obtainable, regardless of the risks involved. If one thing is essential to racing success, it is rational behavior. The determinants of success are the laws of nature—rational and inimitable. Luck provides success only when one's competitors are less competent, less rational. Risk-taking based upon rational assessment is characteristic of confidence and integral to success. Risk-taking based upon greed is irrational and destined to failure.

8. The Skipper's Job

The skipper is responsible for the determination of priorities. He must start with the boat—rigging, tuning, and testing until a peak of performance is reached which can be maintained *with minimal attention during the race.* He must then select and train a crew who will make all trim modifications, perform all maneuvers, and report all needed data without error and *with minimal supervision during the race.* He must then organize the management of the racing so that all necessary information can be collected *with minimal attention.* Because most of all, the skipper must free his mind from the minutiae of racing to concentrate on winning. That is his overriding responsibility.

But sailboat racing is a team effort, and the skipper is part of a team. In many boats he trims the mainsheet, adjusts the traveler, even hoists the spinnaker. Since he may have occasion to do these things because the crew is temporarily unavailable—their performance must become automatic. Insofar as possible, the crew should pull the strings and hike and clean up the mess; the skipper should think, and induce the boat to respond to his thoughts. The latter is done by steering. This is the skipper's job; he must perform it with the same precision he expects of his crew. On many boats and in many situations, steering requires full attention. At the start, at mark roundings, when other boats are threatening, the skipper can be involved in nothing else. In panic situations, the crew must be delegated the responsibility of solving the immediate problem; the skipper must steer so as to minimize the loss. But steering itself, like other crew functions must become automatic; the skipper must be able to think while steering. As information pertinent to decisions regarding strategy and tactics is reported by his crew, he must be able to assimilate this data, so that periodically a quick look suffices to permit a valid appraisal and an appropriate decision.

During the race, the skipper must restrict himself to strategy and tactics and leave boat speed to the crew. The skipper's job is the far more important one; if he neglects it, the race is lost. If a crew member neglects his, the boat merely goes a bit more slowly. Some will assert, "Nothing makes a helmsman look better than a fast boat" (Shorty Trimingham). I prefer, "He who makes the fewest mistakes wins" (Cooch Maxwell).

I practiced what I am herein preaching for the greater part of the 1973 International 14 Spring Regatta. I ignored my crew and the boat (almost) and took every start, led regularly at the weather mark, planed away from the fleet without thought for the outhaul, the Cunningham, or the board, was never farther back than second at the leeward mark. But in almost every race, I managed to throw away my lead (or most of it) at that leeward mark. As my inexperienced crew fumbled with the spinnaker drop, I prompted his every move, and preoccupied with the tangled mess on the bow tank and the sheets dragging in the water, paid no attention to the strategic and tactical demands of the situation. In one race we rounded the leeward mark with a lead of two boat lengths over sharp, young Toby Doyle, while the rest of the fleet was scattered well astern. But Toby, innocent of the need for neat boat tanks, slipped into gear and marched away to a hundred-yard victory as we wallowed along on the wrong tack in successive doses of bad air. Of course, it would have been nicer if the crew could have gotten the jib sheet in and hadn't had to come in off the wire to stow the spinnaker again. But I couldn't have thrown away a hundred yards merely by losing boat speed. I had failed in my job; I was paying no attention to steering—to the wind, the water, and the other boats. I was preoccupied with boat speed; the eighth of a knot lost because the jib was still too far out, the quarter of a knot lost because the boat was lying on her ear, the hundredth of a knot lost because the spinnaker sheet was dragging astern.

When the skipper becomes preoccupied with boat speed at the expense of attention to strategy and tactics, he compounds the crew's defects with his own and insures disaster. The benefits of boat speed are chiefly psychological. Confidence in boat speed produces an attitude that justifies preparation, organization, and concentration. Demonstration of boat speed intimidates the opposition. But boat speed infrequently wins races and rarely wins series. I always remember how fast Brownlow Gray was going when he won the practice race before the 1960 Princess Elizabeth series in Bermuda—which I subsequently swept with four firsts and a second. What little the skipper may contribute to the resolution of a problem of boat speed will be more than offset by the costs of even a brief lapse in attention to strategy and tactics. Buddy Melges says (though whether what Buddy Melges says can be applied to ordinary mortals is questionable) that he pays little attention to boat speed while racing. He watches the wind, the water, and the other boats, and ignores the fine points of Cunningham control. Good skippers are attentive to the skipper's job, let their crews be attentive to the crew's job.

The skipper must concentrate on the elements that matter at each stage of the race, focus his attention on the circumstances which precipitate the major mistakes, the disasters, by which series are lost. He must resist distraction, concerning himself solely with the factors that determine the score. The struggle is between occupation and preoccupation.

The skipper who is preoccupied—with his competitors, with individual boats, with the immediate situation—misses the significant elements of the race. He worries about details: Is the spinnaker properly stowed? Is the right jib being used? Other boats look faster, other helmsmen more competent. Because he is preoccupied he acts impulsively instead of analytically. A decision made is immediately doubted. He neglects the organization which is essential to winning. He starts without a plan, enters the beat without strategic intent. At the same time, a hazy indifference obscures his concern about winning or losing. He presumes, often verbally, that the race "doesn't matter," that he won't care if he loses. Sailing a bad leg, making a bad tack, being passed, are accepted.

Some skippers exhibit this indifference continually. It provides an escape from the pressure, a guarantee in advance of the acceptability of certain defeat. Others start out determined enough, but after the first conflict or the first setback lapse into tunnel awareness, seeing only the immediate minutiae. As soon as one boat works up from a lee-bow position and moves out ahead, the race is regarded as lost. With each head-to-head conflict comes the fear of defeat and the presumption of inferiority. Here is where the skipper earns his keep. He must learn to recognize this fear, to avoid either surrender or indifference. As soon as the thought "He will get me" appears, he must resist it. When the crew points out the imminence of conflict, he must face it. When a threat appears, he must deal with it. Neither preoccupation with other matters nor acceptance of defeat is permissible. Fear must be converted into a determination to win and be replaced by a confidence that losses are temporary and will be overcome.

Head-to-head conflicts must be welcomed as opportunities to demonstrate superiority, with the recognition that most competitors will be adversely affected by the demonstration. A fine line separates the aggressive from the submissive, and this fine line must be exploited. Although each helmsman may expect to resolve a lee-bow situation in his favor, only one will win. In some conflicts, the outcome is predetermined; a loss then must be recognized as inevitable, accepted, and not construed as a demonstration of inferiority. In other conflicts the issue is for a time in doubt; then the most determined succeeds. As soon as a slight gain is made by one boat, the helmsman of the other feels threatened. Unless he possesses the necessary toughness, he becomes paralyzed by the imminent disaster, mesmerized by the threatening boat. His attention riveted upon the topsides of the hull to leeward or upon the roar of the bow wave behind his back, he no longer concentrates on his steering and falls rapidly astern. This dropping back, in turn, reinforces the confidence of the helmsman of the gaining boat, and thereby strengthens his concentration on his steering. Since the differing responses of the two helmsmen may be induced by a fancied gain as readily as by a real one, the preexisting expectation is the major determinative of the result. The winning helmsman is certain of success in advance. His certainty is substantiated by the inevitable result. Thus confidence wins conflicts—and races.

The necessary psychological attributes of the winning skipper, as indicated above are

confidence	aggressiveness
determination	mental toughness
drive	high goals.

In addition, and probably as a prime basis for many of the qualities listed, he must have a sense of guilt. He seeks perfection to avoid the pangs of that guilt. He cannot tolerate defeat. He is driven by that guilt to set high goals. His aggressiveness, determination, and drive are mechanisms for overcoming that guilt. And he must succeed in overcoming it, if he is to achieve the confidence and mental toughness which permit him to deal with a race rationally, analytically, effectively.

Innate or acquired, these are the qualities which determine whether the skipper does his job. They enable him to occupy himself with steering and with the strategic and tactical determinatives of the race. They prevent him from being preoccupied with the jobs of his crew, with the speed of his boat, with the presence of his competitors.

9. The Crew's Job

We were halfway down the long, last leg of the Ice Bowl under spinnaker when Bob Reeves passed us to windward. I maneuvered to blanket him but he was obviously escaping. My incredulous crew said, "He's going faster than we are!"

"Yes," I said, "under spinnaker, he always does."

The crew's reply came loud and clear: "Don't tell me that! I don't want to hear it! Now make this boat go faster than his!"

"Well," I said, "we could try the board up a little higher and our weight a little farther aft and—" We passed him in about three minutes and beat him by a hundred yards. It is said that crews lose races and skippers win them. This is clearly not so: racing is a team effort; each member of the team makes an equal and essential contribution.

The crew member must provide a great deal more than performance. He must be able to think, but to restrict his thinking to factors pertinent to racing success, and he must contribute to morale. Indeed, in the long run, his contribution to morale may be of the greatest significance. But performance must come first. Once appointed to the team he must work to perfect his performance.

Few major sports, if any, are undertaken with less practice than sailboat racing—and consequently, of course, those crews willing to practice can excel. A basic characteristic of the good crew member must be a willingness to practice. Sail handling must become automatic. Spinnakers must be raised, jibed, lowered, and changed in all conditions with an ease which never limits their use. Helmsman and crew must be able to sail the boat around the course without being distracted from their primary mission—winning. Each crew member must have specific duties—all so well understood that they can be performed without thought in the heat of battle—and there should be no doubt under any circumstances about who is responsible for what. Each crew member should know the limitation of his responsibilities, should avoid usurping those of his mates, but should be capable of assuming them in a crisis. Practice must include data reporting and modifications of sail trim as well as performance. It has been well said that poor or incomplete practice results in poor or incomplete performance.

Crews should be selected for their enthusiasm. Once practice is under way and the demands of racing have been met, an assessment of determination can be made. Does each member's enthusiasm hold up under pressure? Practice will perfect performance, and experience can provide understanding, but there is no substitute for determination and desire. The other essential attribute of a good crew is stability under pressure, and unfortunately no amount of desire and determination can make up for a lack of that stability. Fumbling and confusion in times of crisis destroy more than the immediate situation. If confusion undermines precision, or if the desire to win is not clearly paramount, a replacement is in order.

The owner/skipper/helmsman must be willing to include the crew member in all possible preparations and decisions. If he is to be a part of the team, he must be given the opportunity to contribute to it on every occasion. The boat should be set up so as to enhance his efficiency. The best way to achieve this is to allow him to participate in the construction of the running rigging, and to arrange it as he deems appropriate. His contributions must be recognized, the excellence of his performance appreciated. When the boat wins, the crew member is as responsible as the skipper; he deserves the same satisfactions as the skipper. His enthusiasm for sacrifice will depend upon his own perception of the significance of his contribution.

And sacrifices must be made. For the satisfaction of being part of a winning team, for the satisfaction of being the best possible crew member on a winning team, he must be willing to endure not only discomfort but pain. He must forgo the pleasure of watching the race, of appreciating the beauty of the sky and the water, of analyzing the determinants of strategy. He must concentrate on the jib telltales, the spinnaker luff, the compass, knowing that to look away is to let down the team. He must tolerate—he must willingly accept—the skipper, the skipper's anxieties, the skipper's complaints, occasionally the skipper's profanity. He need not enjoy pain and disparagement, but he must accept them too if by doing so he improves the chances of winning.

However, the great crew member rises above mere acceptance. He does not think in terms of sacrifice; he delights in adversity for the opportunity it provides to make an even greater contribution. By being indefatigable in his own efforts, he establishes a standard that demands the utmost of the other members of the crew. His only question is, Are we doing our best? He believes wholeheartedly, unquestioningly, in victory. He not only accepts the leadership of the skipper, he insists that his authority be maintained. He supports the skipper, encouraging him even—particularly—when things are going badly. Since the accomplishments of the team, the performance of the boat, depend to a major degree upon the skipper's psyche, reinforcing that psyche may be the greatest contribution to victory that the crew can make. The great crew member senses the skipper's mood, his response to the situation, and complements, restores, or re-creates the attitude appropriate to victory. He never deprecates the skipper or his decisions and their consequences. Critiques are held ashore or after the race, never while it is going on.

Racing success is the consequence of a team effort, or more precisely, a mutually supportive coordination of skipper and crew. The inefficiency of the poor crew preoccupies the skipper, diverting him from his primary responsibilities. To the extent that his crew is competent to keep the boat at top speed, manage her maneuvers without a flaw, and provide the data for appropriate tactical and strategic decisions, the skipper is freed to concentrate on his own job. To the extent that the crew by an example of confidence, enthusiasm, and indefatigability transmits similar feelings to the skipper, the crew determines the behavior of the skipper and increases the likelihood of victory.

10. A Classic Example

By watching a race—a race involving one's own usual competitors —one can obtain a clear demonstration of how racing success is determined. I commend such observation to all racing sailors. The perspective available to a participant is markedly limited both by his preoccupation with his own success and by his misapprehension of the behavior of his competitors. There is a tendency to view the entire race as if one were its central determinant, as if success were dependent on one's own talents, and failure on one's own deficits. In reality, as any uninvolved observer will affirm, most competitors take themselves out of the running by making mistakes. The winner is merely the one who makes fewer mistakes, by virtue of a more single-minded concentration on the things that matter. I recently watched (from a whaler, close to the action) a race of a major Soling regatta on Long Island Sound in mid-May. The best of my East Coast competitors were there, and their behavior was most revealing. The following is an entirely accurate description of the race, but names are omitted to protect the guilty.

The race (the third in a series of five) was started at 1:30 P.M., about twenty minutes after the appearance of the local Long Island

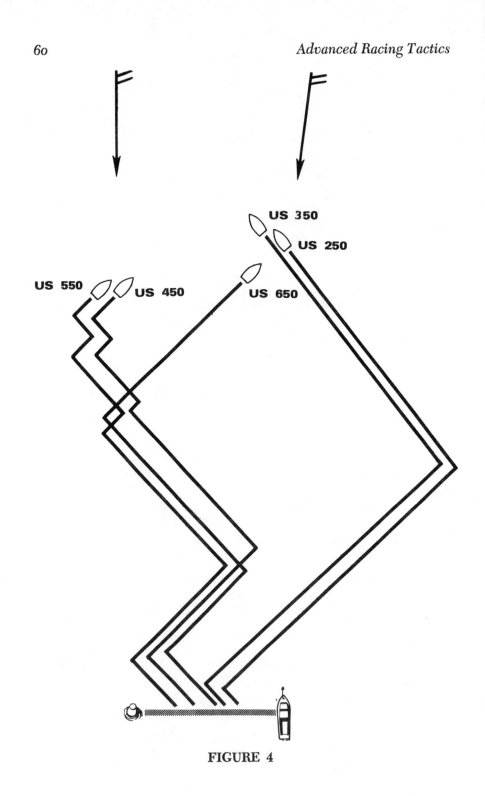

US 350

US 250

US 550   US 450   US 650

FIGURE 4

Sound sea breeze (Figure 4). The predicted northerly had never reached the surface and the local sea breeze had been delayed both by a subsidence inversion and its accompanying cloud cover and by the conduction inversion above the cold water. As the sky cleared, the sea breeze filled in; at the start, it was blowing 6–8 knots from 210°, and it was steadily increasing in velocity. A 10°-to-15° veer could be expected within the next half hour as its velocity increased. A significant fan effect was not likely to be evident this far from shore (more than two miles), and the current was uniform across the course. The line was square to the wind, but although the fleet was well spaced, the "hotshots" were concentrated at the weather end. I presumed this meant that they were as aware as I of the need for an early tack to port.

U.S. 550 had the ideal start, right against the committee boat with the gun. U.S. 350 and U.S. 250 hung back to start late at the weather end, and both tacked to port as soon as they crossed the line. U.S. 550 continued on starboard, presumably covering U.S. 450, which was essentially tied with her for the series lead. Within three minutes, the majority of the fleet was on port. When U.S. 650, which was apparently doing the best of those on starboard, tacked, U.S. 450 and U.S. 550 tacked beneath her. These three seemed to be in the lead. Within a quarter mile U.S. 550 worked up under both U.S. 450 and U.S. 650, and disregarding the expected veer, tacked. U.S. 450 was forced to bear away astern and U.S. 650 was forced to tack on U.S. 550's lee bow. Subsequently U.S. 450 also tacked to starboard and these three continued offshore as the majority of the fleet held to port. When they were two-thirds of the way to the lay line, the expected veer became evident. U.S. 350 and U.S. 250, which had held on port from the line loomed impressively on the horizon. U.S. 650 tacked to port and U.S. 550 followed suit twenty yards to leeward. U.S. 450 was able to tack close on U.S. 550's bow, and forced her back to starboard. U.S. 450 then tacked to cover as U.S. 650 raced for the starboard-tack lay line. It soon became evident that she was far too late. U.S. 350, with U.S. 250 close astern, crossed U.S. 650 by a hundred yards and tacked to cover.

U.S. 650, with the best boat speed in the fleet, had lost the leg by a hundred yards because she had failed to recognize the over-riding need to sail toward the expected veer. U.S. 550 had given up her dominant early position for a short-term tactical advantage, had subsequently lost that advantage, and had been forced far to the left. U.S. 450, busy covering U.S. 550, was faring little better than her rival. U.S. 650, by setting off determinedly to the right once she recognized her error, had salvaged third. But U.S. 350 and U.S. 250, occupied with the persistent shift that mattered, rather than preoccupied with tactical trivia, had developed nearly insurmountable leads.

U.S. 550 eventually found herself on the port-tack lay line and rounded the weather mark eighth, with U.S. 450 sixth. These two moved up on the reaches, but U.S. 450 managed to become involved in a luffing match. At the leeward mark, U.S. 350 and U.S. 250 had doubled their lead over U.S. 650, and she was seventy-five yards ahead of U.S. 450. U.S. 550 was in sixth, behind U.S. 150. On the second beat, U.S. 350 tacked twice to cover U.S. 250, and then both took off side by side to the right, with U.S. 650 following. U.S. 550 tacked to starboard and U.S. 450 tacked to cover her. Since there was little evidence of a persistent shift in this leg (perhaps a slight back as the wind began to die), boat speed was the major determinant of success. U.S. 550 worked through both U.S. 150 and U.S. 450 to round the weather mark fourth, close behind U.S. 650, and to gain significantly on the leaders. She was now within striking distance, but—as she had done on the first beat—she soon threw away all she had gained.

U.S. 450 and U.S. 150, rounding close astern of U.S. 550, jibed to port and took off to the left of the run. U.S. 550, disdaining to cover and ignoring the likelihood of a significant back in the dying air, followed the leaders on starboard. The wind did back, however, and U.S. 450 and U.S. 150 to the left had a far better sailing angle into the mark than the four leaders, all of whom had continued on starboard. U.S. 450 was forced to jibe sooner than U.S. 150, which retained an inside overlap at the mark and rounded third, close astern of U.S. 250. U.S. 550, having sailed the latter part of the leg at a poor angle, was now back in sixth, just astern of U.S. 650.

In the backed wind the weather mark (moved for the second beat because of the earlier veer) was considerably to the right of upwind. U.S. 350, leading by a mere fifty yards, took off on the obviously favored port tack, and her closest contenders, U.S. 250 and U.S. 150, doing the right thing, followed. U.S. 550 again tacked to starboard, taking what was the minor tack, and in the now increasing wind, the tack away from the probable veer. U.S. 450 again covered. The race was no longer in doubt. U.S. 350 increased her lead, and U.S. 150, sailing higher than U.S. 250, worked into second.

U.S. 450 was a distant fourth; U.S. 650 was fifth; and U.S. 550, which had thrown away opportunity after opportunity, sixth.

The boat speed of U.S. 350, the winner, may have been equal to that of her competitors, but it was certainly no better. She won the race by doing the strategically right thing on the first leg and then, with clear air, maintaining her lead as most of her competitors took themselves out of contention. U.S. 250 and U.S. 150 sailed smart races, doing what was correct again and again. Instead of tacking or jibing away in the vain hope of finding an advantage contrary to reasonable expectations, they followed the leader when she was (usually) doing the right thing. U.S. 650 and U.S. 550, with the best boat speed in the fleet, by seeking immediate tactical advantage or the chance to recover in a single gamble all they had lost, repeatedly gave up their excellent positions. U.S. 450, preoccupied with her relationship to U.S. 550 in the series standings, covered her so assiduously that she fared little better. It is reassuring to find that our competitors make the same foolish mistakes that we do, and, more important, to recognize that merely doing the right thing in a few obvious situations will usually bring victory.

II. *Tactical Principles*

11. Clear Air

We raced International 14's in dead light air in a multiclass regatta at Cambridge recently. As we approached the second weather mark, we had lapped the late-starting fleets and were confronted with a mass of drifting Penguins and Comets. I was leading and carefully covering Bob Reeves from a position two hundred feet abeam to windward as we neared the starboard-tack lay line. In the fluky air I wanted to be certain to tack ahead of him, as I knew that otherwise he might slip past to windward or to leeward. I watched his every move through the mainsail window, and we were about as soon as his jib sheet was let go. Unfortunately, however, his was a false tack intended to send us (slightly under the lay line) directly into the mass at the mark. In the drifting conditions I didn't dare tack back immediately, so instead I held hopefully on into what seemed to be better air ahead. I slipped past boats without steer-ageway, preserving my own speed as carefully as possible, struggled through the melee at the mark, and finally squeezed between two Penguins which had hit it and were rounding a second time. When I emerged (I thought triumphantly), there was Bob Reeves sailing gaily by, two boat lengths ahead, to windward of all the confusion.

In the 1969 International Team Match at Kingston, Canadian Bruce Moyle had us trapped on the lay line, dead to leeward of him. He and his crew sat on their gunwale leaning inboard with their sails flapping. My crew and I were fully hiked out, working against the leverage of full sails in a 15-knot breeze—and going no faster than our opponent. During a recent team race on the Chesapeake, St. John Martin and I each took on a following opponent, sat on his wind for an entire weather leg, and brought our last boat from a leg behind to a winning 2–3–4 combination. Bad air can be very bad.

I can remember four separate incidents in a two-week period when I picked up one or more positions by rounding a weather mark into clear air on a run. The key is, of course, to do it differently from the others. Watch the boats ahead (and astern). If they swing wide before jibing, go inside and blanket them; if they go off on starboard jibe, each in the other's bad air, try port; if they luff, go to leeward; if they bear away sharply, reach over to windward of them.

The leeward-mark approach is fraught with the dangers of wind interference. Indeed, in an adverse current an entire fleet may be stopped in its tracks, with the only remaining wind off to the sides, where it is not obstructed by the cloud of Dacron. As the fleet condenses after the wide spacing on the run, it congeals. I remember a light-air finish in a team race in Bermuda in which four boats came down the run abreast. The outer boat on each side headed up abruptly near the finish line and reached across in front of the two middle boats, which had sailed the straight-line, shortest distance. Walt Lawson in his Penguin days, was noted for reaching in under the fleet from a position far to the side. He would often pass ahead of an entire group whose members thought they had an inside overlap at the leeward mark. Separation from the disturbance produced by the fleet provides an advantage in speed that easily compensates for the extra distance sailed.

An air flow is disturbed by any object in its path. It is forced to lift over, deviate around, or eddy through an obstruction. It is reduced in velocity, it has been deflected from its true direction, and worst of all, instead of flowing smoothly it is filled with eddies. Because it attaches poorly to the leeward surfaces of sails, it produces a much-reduced aerodynamic force. Disturbed air is of two types—that caused by general interference with the air flow by the fleet as a whole, and that caused by blanketing and backwinding by neighboring, individual boats. The presence of an entire fleet causes the air flow to lift, deviate, and eddy so that the boats within the fleet receive nothing but disturbed air and only boats separated from the fleet receive clear air. The dense massing of the fleet at the starting line creates a disturbance that slows individual boats for a prolonged period. The air is so disturbed by boats coming down the second reach that boats on the left side of the beat are adversely affected. The presence of the fleet always produces a disturbance, but the effect is particularly severe in light air. Separation from the fleet is always desirable; the best way to separate, of course, is to get ahead. The leaders keep moving farther and farther ahead, in part because they are separating from the fleet.

Each boat continually disturbs the air flow that reaches her, and the result is a blanket zone to leeward and a backwind zone aft and to windward (Figure 5). The blanket zone is a rapidly narrowing cone of turbulent air extending dead to leeward (in the direction of the apparent wind); at its base it is the width of the boat's sails, and ends in a point, approximately five boat lengths away. Even three boat lengths to leeward, the zone is so narrow that a leeward boat can traverse it without much harm. If, however, the weather boat bears away as the leeward boat enters the zone (the masthead fly indicates when this occurs), she can trap her, slow her, and keep her astern. The backwind zone is larger, extending to windward for a boat length and aft for three to five boat lengths, with only gradual narrowing. Within the zone, the air flow is not only turbulent but deviated so that it will head a following boat. The backwind zone is not more turbulent than the blanket zone; its greater harmfulness is occasioned by its position. The blanket zone extends *across* the course of a boat to leeward and can be easily traversed. The backwind zone extends for many boat lengths *along* the course, so a boat astern or astern and to windward must remain in it continuously. Once an opponent has acquired an ahead and to leeward position, the windward boat can only escape by falling back, which means losing two to three boat lengths, or by tacking or breaking through to leeward. The backwind zone parallels the sail trim (the sheeting angle), and therefore extends farther to windward on a close-hauled course than on a reach. On a beam reach the windward boat may be able to maintain a position with her bow to the stern of the leeward boat, but this position is impossible to maintain on a beat. Since the boat affected by blanketing or backwinding can progress at a speed no greater than that of the boat

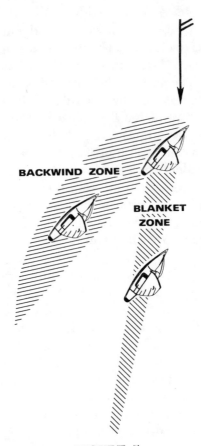

BACKWIND ZONE

BLANKET
ZONE

FIGURE 5

causing the disturbance, it is more of a disadvantage to be blanketed or backwinded by a slow boat than by a fast boat.

The great challenge of sailboat racing lies in identifying the
more beneficial or less harmful of two possible solutions. The simple
act of tacking away from a boat on the lee bow way result in the
loss of the race (especially if she sails on into a header). On the other
hand, if one sails continually in bad air, one will soon see the leaders
(in any decent-sized fleet) move completely out of reach. An essential element of a starting plan is a means of acquiring clear air. And
throughout the remainder of the race, retaining clear air must be a
constant concern. The need to choose between the strategically
advantageous course and clear air constantly recurs. The boat that

is able to sail the greatest portion of the race in clear air while going in the right direction wins. Sailing in the right direction must always come first, but each segment of the course must be selected so as to be as free as possible of the disturbance created by other boats.

Careful advance planning of each leg should permit progress in the right direction without significant interference. But at some point other boats, whether intentionally or not will be in a position where they disturb the air. If there is no *major* advantage to continuing in the disturbed air, separation should be attempted as soon as the disturbance is recognized. The standard techniques of escape from disturbed air are as follows:

Start:	Tack to port
	Bear away and foot through to leeward
Windward Leg:	Tack
	Bear away and foot through to leeward
	Point higher and lift above
Windward Marks:	Overstand and reach in
	Approach on port and tack beneath, close to the mark
Reaches:	Sail high (in gusty or increasing winds)
	Sail low (in steady or decreasing winds)
Runs:	Luff
	Jibe
Leeward Marks:	Sail wide and reach in high on the wind

There are three harmful misconceptions concerning wind interference. One is the belief that blanketing is the significant cause of this difficulty. Actually, blanketing is of only minimum significance to windward; then backwind extending aft from an opponent's weather quarter or stem is the real threat. Backwind is the significant danger on the reach as well; only on the run is blanketing a practical weapon or frequent hazard. (Bearing away from a position close aboard an opponent's weather bow while beating is, of course, an extremely effective slowing maneuver in team racing, but it must be done from very close aboard.)

The second misconception is that major wind interference occurs only in light air. It occurs in all winds and is significant in all airs. Because we spend more time on the course in light air, we have more time to detect its effects in that situation (and disturbed air moving at low velocity is less capable of attached flow than disturbed air moving at high velocity). But think how the fleet spreads out immediately after the start, how it bunches on the mark approach and spreads again after the rounding, how the leaders always get farther and farther ahead. Clear air makes the difference —in all winds.

And finally, just as blanketing is not the major cause of bad air, so a position to windward is not its necessary cure. If we look at the water when the wind begins or on a gusty or fluky day, we can detect patches of wind on its surface. These patches obviously have windward sides; i.e. it is possible to be to windward of them. In the same way, better air may be present to leeward of the fleet. The natural variations in wind distribution may mean that a boat a hundred feet to leeward will have wind when those to windward do not. We lost one great chance to beat the (eventually) undefeated English team at the 1969 International Team Match when the boats in our 2–3–4 combination sailed into a hole on the penultimate (windward) leg of a ten-leg course and watched Johnson Wooderson sail past 150 feet to leeward. We hadn't thought to cover to leeward.

12. Shifting Gears

I am impressed by the remarkably similar ability of boats which gather from many different fleets and sailing experiences for a world's championship. In no other situation do twenty boats of almost identical windward ability meet each other overlapped at mark after mark. This is a great opportunity to learn tactics, since tactics are most significant among boats of equal ability. The fast boat has little need for tactics; there are no competitors nearby to contend with her. ("Nothing makes a helmsman look better than a fast boat.") And the slow boat needs them even less; she must avoid maneuvering with other boats. She relies upon daring and takes the big risk to win occasionally. Among boats of equal ability, however, tactics determine the outcome. Tactics at the start determine whether or not a boat will finish in the first ten. Tactics on the beat to the finish determine which place among the first ten the boat will secure. And the effectiveness of tactics ultimately depends upon boat ability—the ability of the skipper to obtain the kind of boat performance optimal for the situation. In a long series no amount of tactical skill can compensate for an inability to modify performance appropriately. The helmsman must be able to "shift gears," to in-

duce the boat to go when he wants it to go, point when he wants it
to point, make less (or more) leeway as he chooses.

At the 1973 Soling World's Championship series at Quiberon it
was evident that the helmsmen who could "shift gears" appropriately and immediately, when necessary, came out on top and that
those (including me) who were less able to do so fell astern. In
my chartered boat I could attain speeds and other performance
responses as well as the best who were present. But there was
always the lag, the time required to retrim, measure the effect
achieved, and retrim again. The Danes, who came fully prepared
after weeks of training, seemed able to "shift gears" instantaneously
(and finished first and second). The Dutch, who had trained in
similar fashion (perhaps less assiduously), and the experienced
Swedes took a little more time to make adjustments and occasionally, for long periods, were unable to do so (despite the potential,
frequently demonstrated, of being as fast as the Danes). The de-
siderata of performance must have been clearly recognized by all of
them—and given the time all could reach the optimal "speed made
good" (Vmg), to windward, the ideal combination of the three
determinants of windward performance—speed, pointing, and leeway. Their training had undoubtedly provided them with an understanding of the hull and sail trim that would, in the absence of
other boats, enable them to obtain the ideal combinations of high
speed, high pointing, and low leeway for the various conditions
(caused chiefly by alterations in wind velocity and wave characteristics) that they would meet. Differences in the rate and success of
response by the competitors to changing conditions determine the
outcome of most regattas, but at the World's the ability to adjust
performance to tactical purposes was the ultimate determinant. And
this the Danes could do. The Swedes could point, the Dutch could
go, and other may have dealt with leeway as successfully, but only
the Danes seemed able to get whatever they wanted *whenever* they
wanted it.

Usually the best result to windward, tactically and strategically,
is achieved by seeking the optimal performance combination (the
best Vmg). On many occasions, however, it is better to sacrifice a
little Vmg, better to sacrifice one element of windward performance, in order to enhance another and thereby deal successfully
with a neighboring boat. The fastest boat (the one with the greatest
potential or even actual Vmg) will not reach the weather mark first
if she spends the beat in dirty air or is forced away from the ad-

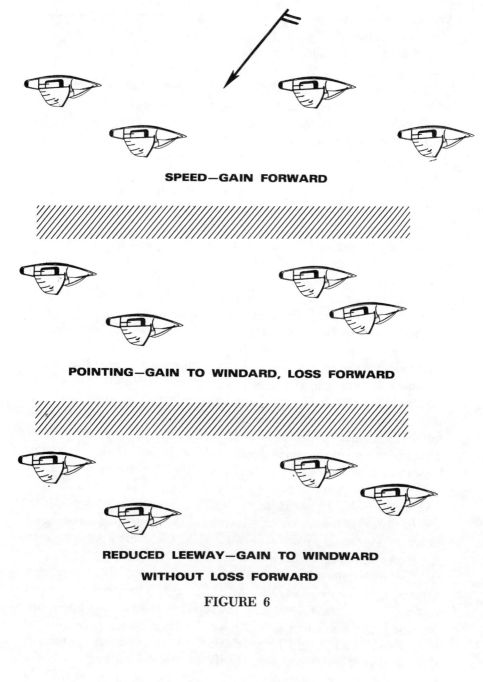

SPEED—GAIN FORWARD

POINTING—GAIN TO WINDARD, LOSS FORWARD

REDUCED LEEWAY—GAIN TO WINDWARD
WITHOUT LOSS FORWARD

FIGURE 6

vantageous side of the course or has to tack repeatedly to obtain clear air. At one time a boat may need to go, at another to point, at still another to reduce her leeway for a specific purpose—to pass a neighboring boat or to avoid being passed (Figure 6).

Sometimes speed is all that matters. Clearly this is true at the start; the boat that attains speed sooner than her neighbors, and can reach a speed greater than that of her neighbors, obviously wins the start. After completing a tack or hitting a large wave, reattainment of this speed sooner than the neighboring competitors is the only concern. Under these circumstances pointing is of little consequence. Once the boat is up to speed, in most conditions pointing and leeway become more significant than speed; but until then, the greatest relative gains derive from attaining additional speed. The "gear" for starting or for the reacquisition of speed which has been lost is "starting gear." The trim for this "gear" includes draft full and forward, marked twist, and loose leech. This trim results in a full leading edge to induce attached flow, a low angle of incidence to maintain attached flow, and a total aerodynamic force well aligned with the heading of the boat. To achieve this trim, the jib leads should be inboard, the jib sheet eased, the jib luff tension released, and the jibstay allowed to sag through minimal mainsheet and backstay tension; the main boom should be to leeward of the midline, the mainsheet eased, the mast relatively straight, and the Cunningham tensioned. It may not be necessary to modify the main luff tension directly during a start, since alterations of mast bend achieved by hiking in small boats and by the addition of backstay tension in large boats automatically modify it appropriately. As the boat comes up to speed and the crew begins to hike more and more (which they should avoid doing until the boat is moving well) or the backstay is tensioned progressively, the increasing mast bend provides a gradual aftward movement of the draft appropriate to the increasing speed (Table 1).

The real determinant of starting success and the "lever" for shifting into the "go gear" is the mainsheet. The helmsman must restrain his impulse to pull it in too soon. As the starting line is approached, the helmsman should have the main traveler-control line in his hand, and should be gradually pulling the carriage toward the midline. Then from a markedly twisted condition, the main leech must be very gradually tensioned with the mainsheet. Early leech tensioning (at a low speed) increases total aerodynamic force chiefly in the form of side (heeling) force and thus increases leeway

TABLE 1

SAIL TRIM FOR VARIOUS "GEARS" IN MODERATE AIR

"GEAR"	MAIN					JIB			
	SHEETING ANGLE (BOOM POSITION)	MAST BEND	DRAFT	DRAFT POSITION (CUNNINGHAM)	TWIST (MAINSHEET)	LEAD (LATERAL)	LEAD (FORE AND AFT)	SHEET TENSION	LUFF TENSION
"Starting"	Wide	Minimal	Full	Forward	Marked	Inboard	Forward	Minimal	Minimal
"Go"	Close	Moderate	Moderate	Aft	Minimal	Intermediate	Intermediate	Moderate	Moderate
"Pointing"	Midline	Increased	Decreased	Aft	*Very* Little	Inboard	Aft	Marked	Minimal
"Low Leeway"	Wide	Marked	Flat	Forward	Moderate	Outboard	Aft	Moderate	Marked

and hull resistance to a greater extent than forward thrust. Not until the boat has attained full speed should this "gear shift" be completed—the mast bent, the leech fully tensioned, the traveler and jib leads moved outboard to the extent appropriate to the conditions. Proper execution of this gradual shifting of "gears" is what distinguishes the successful starter and permits his boat to jump out of the pack into clear air.

Sometimes leeway is all that matters. Leeway and speed are opposite faces of the same coin. It is the movement of the boat through the water, its speed, that produces the hydrodynamic side force necessary to balance the aerodynamic side force. Thus when the boat is moving at high speed, leeway is minimal, but when it is moving slowly, particularly when it is moving slowly compared to the wind speed (high aerodynamic side force requiring a high hydrodynamic side force), leeway has a major influence on performance. Leeway is of paramount concern in very light air and in very heavy air. The situations which require a shift to "starting gear"—starting and the reattainment of speed after slowing—require attention to leeway. Fortunately, the trim appropriate to the reacquisition of speed, particularly the loose, open, twisted leech (on both main and jib) results in little leeway. Particularly in *very* light or very heavy air, a reduction in leeway requires, in addition, the flattening of the sails—marked mast bend is the best technique—and their sheeting well off the center line. It is often amazing, even to the initiated, to see a boat in "low-leeway gear" move through and over a fleet of tight-leeched, full-sailed, closely trimmed boats in a glassy calm—just as she will in a gale.

Sometimes pointing is all that matters. The fourth "gear" is the "pointing gear." Once the boat is out on the course and moving in clear air (except when the air is very light or heavy), pointing produces the greatest dividends for the sacrifices required. In moderate air, variations in speed (among boats of reasonably comparable ability), limited by the severe restrictions of wave making, are slight, but variations in pointing may be great, and at 35°–45° to the desired course they result in major differences in the distance sailed. Tactically, pointing is an extremely useful weapon. *It should not be employed, however, when conditions demand the acquisition of speed or a reduction in leeway.* Because pointing is attainable only at the expense of an increase in leeway and/or a loss in speed, it is disastrous at the start, during an attempt to regain speed, or in very light or heavy air. When tacking on the lee bow of an opponent, pointing should not be attempted immediately; first the boat must be brought up to speed in "go gear."

Pointing is the "gear" that sorts out the boats on the beat to the finish. The boat which can point can force her rivals about and successively tack back beneath them until they are driven to or beyond the lay line. In moderate air trim for pointing requires movement of the draft aft (through increased mast bend), minimization of twist through increased mainsheet tension), and movement of the leads inboard. A boat that is up to speed can be shifted as circumstances require from "go gear," with relatively full, moderately loose-leeched sails, to "pointing gear," with flattened, tight-leeched sails. When a boat is attacked on the lee bow, if the main-sheet and the backstay come in *together,* the boat, though slowing slightly, will move up to windward out of the backwind of the attacker. The essential point is that nothing can be obtained without some sacrifice; merely tightening the leech would mean that the resulting increased leeway would offset the improved pointing. The loss in speed due to the flattening of the sail is accepted as the price of the improvement in pointing.

Fifteen seconds before the start you are in "starting gear," draft forward, leads inboard, leech twisted. As you cross the line you are shifting gradually into "go gear" (optimal Vmg); the draft is coming aft, the leech is being tightened, the leads are moving outboard. You hit a big wave and shift back to "starting gear." The wind velocity drops dramatically, and you shift to "low-leeway gear"; the leech is eased, the mast is bent, the leads are moved farther outboard. The wind increases again, and you shift through "starting gear" up to "go gear." As you approach the finish line, you spot a threatening boat on your weather quarter. You tack and then tack again on her lee bow. At the completion of the tack you momentarily shift down toward "starting gear," with eased leech and straightened mast. Then as speed is regained you gradually shift into "pointing gear," with the mainsheet and the backstay tightened to produce a tight leech without excessive side force and leeway. You move up across her bow and she is forced to tack.

13. The Utilization of Wind Shifts

A persistent shift is one in which the wind changes direction and during the period of the leg being sailed does not shift back to its initial direction. It may shift abruptly to a new direction and not vary thereafter (a completed persistent shift), or it may progressively or erratically shift further and further from its initial direction (a progressive persistent shift) (Figure 7). An oscillating shift, on the other hand, is one in which the wind shifts from its initial direction and then returns to (or beyond) it (Figure 8). A wind flow that oscillates between two extremes every five minutes will result in a persistent shift during a four-minute beat. The appearance and disappearance of a sea breeze during an afternoon will create two persistent shifts for one-design sailors racing on beats of twenty-minute duration but will constitute a set of oscillating shifts for a cruising-boat sailor in a long-distance race. The management of the shift is determined as much by the duration of the beat as by the origin of the change in the wind flow.

Rules for Windward Strategy

I. A persistent shift is of paramount importance.

    A. If a persistent shift is expected (has not yet appeared or

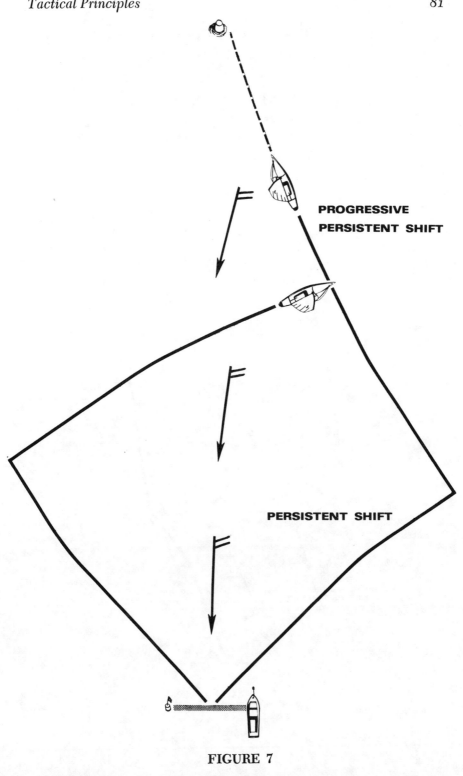

PROGRESSIVE
PERSISTENT SHIFT

PERSISTENT SHIFT

FIGURE 7

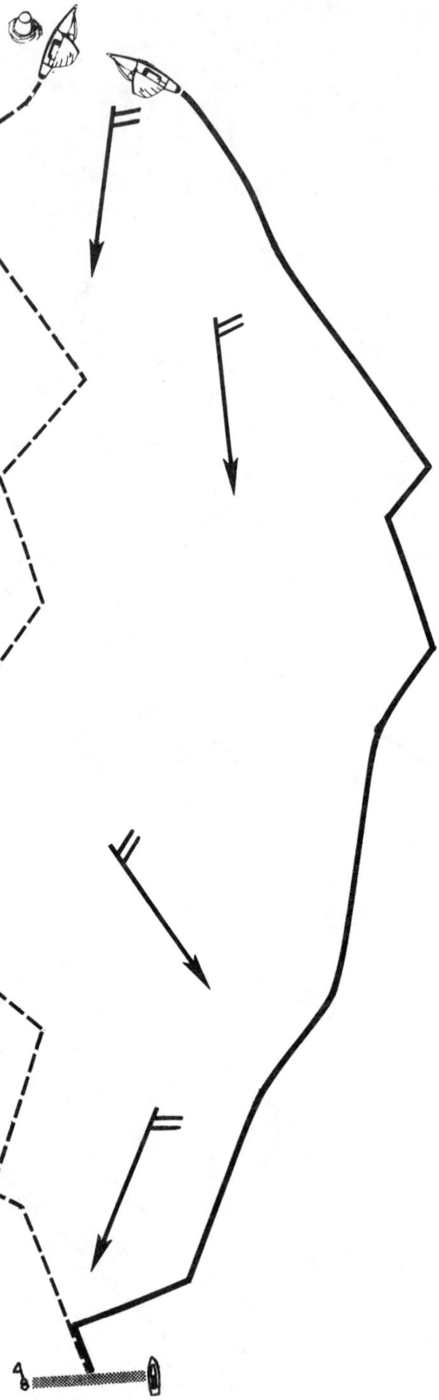

FIGURE 8

can be expected to progress further), the optimum course is the headed tack toward the shift and *then* the lifted tack toward the mark. To achieve this course,

1. Tack toward the shift.
   a) Avoid the lifted tack initially, since it is directed away from the shift.
   b) Tack from the lift toward the shift (into a header) as soon as it is recognized. The farther one sails away from a progressive persistent shift the more one loses.
   c) Beware of a lift significantly beyond the range of lifts observed before the start or during preceding beats.

2. Continue on the headed tack until nearer to the new lay line (the lay line in the new, shifted wind) than any competitor, then tack.
   a) The length of the initial tack toward the shift will be inversely proportional to the degree of the shift. The lay line is reached at the starting line when a 45° shift occurs at the start, whereas if a 20° shift occurs after the boat has sailed a major portion of the distance toward the original lay line, the new lay line may have already been reached.
   b) The boat that makes her final approach tack on the new lay line will sail the shortest course to the weather mark.
   c) If the shift progresses, the new lay line will be a curved line providing a progressive lift into the mark. The approach tack should then be made short of the apparent lay line.

3. Keep inside and to windward of competitors for the final approach tack to the mark. However, overstanding is always detrimental and therefore one should never risk overstanding in order to be inside and to windward. When in doubt, particularly when the mark is still distant, tack ahead and to leeward of the competition, so as to avoid overstanding.

B. *If a persistent shift has ceased to progress (if the conditions which caused the shift have reached their maximum effect), the most likely subsequent shift will be an oscillating shift, in the opposite direction.* Tack away from the direction of the shift.

II. Oscillating shifts may appear in the presence or in the absence of a persistent shift. If oscillating shifts are detected (by compass observation prior to the start, or by direct observation),

  1. Keep to the lifted tack—sailing toward an expected header.
    a) Determine (by the compass) the range of variations in the wind direction and keep to the tack that is lifted relative to the median wind (midway between the extremes). Sailing the lifted tack in each shift shortens the course to the weather mark.
    b) Tack, when the course is headed relative to the median wind. Usually a significant header is presumed and tacking is justified when the compass shows a heading 5° below the median.

  2. Keep ahead and to leeward of competitors.
    a) From this position, in a lift, one is always sailing toward the next expected header, since in a randomly oscillating wind the next shift after a lift will eventually be a header.
    b) From this position, when a header appears, the boat will be farther to the side of the course than her competitors—in the position that results in the greatest gain from a single shift (as in a single persistent shift).
    c) Avoid reaching either lay line until very near the mark. A shift cannot shorten the course of a boat on the lay line (a straight line to the mark) but may shorten the course of any boat below the lay line. The farther the lay line lies ahead the greater is the time available for another, beneficial heading shift to appear.
    d) Cover from ahead and to leeward and, if possible, inside on the tack toward the rhumb line. Avoid continuing a tack away from the rhumb line unless it is clearly lifted to the median wind (midway between

the previously noted extremes). Tack back inside and to leeward of competitors when in doubt.

e) When a competitor (or competitors) ahead and to leeward receives a heading shift, continue the tack in progress until
  (1) Headed beyond the median wind
  (2) Headed as much as that competitor
  (3) He tacks
  Thereafter tack ahead and to leeward of him.

f) Covering from dead to windward results in a loss with every shift (whether a lift or a header) and therefore should not be undertaken except in the final stages of a beat.

3. Bear in mind that a shift will cause the greatest gain or loss when boats are aligned laterally across the wind, as they are at the start. It is therefore particularly important to be on the lifted tack at the start and to be able to tack to the lifted tack at the time of the first shift after the start.

4. When in doubt, don't tack. It is better to continue on a tack through a header so as to be farther to the side of the course in the next expected header than to tack inadvertently away from the next expected heading shift.

5. Be alert for a persistent shift even while tacking in oscillating headers.

a) If the compass indicates a lift beyond the range of the expected oscillations, suspect a progressive persistent shift and tack toward it immediately.

b) Sail through minor headers so as to move to the side of the course from which a persistent shift is expected.

Rules for Downwind Strategy

I. Assume the jibe which at the predetermined ideal sailing angle is closest to the rhumb line unless
  1. A major advantage in the form of reduced adverse or increased favorable current, stronger wind, or larger waves exists on the opposite side of the course, or

2. A persistent shift is expected.

II. A persistent shift is of paramount importance. If a persistent shift is expected (has not yet appeared or can be expected to progress further),

1. Assume the jibe away from the shift and continue on that jibe until just short of the new lay line (the lay line at the optimal sailing angle in the new, shifted wind). A jibe away from the persistent shift at the optimal sailing angle carries the boat into an increasingly advantageous position for the return jibe to the mark. If the persistent shift is progressive, the return jibe to the mark, initiated from a position just short of the new lay line, will provide an increasingly advantageous course, higher and higher on the wind (Figure 9).

2. Early in the leg, avoid the jibe that is progressively headed if the heading appears to be consequent to a persistent shift.

3. On the final approach jibe, keep outside and to leeward of competitors if a progressive persistent shift is occurring.

III. When in doubt as to whether a persistent shift will occur, sail so as to avoid major losses.

1. Jibe back toward the rhumb line early so as to be in the middle of the course about a quarter of the way to the leeward mark.

2. Keep alert to the possibility of a persistent shift. Observe the other boats to detect persistent shifts affecting the extremities of the course. When boats on the opposite jibe are being lifted (sailing at an optimal sailing angle greater than yours), or boats on the same jibe are being headed (sailing lower than you are), jibe. They may be experiencing a persistent shift, and you are sailing toward it.

IV. Oscillating shifts may appear in the presence or in the absence of a persistent shift. If oscillating shifts are detected

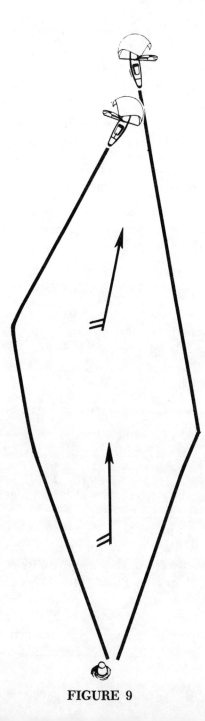

FIGURE 9

(by compass observation prior to the leg, or by direct observation), or a persistent shift has been completed,

1. Keep to the headed jibe—sailing toward an expected lift.

2. Keep the sails trimmed for the optimal sailing angle and continue on the jibe until the boat is lifted beyond the optimal angle to the median downwind line. Then jibe, and continue on this opposite jibe until once again the boat is lifted beyond the optimal angle.

General Rules for Sailing the Course

I. A persistent shift affects the sailing angles for all legs:

1. Windward legs may become one-leg beats. Keep to leeward on the major tack.

2. Know which sails (jib, large spinnaker, small spinnaker, reacher) will be appropriate to the changed sailing angles of each reach.

3. Sail the course to the next mark (check the compass); don't be misled by the change in sailing angle.

II. Oscillating shifts affect the strategy of windward and downwind legs particularly but should be detected on all legs. Decide the advantageous tack or jibe for the initiation of a subsequent beat or run by determining the direction of the last oscillation on the preceding leg.

III. When two winds are present simultaneously,

1. Sail so as to obtain maximum benefit from the wind (new or old) which will be present at the next mark when you arrive there.

2. When the new wind will be present at the time of arrival at the next mark,
   a) If its presence will cause the leg to become a beat, sail directly toward the new wind so as to be to windward of the fleet upon its arrival.
   b) If its presence will cause the leg to become a reach, run, or one-leg beat, sail away from the new wind so as to be to leeward of the fleet (at the best possible sailing angle) upon its arrival.

14. Light Air

Racing in light air requires daring, the courage of your convictions. It can be exciting, challenging, intriguing—*if* you acquire a talent for it. In no other aspect of racing is there a greater demand for drive, determination, and self-confidence. With the exercise of these traits, success in light air can be regular; otherwise frustration and failure will be inevitable. Light-air racing requires a single-minded resolve to carry on in accordance with the game plan regardless of shifts or variations in wind strength. Since there is an overabundance of variables in light air, the plan should not introduce any more. If the same plan is utilized weekend after weekend, the percentage of success will be far higher than if continuous modifications are attempted in response to each variation in wind strength or direction. (A clock that is stopped provides the correct time twice a day; a clock that is malfunctioning may never be correct!'

The worst race that I can remember (a race that I wish I could forget) was one in which each attempt to correct an error resulted in a sequence of additional errors. I was sailing my Soling in light air at SPORT; we ultimately got so far behind that we began to giggle. (I can't remember any other time that I rounded the weather mark last—and this was by a hundred yards!) My self-confidence had undoubtedly been shattered by our poor showing the day before and by the boat on our lee bow which forced us about shortly after the start. We headed for the left side of the course with a number of other good boats but without any clear purpose that I can remember. The majority of the fleet crept away on port. They soon experienced a slight increase in wind strength and a distinct veer. We decided that this was a progressive persistent shift and that we had better catch up with it. Having sailed the first quarter of the weather leg in the wrong direction, we were now about to consolidate the gain of all those who had been correct initially. By the time we reached the rhumb line the wind began to die and back. We now concluded that our original move had been correct, that we should have continued to the left, and that now, in another progressive shift, we should go back where we had come from. By this time, of course, the early port tackers were crossing hundreds of yards ahead on starboard, and as we limped back to the left, the early starboard tackers were crossing far ahead on port! I had treated each shift as progressive and persistent while boats from each side of the course, with the courage of their convictions, had sailed by in a series of oscillations.

From this elementary experience can be derived most of the principles that determine the outcome of light-air races.

Head for the advantageous side (the side with more wind)—with conviction.

1. Avoid the middle.

2. When in doubt, head for the shore.

Keep moving.

1. Stay away from other boats.

2. Check wind direction continuously.

3. Adjust sail trim continuously.

Continue the planned course.

1. Don't tack to chase patches of wind or wind available to other boats.

2. Assume that detected shifts are oscillations, until the expected major advantage is obtained.

3. Tack only when
   a) The expected advantage is acquired.
   b) A major increase in wind (with or without a shift) on the opposite side of the course is detected.

Look around continuously.
Keep to leeward on reaches and runs.

1. Sail away from a new wind so as to have a better reaching angle when it arrives.

2. Deviate toward a new wind only when beating.

The first lesson is that although it pays to select the correct direction before the start, if the leg is reasonably long, it doesn't matter very much which way you go so long as you keep going. Here is where determination and self-assurance are so necessary. It is very easy to be intimidated by an early reversal, to assume that you've "blown another one." *In light air, shifts are so unlikely to persist, unless they are accompanied by a major increase in wind, that they can be treated as oscillations.* With or without the confidence that you are doing the right thing, there is so much to be lost by "bailing out," so much to be gained by continuing, that the only practical solution is to assume that the wind will shift back, to continue in a lift.

Second, it pays to head for one side of the beat or the other. The advantage that should be sought, above all others, is more wind; in light air, major differences in boat speed are possible, and these depend upon wind velocity. More wind will be found not in the middle of the course but to one side or the other (along with advantages from the current and from persistent shifts, if any). A course in the middle of the fleet will be a course in air disturbed by the boats on each side and will require frequent tacking and consequent slowing. Most important, however, are the effects of any shifts that may occur. In each oscillation the boat farthest to the side of the course (toward the shift) gains the most.

Of course, if you can choose the advantageous side, so much the better. A careful consideration of the ODSSSIC factors will usually indicate the side toward which the boat should be sailed from the start. When in doubt, you should select the side toward the shore. The sea breeze appears first at the water's surface along the shore, and the offshore weather-system wind persists longest near the shore. Stable conditions over cool water isolate the wind aloft, while thermal turbulence over warm land brings it to the surface.

The advantages of being to the side are obtained only by continuing. And the opportunity to continue, free of disturbed air from boats ahead, depends upon the success of the start. Hence, a good start in clear air—on port tack and/or away from other boats—is extremely important in light air. Once on the presumably advantageous tack, you should continue farther to the side of the course than your competitors. If there is an advantage, you should seek the best of it, but not by chasing someone else's wind. For by the time you have reached the spot where a patch of wind appeared, it will usually be gone. Since in light air the wind is randomly distributed in any given area, the fact that it has already appeared at a particular site may mean simply that it is less likely to appear there again.

Third, look around—continuously. Although it is usually best to carry on regardless, ignoring the competition, the wind on the water, and the compass, you should be the first to detect a significant change when it does occur. A calm is a temporary condition ("Be a long calm spell if it weren't!") often due to the conflict of two present and active wind sources, or to an inversion which could dissipate at any moment. If the wind does appear in strength, you must be positioned to obtain the first and greatest benefit from it. Look around; watch boats on both sides of the course, boats in other fleets, cruising boats on the horizon, smoke ashore, color changes on the water's surface. Don't chase off to the opposite side of the course until sure that a suspected advantage will be there when you arrive, but be on the lookout for it.

Fourth, tack when you have obtained what you expected—a significant advantage over all the boats that stayed in the middle and should have lost and over all the boats that went to the opposite side of the course and might have gained. "Take what you've got when you've got it." But don't be hasty; keep going until you are sure you've got what you expected. (Remember that boats on your weather quarter are actually better off than they look, since in light air you cannot tack in 90° to cross them.) The only circumstance that warrants a tack prior to the acquisition of a significant advantage (or to reaching the lay line!) is the presence of a clear and major increase in wind strength on the opposite side of the course. If this increase in strength is accompanied by a shift toward the other side of the course, a progressive persistent shift must be presumed, a major loss must be accepted, and an immediate tack to avoid further loss must be undertaken. However, unless a distinct increase in wind strength, different from the variations previously noted, is detected, any accompanying shift should be presumed to be an oscillation. Then, with a heading shift a major gain (the expected advantage) will be noted in relation to boats on the weather quarter and the boat should be tacked. With a lifting shift the tack should merely be continued, in expectation of a subsequent shift back and a later advantage.

The same principles hold for reaching and running. Decide in advance whether it will pay to go to windward or to leeward on a reach, whether it will pay to assume starboard or port jibe on a run; then take off in the desired direction and keep going. Again, the worst place to be is in the middle; the advantages of clear air and an earlier arrival of the wind will be enjoyed by those on the extremities of the fleet.

Recently, during a long-distance race at the mouth of the Severn, we spent over an hour on one long, light-air reach. The boats that deviated toward the shore (to leeward) gained the most, but the boat that deviated to windward won the race. Those that stayed in the middle, alternately heading up or heading down to protect themselves from being passed or to catch up with an ephemeral patch of increased air flow, were passed on both sides. It takes courage to do well in light air. You must be willing to ignore the gain made by another boat, which spurts ahead during an evanescent localized increase in air flow. To chase it is to be absent when random variations in wind distribution bring air to your own position.

At the start of the final race of the 1974 Soling Bowl, Jonathan Ford and I were essentially tied for the lead far ahead of the twenty-six other competitors. The northerly was dying as a sea breeze attempted to lift it from the surface. Jonathan was over early at the congested leeward end when we broke free from the middle of the line. We continued on port into the favorable offshore current, covering Jonathan, who was a hundred yards astern and to leeward. We took two tacks to establish a position abeam to windward, between him and the mark, and when we were clearly laying it, tacked away. Jonathan continued, and as we approached the mark he was at least a quarter mile astern. But the wind had almost completely disappeared in the vicinity of the mark. It persisted to the north a few hundred yards to windward of the starboard-tack lay line, and far up the river to the west. We rounded the mark and slipped ahead on port jibe in fingers of veered air which periodically penetrated into the course from the north (Figure 10). Jonathan rounded the mark still a quarter mile astern and headed off to the west at 30° to our course. When he started to move, we jibed to cover; when he died, we jibed toward the wind, where boat after boat was slipping by, far to the east of the rhumb line. When the wind died in the east, it began to increase in the west and Jonathan began to move. We jibed back toward him, and from a position a hundred yards ahead jibed away again as the wind strengthened to the east. We were continuously just beyond the border of the surface air flow which was inexorably bringing Jonathan down to us. Finally, as we flitted to the east, the wind filled in the west—and Jonathan, the race, and the series slipped away.

As helmsman, I had violated the basic rules: head for one side or the other, keep going (on the same side of the course), and sail away from the wind on a run so as to be to leeward when it arrives. I had justified my technique by my presumed need to cover my single rival. What I had demonstrated was that, regardless of the lead and regardless of the excuse, in light air you cannot be successful if you flit from side to side. As the wind fills in from astern and the fleet overtakes from all sides, you must acquire the best potential position—not in the middle, where the air is all cut up, and certainly not in a spot which will require a dead run to the mark. *Distance may be lost, but position need not be.* Both the boats that continued to the east with an early wind advantage and those that had doggedly held off to the west for a later wind advantage eventually passed us.

My error was more fundamental, however. I had substituted caution for daring—a cardinal sin in light air. I was concerned with retaining what I had instead of utilizing the opportunities that were evident. This is a characteristic behavior pattern of the helmsman in the lead—and one that is totally inimical to success in light air. At the start, each helmsman is determined to break away for clear air and position without regard to his competitors. The farther he moves ahead, the more he looks back, and the more he becomes concerned with defense rather than attack. The advantage shifts to the opposition, as the leader sacrifices opportunity after opportunity in order to stay between his competitors and the mark. How much more threatening is the competitor gradually gaining from a hundred yards astern than one just overtaken but only a few feet astern? Protectionism is sensible in moderate and heavy air, when gains and

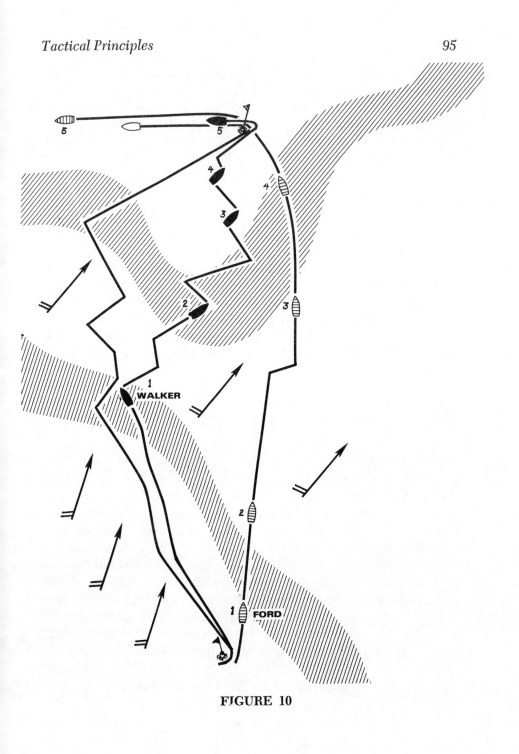

FIGURE 10

losses are usually gradual and limited, but it is disastrous in light air, when gains are dramatic and limitless.

The final element of light-air success is boat speed. Because in light air major variations in speed are possible, attention to speed can be extremely rewarding. And because in light air it is almost always desirable to maintain an unvarying course, boat speed can be given full attention. Becoming tactically involved with other boats is not only unnecessary but highly undesirable. Indeed, one of the most important determinants of boat speed is clear air, separation from other boats. Speed depends upon the maintenance of attached flow on the leeward surfaces of sails. But light-air sailing consists of a series of accelerations and decelerations which interfere with this maintenance of flow. Also, when the wind varies widely in strength and direction, the sails are frequently not sheeted correctly or shaped properly to initiate the attached flow. The superimposition of a disturbance created by neighboring boats markedly delays or completely prevents the establishment of the organized flow necessary to acceleration.

Since most boats are poorly prepared for the receipt of what little wind flow exists in light air, attention to sail trim can pay large dividends. It is first necessary to have a sensitive wind-direction indicator. Many use smoke (from cigarettes, pipes, or the like). Henry Fierz, the light-air wizard of Kingston, has been known to mount a smudge pot on his bow and slip through the fleet trailing a smoke screen (and those sensible enough to follow him). An ideal technique I have recently discovered is to toss dried thistle seeds into the air. These will remain aloft for a remarkable period, indicating the vagaries of the low-level air flow. The jib is a neglected wind indicator. It should be held by the clew and constantly moved to insure the correctness of its trim and the establishment of attached flow as indicated by the leeward telltales. Unless the air flow has been established, the spinnaker should be stowed; sail shape is needed to initiate attached flow, and spinnakers have no inherent shape. The boom may have to be held aloft to prevent it from hooking the mainsail leech. Both sails must be adjusted continuously without disturbing the trim of the hull to assure that whatever wind arrives is utilized.

In light air, decide where you want to go, get away from other boats, and keep going—as efficiently as the minimal, fluctuating air flow will permit.

15. Heavy Air

Heavy air sorts out the men from the boys—or more precisely, the good crews from the poor ones. Coordination and precision make it possible to exploit the forces available; the lack of these qualities results in disaster. The outcome of races in light air depends largely upon strategy. In moderate air, boat speed is what matters. In a breeze, boat-handling skills determine the results. Speed is still important, however. The mishandled boat, poorly trimmed, poorly balanced, is so much slower than her neighbors that the race is over in the first few yards. Of the three determinants of upwind performance—speed, pointing, and leeway—leeway is most important in heavy air. The mishandled boat not only moves ahead more slowly, but because of heeling, lack of balance, and lack of speed is unable to achieve a lift from her underwater surfaces sufficient to counterbalance the great aerodynamic side forces. With every gust, she slips to leeward. Poorly balanced, she may require excessive rudder angulation merely to remain on course, and when going downwind, slight variations in wind direction or wave conformation may send her yawing into a disastrous broach. Speed and proper management go hand in hand. The boat must be so trimmed that with a gust she surges ahead, with minimal heeling, minimal yawing, and minimal rudder angulation. No tactical or strategic advantages can compensate for a lack of trim.

Because speed is as essential to reduction in leeway as to forward progress, tactical considerations revolve around the maintenance of speed. The proximity of other boats must be avoided not only because they disturb the air flow (greatly if their sails are flogging) but because they interefere with maintenance of the desired course. Boats to leeward must be particularly avoided; on a windward leg they necessitate pinching, a major cause of increased leeway, and downwind they prevent bearing away, the only satisfactory response to a gust when reaching or running. If the precarious balance that maintains speed and prevents leeway and yawing is not to be lost, maneuvers must be made gradually, sail adjustments synchronously. Thus closeness of other boats may require abrupt maneuvers, and these always result in slowing and sometimes result in broaching or capsizing.

Speed is as essential at the start as at any other time during a heavy-air race. The large lateral aerodynamic force produced as the sails are sheeted in readily overcomes the minimal hydrodynamic side force produced by the fins at low speed. The boat that approaches the line slowly must therefore bear away for a protracted period to attain speed; otherwise she will suffer marked leeway. The boat that is luffing on the line before the gun will still be there long after, while the boat that started at speed has surged far ahead. Abrupt maneuvers—tacking or jibing—should be avoided late in the starting sequence, since the reacquisition of speed may be long delayed. A long approach is indicated. The approach tack should be initiated farther from the line in heavy air than in any other condition. A long, swooping approach on a close reach to a starting site in the middle of the line is the safest route. This permits the maintenance of speed while allowing for necessary time–distance adjustments, and avoids the probable congestion at the favored end of the line. Boats intruding ahead should always be passed to leeward so that speed is retained and a lee-bow position acquired. When close to the line, an opening to leeward must always be sought. The presence of a boat to leeward hinders the initiation of speed by means of bearing away and may subsequently necessitate a course higher than optimal, resulting in excessive leeway and a major loss to the fleet as a whole. A port-tack start may be appropriate in heavy air, since it permits an approach and a departure free of the hindrance of boats close to leeward. If the line is sufficiently long, an opening can always be found. A port-tack start is clearly the technique of choice if the starboard side of the course is favored; it results in emergence in undisturbed solitude, and permits the advantageous initial tack to be continued. A barging start, unsafe in most conditions, is sometimes useful in heavy air. The fleet, approaching the line at less than full speed, often makes greater leeway than expected, leaving room at the weather end for the barging boat to escape with little constraint. Whatever the planned start, it should be arranged to permit the continuance of the initial tack, so that the first tack need not be made until separation from the mass of the fleet has been achieved.

Once on the beat, tacking should be avoided—particularly frequent tacking and tacking in the company of other boats. Except in smooth water, an early tack is justified only if there is a major oscillating shift or clear evidence of a progressive, persistent shift to the opposite side of the course (or, of course, if the boat's present position is made unacceptable by the disturbed air of neighboring boats ahead). Persistent shifts should be suspected when there is a major alteration in wind velocity, when a squall appears (in the presence of a major low-pressure system), or when a shoreline is close by. (The subsequent appearance of a sea breeze or an inversion breakthrough need not, of course, be anticipated in the presence of heavy air.) A difference in current across the course is as significant in heavy air as at any other time; the route up the beat should be planned in advance to utilize the variation. In the absence of a clear indication to tack, the best strategy (as in light air) is to continue; the result will be fewer tacks and fewer neighbors. A careful lookout should be maintained for boats on the opposite tack, since an abrupt last-minute response may be not only slowing but dangerous. Be prepared to ease the mainsheet so as to bear away and pass astern of a crossing boat. Avoid tacking to a close lee-bow position. Unless the tack is perfectly accomplished, the opponent may be able to drive over as your underwater lift fails and you slide to leeward. The best control position is on the weather quarter; the boat ahead will then have to gain considerably before she dares a crossing tack. A tack should be made back to the rhumb line from a position well short of the lay line. The congestion near the lay line, particularly the starboard-tack parade, should be avoided for as long as possible.

Broaching

In one Bermuda International Race Week, Bob Mosbacher planed a Soling under a small chute from twelfth at the jibe mark to third at the leeward mark and gained a quarter mile as most of the fleet broached repeatedly under jib alone. In a previous series in a 35-knot northerly, we had come from fifth to second on the run and gained a quarter mile on the leader, only to lose half of this gain— and second place—in a broach while jibing. In St. Petersburg in a 30-knot northwesterly, the Soling fleet Yo-Yo-ed on the reaches and runs, with boats going from second to eighth and back again, depending upon how well they were prepared for the 40-knot gusts and how often they broached. In the 5.5-meter World's Championship series at Copenhagen in 1966, Ted Turner led the fleet to the jibe mark, broached, and then headed back up the course while half the fleet roared by! In this same series the Finnish entry, after broaching with both guy and sheet released to their stopper knots, filled the spinnaker sixty feet to leeward, and sank.

Broaching is an extreme consequence of a common phenomenon, the misalignment of the basic forces which determine yacht performance (Figure 11). Lateral equilibrium and forward motion re-

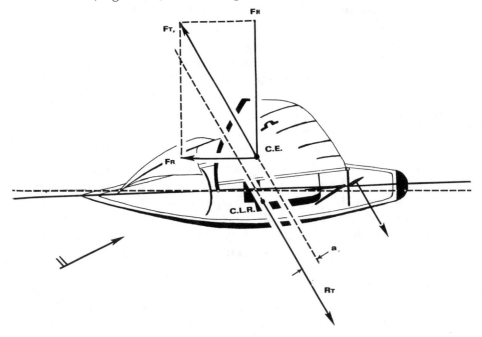

FIGURE 11

quire that the aerodynamic force produced by the sails, acting through their center of effort (C.E.), be matched by an equal and oppositely aligned hydrodynamic force produced by the hull and its fins, acting through their center of lateral resistance (C.L.R.). A turning, or yawing, moment results whenever the forces are misaligned so that a lever arm exists between the directions of action of the aerodynamic and the hydrodynamic forces. The force applied to that lever arm varies with, and is usually considered to be equal to, the horizontally acting portion of the aerodynamic side (or heeling) force. Ordinarily, the hydrodynamic side force from the hull and main fin alone acts forward of the aerodynamic force (acting through the center of effort) and a lever arm exists unless and until an additional hydrodynamic force, acting farther aft, is created by angulation of the rudder. The angle of incidence of the rudder is adjusted until the hydrodynamic force farther aft is sufficient to eliminate the lever arm and align the total hydrodynamic force with the total aerodynamic force (Figure 12). If equilibrium can be accomplished at a relatively small rudder angle, very little resistance or reduction in boat speed results and the boat is said to be well "balanced." If marked rudder angulation is required, the maximum angle of incidence which the rudder will tolerate may be exceeded, the rudder will stall, the hydrodynamic force produced by the rudder will diminish rapidly, the site of action of the hydrodynamic force will move forward, the yawing moment will be unequilibrated, and the boat will broach out of control. Equilibration of yawing moment is achieved by realignment of misaligned aerodynamic and hydrodynamic forces to eliminate the lever arm, and/ or reduction in the heeling force. Because the heeling force increases by the square of the wind velocity, it is by far the most significant element of the yawing moment. At low wind velocities even a large misalignment is readily overcome by the hydrodynamic lift force created by modest rudder angulation; at high wind velocities even a small misalignment will require a large rudder angulation, which will produce a marked increase in resistance and marked slowing.

To decrease the windward yawing moment and the tendency to broach, the center of effort of the sails must be displaced forward and the center of lateral resistance of the hull and fins displaced aft. The lever arm must be shortened by a reduction in heeling and by constriction of the sails toward the center line of the hull. The heeling force must be decreased by reductions in both the camber and angle of incidence of the mainsail and the spinnaker. (Opposite ad-

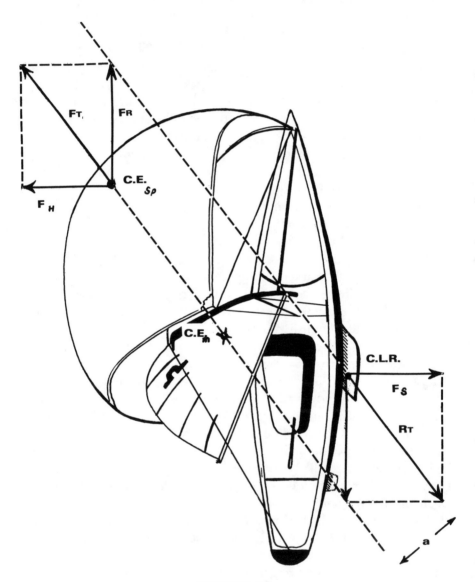

FIGURE 12

justments of the C.E. and C.L.R. are, of course, appropriate to the control of leeward yawing moment, a common problem in small centerboarders.) The techniques employed may be summarized as follows:

MOVEMENT OF THE CENTER OF EFFORT FORWARD AND INBOARD

Mainsail:	Set flat, with draft forward at a low angle of incidence
Jib:	Set full, at a high angle of incidence
Spinnaker:	Set flat, with draft forward at a low angle of incidence
	Small, flat design
	Trimmed flat horizontally and vertically
	Carried close to the boat at the least attainable angle of incidence
	Pole set down (to stretch luff) and parallel to the center line
Mast:	Raked forward

MOVEMENT OF THE CENTER OF LATERAL RESISTANCE AFT AND TO LEEWARD

Centerboard:	Elevated and shifted aft
Crew Weight:	Shifted aft and to windward
Heeling:	Minimized by hiking and by reduction in aerodynamic force produced (flattening the sails)
Steering:	Bearing away when immersing the bow, setting the spinnaker, or recovering from a broach

REDUCTION IN HEELING FORCE

Angle of Incidence:	Main and spinnaker—reduced to the least attainable
Main Leech Tension:	Reduced (and reestablished as necessary) by modification of vang tension
Spinnaker Sheet:	Released when all other adjustments fail, to prevent an incipient broach

The management of yawing moment and the prevention of broaching have been emphasized here because of their central significance for tactical success. The immense gains characteristic of heavy-air reaching result from the initiation and maintenance of planing or surfing. This requires that the reach be sailed at least partially at the optimal sailing angle *and* at whatever angle is necessary to permit a return to the rhumb line. In many situations these conditions are best obtained by breaking away to leeward at top speed with the confidence that the boat can be brought back up as necessary later. On a tight reach the helmsman who doubts his boat-handling skills has little choice but to limp along the rhumb line or to work to weather of it, under jib alone, until the spinnaker can be set in safety. Meanwhile, the helmsman who is prepared to control the forces involved can be sailing the optimal course with the optimal sail—jib or spinnaker. He is free to utilize the tactics appropriate to the conditions, unlimited by the sailing angle of the rhumb line.

Downwind Tactics

Reaching in heavy air requires first, prevention of broaching or capsizing by means of the trim and methods previously described; second, the maintenance of high speed, by means of these same techniques (avoiding the increase in forward resistance occasioned by heeling and excessive rudder angulation); and third, the utilization of waves to increase speed. The latter requires keeping the boat upright and headed downhill. When the boat is moving faster than the waves, this means avoiding the backs of waves, where the uphill course, the increased hull immersion, the displacement of lateral resistance forward, and the aft movement of the water in the wave combine to retard forward progress. When the boat is moving more slowly than the waves, this means maintaining a position on the wave face, where the downhill course, the decreased hull immersion, the displacement of lateral resistance aft, and the forward movement of the water in the wave combine to accelerate forward progress. The maintenance of the desired position relative to wave crests requires freedom to steer a highly varied course. Therefore, as in sailing to windward, other boats must be avoided. Before rounding the weather mark, a decision should be made as to the initial course to be followed after rounding, one which will provide separation from the other boats, either to windward or to leeward of the rhumb line. And once established, this course should be maintained. The great advantage of rounding the weather mark first is particularly evident in heavy air—freedom to pursue the ideal course, up in the lulls, down in the gusts, and always downhill.

If planing is possible, get planing—and the sooner the better. The optimal reaching course, the one that facilitates planing, is often to leeward of the rhumb line (because the apparent wind moves forward when planing, and heeling is increased as the apparent wind moves forward). Also, the leeward course provides the inside position at the mark. Although it is easier and safer to go high without planing early in the leg, so as to facilitate bearing away and planing later, the early loss means that other boats, particularly boats ahead, remain nearby and continue to prevent the free selection of the optimal course. Because the boat gains stability as it planes and may tolerate a higher course than expected, and because immediate planing permits separation from the neighboring boats (which are left behind), it is better to get planing first. If the spinnaker will facilitate planing, it should be set initially, the boat borne away until planing is achieved, and then gusts and waves utilized to maintain a course as close to the rhumb line as possible. Even if the jibe mark cannot be laid under spinnaker, lowering and/or flogging of the sail as the boat limps up to the mark should result in little loss if properly managed.

Regardless of the approach, the jibe should be made during a wide, gradual turn. The spinnaker should be fully squared, the sheet and guy cleated, the boat borne away under the boom as it is swung across, and the dead-downwind course maintained until the pole is refastened to sail and mast. Main and jib trim should be reorganized and the spinnaker lowered well in advance of the leeward mark. An approach at high speed often results in reaching the mark unprepared, with a consequently poor rounding and a significant loss to leeward as the beat is initiated. An abrupt rounding associated with slowing and marked leeway produces a greater loss than does a wide rounding. If other boats are nearby, demand the widest rounding they will permit. In heavy air, an outside position is often preferable, particularly at the leeward mark, since it permits a smooth speed-preserving turn that more than compensates for the usual advantages of the inside position.

The run, like all other legs, should begin with a deliberate move to the preferred side, and that course should then be maintained until the desirable position for return to the mark is reached. In very heavy air, to avoid jibing under spinnaker, a short move to the preferred side of the course may be made under jib, the boat jibed, and the spinnaker set on an optimal course to the leeward mark. If the main is held down by the vang (to avoid the twisted upper sections that result in oscillation) and the spinnaker well stretched and fully hoisted, neither the near dead: downwind course nor jibing should be hazardous. The boat should be sailed as high as is necessary to permit planing or surfing, but in very heavy air this should be possible dead downwind. Significant deviation from the rhumb line then results in loss. When in doubt, take port jibe away from the weather mark so that the fleet will be met again on starboard jibe. In this way the need for dangerous course alterations at meetings can be avoided. The last jibe should be made well in advance of the mark, and the approach made on the rounding jibe. A 180° turn while jibing in heavy air is disastrous and seriously compromises the preparation for the weather leg to come.

16. Current: Fact and Fiction

There need be no mystery about the relationship of current to racing performance. It produces quantifiable effects in a predictable fashion. In moderate to heavy air, when wind shifts and changes in velocity are unlikely to occur, current becomes the major strategic determinant. In light air (contrary to popular opinion), the possibility of major variations in wind strength and direction means that current becomes less important as a strategic determinant. An adverse current is more significant than a favorable one of comparable velocity because the boat is forced to remain in it longer. Although we become more aware of the current when exposure is prolonged (as in an adverse current, in light air, or on a long leg), it is always producing the same inexorable effect per unit of time. And because it can be readily measured, that effect is far more predictable than the effect of the wind. Consequently, current is often given greater weight in strategic decision-making than is appropriate. It must be considered in every racing plan, however, and if present, reconsidered on every leg of the course.

Current has the following effects which influence the outcome of racing:

1. Current that differs in strength in different portions of the course (or at different times in the same location) will alter the speed of affected boats differently.
   Select the side of each leg that will provide the most favorable or the least unfavorable current.

2. Current will cause all boats to deviate in the same direction and will alter the course that must be sailed when approaching marks fixed to the bottom.
   Allow for the deviation due to current, so that the result is a straight-line course from mark to mark on reaches, and on the lay line, beating or running.

3. As a boat is propelled by the current, her motion through the air creates a "current wind" equal in velocity and opposite in direction to the current, and the velocity and direction of the apparent wind are altered accordingly.
   Allow for the alteration in apparent wind induced by the current wind. Reserve the more advantageous sailing angle for the most critical period of the leg, the approach to the mark.

4. Current will cause an amount of deviation proportional to the duration of exposure to it.
   Plan for a greater alteration in course for a given distance sailed when the exposure will be prolonged (in light air or an adverse current).

When one boat sails in a current of different strength than another, her relative speed is altered by an amount equal to that difference. Differences in current are largely determined by differences in the depth of the water. In relatively open water the current flow is reduced in shallow areas, increased in deep ones. An analysis of the contours of the bottom, as shown on the chart, will indicate whether and where current variations will occur. If the depth varies little throughout the racing area, current will not be a strategic factor. If abrupt differences in depth exist—caused, for example, by a dredged channel or a sand bank—marked variations in current velocity will be present. The course for each leg must then be planned to utilize the side of the leg in shallower water when the current is adverse, and the side in deeper water when the current is favorable. In tidal flows the current may change direction in one area of the course (usually inshore) before it changes in another. In this case one boat may be able to sail in a favorable current while another is sailing in an adverse current. A study of the current tables and the underwater contours may suggest that this situation exists, but only local knowledge can confirm it.

In most races, the current has a significant effect only if differences in velocity exist in different areas of the course. When the flow is equally distributed throughout the course, all boats are moved equally in the same direction at the same speed regardless of their attitude to the current or the wind. In its effects, this uniform current may be likened to the movement of a rug on which a fleet of toy boats has been placed. When the rug is moved, all the boats move together regardless of the size or shape of their keels, regardless of the direction in which they are headed, regardless of whether they are lee-bowing or windward bowing the direction of movement of the rug. Although (as will be shown) their apparent winds are affected differently, there are no attitudes to the movement of the rug that will result in dramatic differences in performance. There is nothing magical about the "lee-bow effect." One tack or one jibe may receive a more advantageous apparent wind than another, but in the absence of wind shifts, each boat will spend the same amount of time on each tack and the apparent wind differences will therefore equalize each other.

The second effect of current, which requires constant vigilance, concerns the relationship of the boats, floating in the current, to the marks fixed to the bottom. A fixed mark may be compared to a powerboat moving at a speed equal to that of the current and in the opposite direction. Boats approaching such a powerboat would be required to adjust their courses to allow for its movement, and in the same way, boats in a current approaching a fixed mark must make an adjustment. When the current is setting toward the line (to windward) the lay line to each end is displaced to leeward, barging is disastrous, and boats on the line must bear away to avoid being swept over. When the current is setting away from the line (to leeward) the lay line to each end is displaced to windward, barging is safe and useful, and boats must stay close to the line to avoid being swept below it. This displacement is the same for the lay lines to the weather and to the leeward marks, and boats approaching them must modify their courses accordingly to avoid overstanding or failing to lay. On reaches, the boat must be headed above or below the next mark if it is to sail the shortest, straight-line course to that mark. The correct course can be simply achieved by sighting a range between the mark ahead and an object on the shore beyond or by occasionally checking position relative to the mark astern. The ultimate danger is, of course, hitting the mark. Prior consideration can prevent such a crisis, but the risk is ever present when sailing in strong current. The proper technique for getting by the weather mark without tacking despite an adverse current is to sail full and bye until just short of the mark and then to luff around it. To pinch on the approach would increase the leeway due to the wind (since a boat moving more slowly has less hydrodynamic lift), prolong the duration of exposure to the adverse current, and decrease the speed available for shooting around the mark.

The direction and strength of the apparent wind of boats sailing in a current is modified by the current wind. The effect of the current wind is inversely proportional to the velocity of the true wind. Figure 13 demonstrates the apparent winds received by boats sailing in a current and in winds from various directions. The wind induced by the forward movement of the boat, an air flow from directly ahead, must, of course, be superimposed to attain a complete picture. The least apparent wind is available to the boat sailing away from the wind (the true wind is reduced by the boat wind) and with the current (the current is taking the boat away from the wind). The greatest apparent wind is available to the boat sailing into the wind (the true wind is increased by the boat wind) and with the current (the current is taking the boat toward the wind). The least apparent wind (regardless of sailing angle and boat wind) is available when the current and wind are moving in the same direction, and the most apparent wind is available when the current and wind are moving in opposite directions. At all other sailing angles and for all other wind directions, the apparent wind is somewhere between the extremes.

For all wind directions acting in the quadrants to the left (as one faces into the current), the apparent wind is backed to the true wind. For all wind directions acting in the quadrants to the right, the apparent wind is veered to the true wind. The diagram is useful particularly for beating and running, where a major difference in apparent wind may be present on each tack or each jibe. To ascertain the effects (1) orient the diagram up-current, (2) pick the wind direction that is appropriately oriented to the current, and (3) select the boat oriented to the appropriate sailing angle. Once that sailing angle has been selected, the alteration in the apparent wind induced by the current can be recognized.

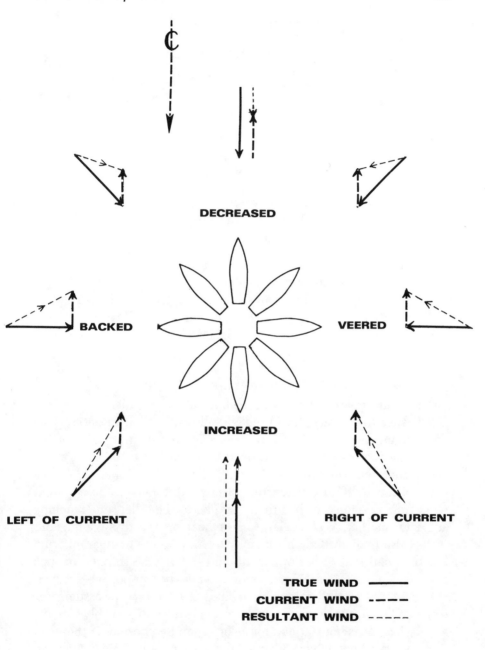

CHANGES IN APPARENT WIND INDUCED BY CURRENT

FIGURE 13

1. True wind and current approximately aligned
       Apparent wind: Velocity—Reduced
                              Direction—Veered for true winds to right of
                                             current
                                             Backed for true winds to left of
                                             current

2. True wind 90° to right of current
       Apparent wind: Velocity—Increased
                              Direction—Veered

3. True wind 90° to left of current
       Apparent wind: Velocity—Increased
                              Direction—Backed

4. True wind approximately 180° to current
       Apparent wind: Velocity—Increased
                              Direction—Veered for true winds to right of
                                             current
                                             Backed for true winds to left of
                                             current

Unless different boats receive currents of differing velocity, alterations in apparent wind due to current are ordinarily of minor significance to the race, for in the end all boats sail at essentially the same sailing angles, both advantageous and disadvantageous for the same length of time. However, everything doesn't come out exactly even, since the true wind varies with time and position. When the true wind is light and the current strong, variations in the apparent wind from one tack to the other, one jibe to the other, one reaching angle to another, become large. If a boat on the disadvantageous tack is also in disturbed air, she may be moving in an apparent wind less than half that of her opponent, and she may be trapped in such a condition for a prolonged period while her opponent escapes. When subsequently the opponent finds it necessary to assume the disadvantageous tack, she may do so in clear air or possibly in more air, so that she is not trapped for a corresponding period. If the wind is dying, the boat which assumes the current-advantaged tack initially gains little in the stronger air, but later loses much on the disadvantaged tack in weaker air. Absolute speed is not what matters; it is relative speed that counts—how much faster one boat is than another.

If, in clear and moderate air, one boat moves at 4 knots and the other at 3.6 knots, the gain achieved is 600 feet in approximately fifteen minutes (the expected duration of a one-mile leg). In disturbed and light air, with one boat moving at 1 knot and the other at 0.6 knots, the same one-mile leg will last approximately an hour and the faster boat will gain 2,400 feet. Thus it is possible for differing gains to be made during a given leg, as the strength of the wind varies. One boat may lose less on a given tack, jibe, or sailing angle early in the leg than she gains on a subsequent tack, jibe, or sailing angle, because—as a result of changes in wind strength—the two segments of the leg differ in duration (Figure 14). In addition, as has been indicated, the presence of disturbed air may result in further variations in speed. In general, therefore, having identified the effect of the current on the apparent wind on a given leg, one should assume the disadvantageous tack, jibe, or sailing angle when other conditions—wind strength, the presence of neighboring boats—are

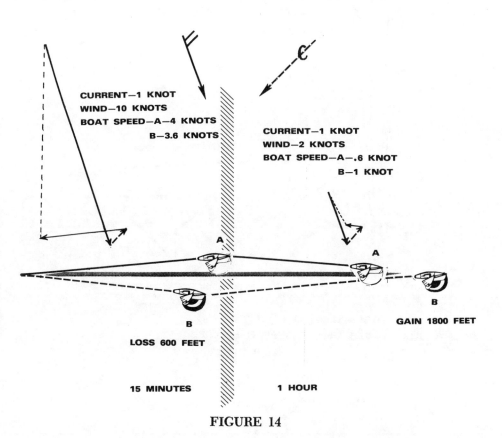

CURRENT—1 KNOT
WIND—10 KNOTS
BOAT SPEED—A—4 KNOTS
B—3.6 KNOTS

CURRENT—1 KNOT
WIND—2 KNOTS
BOAT SPEED—A—.6 KNOT
B—1 KNOT

A

A

B

GAIN 1800 FEET

B

LOSS 600 FEET

15 MINUTES

1 HOUR

FIGURE 14

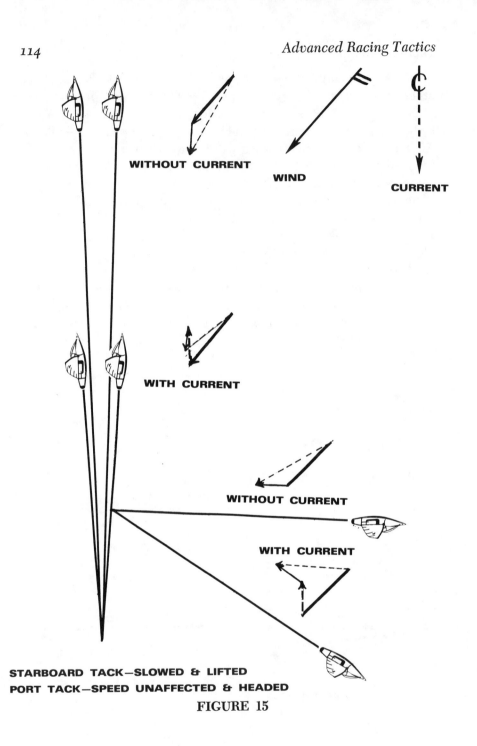

WITHOUT CURRENT

WIND

CURRENT

WITH CURRENT

WITHOUT CURRENT

WITH CURRENT

STARBOARD TACK—SLOWED & LIFTED
PORT TACK—SPEED UNAFFECTED & HEADED

FIGURE 15

most advantageous. The current-advantaged sailing angle can then be saved for use when other boats are at a disadvantage.

In addition to its other effects, current alters the duration of a leg. If a leg (or a portion of one) is prolonged in adverse current, performance differences will become exaggerated. Then the most advantageous sailing angle, the most careful sail trim, and the clearest air must be utilized.

Figure 15 shows the effect of adverse current on the course of boats sailing to windward. The current is presumed to be half the strength of the wind and the boat speed into the current to be reduced by half. Regardless of performance capabilities, all boats on starboard tack will be moving over the bottom and through the air at reduced speed and will be sailing in a veered apparent wind that permits them to point higher. Inherent differences that cause one boat to make ground to windward better than another will appear to be exaggerated. The lateral deviation between two boats sailing at slightly different headings on starboard tack will be greater than expected for a given distance sailed because of the increased duration of the leg. The deviation that would have been present one mile out will be present one-half mile out, suggesting a deviation of one boat to windward by the current, a "lee-bow effect." However, inasmuch as all boats are being set down-current in exactly the same manner (as if they were on a moving rug), no differences in windward performance (except those due to the differing effects of their current wind) can be attributed to the current. There is no "lee-bow effect." A boat on port tack, sailing essentially across the current, will move over the bottom and through the air at nearly the speed of a boat in the absence of current. She will, therefore, receive an apparent wind little changed in strength, but because of the current wind, markedly veered. She will be headed relative to the true wind. The cross-current tack, because of the veer, will be more than 90° to the up-current tack, and the up-current tack, because of the reduced apparent wind, will be significantly slower than the cross-current tack. However, since—in the absence of variations in current or wind—all boats must spend the same amount of time on each tack, none of these phenomena results in an absolute gain or loss.

17. Big Fleets: Basic Requirements

Start: Stick to the starting plan.

Obtain clear air and/or freedom to tack.

Get out where you can see the fleet as a whole and look around.

First Beat: Assume the tack toward the advantageous side of the course; if in doubt, stay with the majority.

Watch the boats on the weather quarter. Tack back when you have gained. Keep inside and to leeward of the majority of competitors during the latter part of the leg.

Be alert for a progressive persistent shift.

Avoid the lay lines as long as possible.

Weather Mark: Avoid the starboard-tack parade as long as possible.

Decide in advance whether to go high or low on the reach. Enter the starboard-tack parade to leeward or to windward accordingly.

First Reach: Go high or low; avoid the middle.

Work to leeward in the gusts, while retaining clear air, so as to be inside at the jibe mark.

Jibe Mark: Manage to be inside. Allow boats to pass to windward if necessary, but break all leeward overlaps.

Second Reach: Go high immediately (unless there is a clear advantage to leeward). Allow no boats to pass to windward, but avoid luffing matches.

Work to leeward in the gusts, but keep your wind clear.

Leeward Mark: Determine in advance the advantageous side of the next beat.

Do not be concerned to obtain an inside overlap unless the left side of the beat is clearly preferable. However, do not allow an opponent to obtain an inside overlap if you are approaching the mark on or above the rhumb line.

Prepare for a good, smooth rounding, and ready the proper sail trim to initiate the beat.

Second Beat: Assume the tack toward the advantageous side of the course; if in doubt, assume the lifted tack.

Watch the boats on the weather quarter. Tack back when you have gained.

Be alert for a progressive persistent shift.

Avoid the lay lines as long as possible.

Second Weather Mark: Decide in advance which jibe you wish to take initially by determining the median downwind direction.

Run: Assume the jibe which approximates the rhumb line at the best sailing angle (and jibe as necessary to continue this relationship).

Reconsider the possibility of a progressive

persistent shift, and if such a shift is in the offing, jibe away from it—unless you are already close to the rhumb line at a good sailing angle.

Maintain speed by sailing up in the lulls, down in the gusts—particularly in light air.

Leeward Mark: Determine in advance the advantageous side of the next beat.

Jibe far enough in advance so as to approach the leeward mark inside and preferably high on the wind on starboard jibe.

Third Beat: Assume the tack toward the advantageous side of the course; if in doubt, assume the lifted tack.

Watch the boats on the weather quarter. Tack back when you have gained. Keep inside and to leeward of close competitors on the tack back to the rhumb line.

Be alert for a progressive persistent shift.

Avoid the lay lines as long as possible.

Consider which boats are in contention, and cover the majority of them.

Finish Line: Tack toward the finish line below the lay line to either end.

Tack to cross the line at the downwind end.

WHEN IN DOUBT, DON'T

Start at the congested end of the line.

Tack.

Pass astern of boats on the major tack (particularly near the lay line).

Set the spinnaker.

THINK AHEAD.

Decide what you will do when the expected happens.

Decide what you will do when the opposite of the expected happens.

Although other tactics may be more appropriate in particular circumstances, failure to follow these basic principles is the usual cause of major mistakes—mistakes which result in a boat's falling behind many competitors and losing significant distance with respect to the leaders. Do not undertake maneuvers contrary to these principles without considering the major risk entailed.

III. *Starting*

18. The Starting Plan

It is not always possible to attain the best start in the fleet, but planning does significantly increase the chance of success. Before the start, a plan must be developed for the race as a whole, for the first leg, and for the start itself. The effectiveness of the plan depends upon the data collection which occupies most of the time before the start. Of course, all plans must be subject to modification as additional data is acquired during the race. But less modification will be required and less error will result if the plan is carefully organized and based upon properly collected data.

Unless the plan for the race is developed systematically, something important will be overlooked. Utilization of the ODSSSIC acronym, insures consideration of all the major strategic factors that will influence the race, the first leg, and the start. Labels on the deck where this information can be recorded, serve both as reminders to collect the data and as references for later perusal. They also remind the person who has been assigned the responsibility that he should check the course as displayed on the committee boat—and record it. The race instructions should have been thoroughly examined before going afloat, but the restrictions pertaining to the course

—government marks that must be left on a specified side, methods of shortening the course, and the like—and the character and location of the marks should be reviewed just before the start. The prevention of major mistakes should be specifically assigned to particular crew members. Also, a crew member should be responsible for determining which sails will be used and approximately what trim will be required on each leg. Without specific orders, he should set up the gear in accordance with the plan; the helmsman should be free to concentrate on strategic and tactical considerations.

Next, a plan for the first leg must be formulated. A review of the ODSSSIC factors is necessary. Is the wind stable or unstable? Will there be oscillating or persistent shifts? Is the wind dying (and backing)? Will a new wind—a sea breeze, a squall—appear during the first beat? Will a nearby shoreline cause a change in wind direction over some portion of the first leg? Will an inversion break through or redevelop during the leg? Is there a significant current and will it vary in velocity or direction in some portion of the leg? In view of all these factors, as they weigh one against the other, which side of the beat will be preferred?

The plan for the start is shaped primarily by this determination. A start from the more upwind end of the line may be desirable, but the direction in which the boat must be taken depends upon which side of the beat has been chosen. Will starboard tack be continued to the left, or must the boat be started on—or immediately tacked to—port? Will conditions be appropriate for a port-tack start? Should the extreme end of the line be avoided? How should the starting tack be approached, and how much time should be allowed between the assumption of the starting tack and the start? The answers to these questions depend upon the data collected and the size and character of the fleet.

The Data

Data collection begins on the way to the start. With the help of prior evaluations of printed information and previous observations, the origin of the existing wind should be determined. Knowing the origin of the present wind, one can better predict whether it will persist, and if not, what wind will replace it. Compass headings should be repeatedly obtained on the way to the start and in the starting area up to the last possible moment, to facilitate detection of a persistent shift and to determine the range of oscillations. Success on the first beat will largely depend upon whether shifts are treated as oscillations or as persistent variations. Compass headings on starboard and port tack, together with the time they were obtained, should be recorded on the deck to determine if a trend in one direction is developing. In fluky conditions it is wise to translate such data into wind directions and to have the crew call out actual wind directions thereafter. Again, if previous data is available this may indicate the imminence of development or deterioration of the sea breeze, an inversion breakthrough, or a velocity shift. On a two- or three-man boat one person should be continually asking for a luff head to wind or a close-hauled course to check wind direction while the rest concentrate on gear arrangement, course determination, and the like. Prior to the start, the accumulated data must be translated into a prediction of the wind to come; in particular, the imminence of a persistent shift which might appear during the first leg must be recognized.

The current should be checked at the starting line and, if time permits, at other sites on the course. If the current is due to a changing tidal stream, it should be rechecked at a time as close as possible to the start. A current stick is a far more accurate means of estimating current than the mere observation of the wake of a buoy. The stick can be easily made from a three-foot pole weighted at one end to induce it to float vertically with a few inches protruding above the surface. This arrangement results in minimal windage, so that when the stick is dropped near an anchored mark, its course will be entirely dependent upon the current. The tip should be painted a bright color to facilitate retrieval in heavy weather. The stick is dropped at a mark, the stopwatch is started, and the boat is sailed in a circle for one minute. At the end of this period, the distance in feet that the stick has traveled should be estimated and its course direction determined by sailing on a heading that aligns the stick with the mark beyond. The current velocity in knots is the distance traveled in one minute divided by 100, and the current direction is the reverse of the boat's heading when the stick is approached in line with the mark. A significant variation in velocity or direction at different sites or at different times will have an important effect on the outcome of the race.

When the committee boat posts the course, each leg should be translated into a compass heading which is then recorded in a designated location on the deck. If the course is between fixed marks set out to create a standard course (Olympic, Gold Cup, equilateral triangle, or the like), the compass heading to the first mark is usually posted. With this data and simple arithmetic (or a disc course computer) the direction of each leg can be determined, and recorded. In boats which gain significantly from tacking downwind, headings 10°, 15°, or 20° either side of dead downwind should be recorded to serve as a gauge of shifts occurring on the run.

The starting line must be checked to determine which end is farther to windward, and whether its length is adequate. Usually the upwind end can be detected by luffing head to wind and sighting the angle between the heading and the line. A more accurate method is to sail from beyond one end of the line on a heading which aligns the marks and to compare this heading with multiple wind readings (Figure 16). With the base data provided by this technique, one can subsequently determine the upwind end merely by identifying the wind direction. The length of the line should be

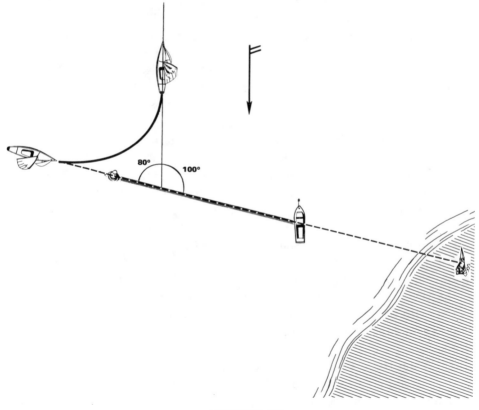

FIGURE 16

considered in relation to the size and quality of the fleet. Will the line be crowded? Will the favored end be packed with talented starters? Should a position more conservative than the extreme end be selected? The third matter to be determined with respect to the line is a means of ascertaining when the boat is on the line. If possible, someone other than the helmsman should be responsible for the sighting, and he needs a range if it is to be done accurately. This can usually be obtained while determining the compass direction of the line from an extension, by noting the alignment of the starboard end (usually the flag on the committee boat) with an object on the shore beyond. The identification of such a range will permit the responsible crew member to determine at the start when the boat is on the line. He must remember that the bow reaches the line ahead of the sighting position.

The Starting Plan

1. Which side of the beat is preferred determines
   a) The starting tack or
   b) The need for starting in a manner which permits an immediate tack.

2. Which end of the line is upwind determines the general location of the approach tack.

3. The size of the fleet, the angle of the line, the wind velocity, the current, the presence of oscillating shifts, determines
   a) The exact location of the approach tack,
   b) The base leg and the sailing angle required to reach the approach-tack position, and
   c) The speed on the approach tack.

Starting Patterns in Large Fleets

I. STARBOARD-TACK STARTS
   Line Square or Starboard End Upwind

   1. Start at starboard end if
        Freedom to tack is essential
            Oscillating winds
            Persistent shift probable but direction undetermined
            Very light air
            Right side of course advantageous
        Current is setting to port (or to leeward)

2. Start between midline and starboard end if
    Starboard tack is to be continued
        Very light air
        Left side of course advantageous
    Very heavy air

Line Square or Port End Upwind

1. Start at port end if
    Starboard tack is to be continued
        Very light air
        Moderate air
        Left side of course advantageous
    Current is setting to starboard (or to windward)

2. Start between midline and port end if
    Freedom to tack is essential
        Oscillating winds
        Persistent shift probable but direction undetermined
        Right side of course advantageous
    Very heavy air

II. PORT-TACK STARTS

Line Square or Port End Upwind
    Oscillating winds
    Very light air
    Right side of course advantageous

19. Starting Technique

The plan for the start should be formulated prior to the ten-minute gun. Data collection must continue, however, to assure that the premises of the plan are correct. The last current check may be made a few minutes before the warning signal, but unless the wind has been previously determined to be unusually steady, it must be tested repeatedly right up to the start. This testing should be accomplished without luffing ahead to wind, as this maneuver would disturb the starting pattern. Close-hauled headings on either tack are equally useful and the attitude of other boats which are testing can be revealing. In light air or oscillating wind, the detection of a shift a few seconds before the start may result in an immediate and insuperable lead. And if you can maintain speed, position, and control while continuing wind surveillance—identification of changes required in jib trim, observation of the sailing angles of other boats —no risk is engendered. Look around, watch the other boats; they are the best wind indicators ever devised. Which end of the line do the top competitors appear to be favoring? Don't dismiss summarily the evident belief of the majority, but don't disregard clear indications that they are wrong. If your previous data collection has been accurate and unhurried, you should know better than they.

Don't sail too far from the position from which you intend to commence your starting pattern (particularly in light air and big fleets). While changing sails, don't drift far from the line, particularly before a second (or third) race whose exact starting time is unknown. Don't allow yourself to be swept away from the line in strong current or to be drawn into a position from which a difficult tack or jibe will be required in heavy air. Acquire a position on your planned base leg for the approach well in advance of the required time; you can always slow down. The desired position for the approach will have been determined in the starting plan, which takes into account the preferred side of the course, the favored end of the line, the current at the line, and the presence of oscillating shifts. In addition, the size of the fleet must be considered in relation to the angle of the line to the wind. If one end is greatly favored and the fleet is large, the preferred end will be heavily congested. The starting plan includes a base leg (the means of reaching the approach-tack position) which will either be parallel to the starting line, on a broad reach, on a close reach, or close-hauled (Figure 17). In many circumstances the approach from to leeward on a near close-hauled course provides the ideal base leg, since it preserves speed and permits control over neighboring boats.

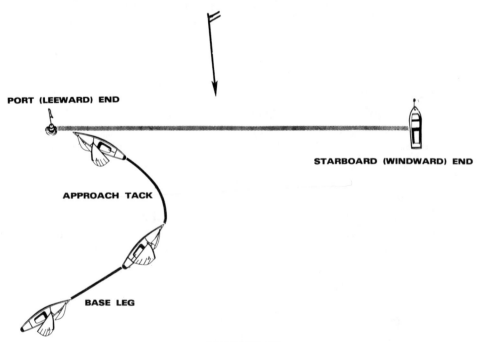

FIGURE 17

The ultimate success of the start depends upon the management of the approach tack itself. The speed that will be utilized on the approach must be adjusted to the wind velocity (the less the wind the faster the approach, since the rate of reacquisition of speed is reduced in light air). Timing tests should be undertaken at the line before the preparatory signal. A feel must be acquired for the time needed to sail a given distance at the speed planned for the approach tack in the conditions prevailing. Reaching the right location for the start is simple enough; being there and moving at full speed as the gun fires is the difficult part. The latter requires a precise feel for the time and distance remaining, so that speed can be increased (or decreased, occasionally) at the right instant—or at least with an accuracy in excess of that achieved by helmsmen of neighboring boats.

In a large fleet, obtaining the position necessary for a good start requires careful organization within the crew. Each member must have assigned duties which require no explanation and no unnecessary orders. Except in single-handed boats, one crew member should be responsible for calling the time remaining, announcing it at steadily decreasing intervals, with the final countdown in seconds. In addition, the helmsman should wear a watch, so that he can see for himself how much time remains. Another member of the crew (if available) should be responsible for calling the distance to the intended position on the line, at first in boat lengths and toward the end in feet (or meters). Thus time and distance are being announced without special requests and without interruption while the helmsman concentrates on steering. All of the sail-shape controls should be set for "starting gear" in advance, so that during the starting sequence trimming will not be required except for the jib sheet and the mainsheet (or preferably the main traveler if sufficient range is available). The only orders needed will be those pertaining to the jib-sheet trim, since the helmsman should handle the mainsheet or traveler himself. The helmsman may have to request information concerning the position of other boats on the base leg, but he should be sufficiently aware of his neighbors on the approach not to require additional reports about them. The only problem that he may not foresee is the appearance of a boat charging in from astern with a good head of steam. One member of the crew should be assigned responsibility for detecting such boats and for apprising the helmsman of their imminent arrival. With the boat thus freed of extraneous conversation, the orders regarding critical changes in jib-sheet trim and the announcements of time and distance remaining are readily audible, and data essential to the helmsman's decisions can be transmitted without interference.

In large fleets, starting success ultimately becomes a two-boat affair; there is always at least one other boat attempting to start at the site selected. The solution cannot be viewed in terms of obtaining simply a better start than that of the nearby opponent. The alternatives are more extreme. A good start for one boat means a disastrous one for the other. This fact of starting life permits no compromise. The opponent must be hurt.

In the final thirty seconds and after the gun the *sine qua non* of success is the ability to bear away to gather speed. Another boat close to leeward blocks such a maneuver. The windward boat must luff to avoid contact with the boat to leeward, and as the leeward boat moves progressively ahead, must continue luffing until the leeward boat escapes clear ahead. The luffing boat, developing little if any hydrodynamic side force, makes marked leeway, while the moving boat to leeward makes little. Consequently, the windward boat is forced to luff higher and higher to keep clear as the leeward boat progresses through her lee, and may be stopped almost head to wind by the time the leeward boat breaks away ahead. The result is that as the gun fires, the windward boat is standing still, and being in the midst of the fleet, with disturbed air all around her, she may be unable to reacquire forward motion for a prolonged period. Boats with clear air may be hundreds of yards ahead before the luffing boat is up to speed. The situation of that windward boat must be avoided.

The vast majority of the helmsmen in most large fleets commit themselves to a position on the line early in the starting sequence. They expect to luff along in the front row, gradually, working down the line through leeway and minimal headway. Each of these boats attempts to press up close to a neighbor to windward so as to require her to slow by luffing. If the boats are near the line and approximately bow to bow, the windward boat will be unable to escape by speeding up and bearing away across the leeward boat's bow. Even if this maneuver is attempted early enough to permit getting back behind the line before the start (an unacceptable solution if the "one-minute" rule is in effect), it results in an excess of speed which in turn cannot be dissipated by a sharp luff without crossing the line. Too much speed is disastrous at the front of a packed line because it forces the boat to move farther down the line and into close apposition to the next leeward boat while awaiting the start—

and that leeward boat with a minimal luff stops the weather boat in her tracks just before or immediately after the gun fires. To avoid this succession of disasters, a windward boat is usually content to respond to the first luff of a boat to leeward in hopes that eventually the latter will drive off to leeward and leave her alone. The windward boat is, of course, simultaneously trying to manage her partner to windward in the same manner (and a boat farther to leeward is attempting to do the same thing to the leeward boat). The boat obtaining the best start will be the one that presses the boat to windward the hardest, leaving herself with the largest gap to leeward. She must also, of course, accurately time her bearing away (and the consequent release of the boat to windward) so as to arrive at the line with better speed than her neighbors just as the gun fires. It is possible for one of a group of boats hovering near the line to obtain a good start in this manner, but only if the boat to leeward lacks aggressiveness.

A technique more certain of success is to avoid the front row of luffing boats until the final thirty or forty seconds (Figure 18). A boat coming into the front row early is a sitting duck, waiting to be trapped by a boat coming up fast to leeward. A boat that assumes a base leg below the line can either tack into or head up onto a close-hauled course when a sparsely populated section of the line appears. Once all the other boats in the vicinity have committed themselves to the line, the boat astern and to leeward is in control. She need fear no other boat appearing to leeward, and is at no risk of being luffed, slowed, stopped. Her speed can be controlled by variations in course or sail trim. She need only place her bow just to leeward of the transom of a boat luffing near the line, when approximately twenty seconds remain. The boat selected should be so close to the line that she cannot escape by sailing ahead in advance of the gun. If she is close to the line thirty seconds before the start, she will be barely moving when attacked. Once an overlap to leeward has been established, the weather boat is forced to hold her course. Although she can no longer fall off to leeward, she is still making leeway. Hence, to maintain her position, she must aim higher and higher, luffing more and more—until she is stopped. The leeward boat on the other hand, although she must stay close to leeward, can continue moving and get her bow ahead of the windward boat by the time the gun fires. She must establish her overlap with enough speed so that her momentum will carry her through to leeward of the luffing boat. After the overlap has been established, she can slow

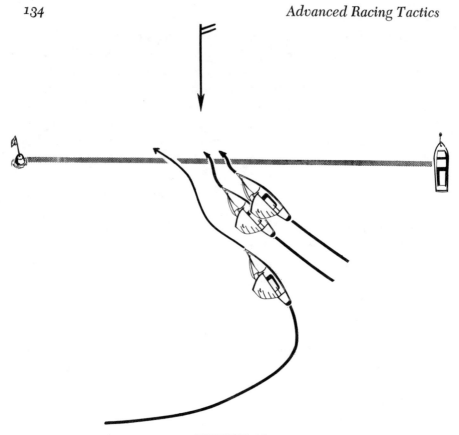

FIGURE 18

if necessary by ragging her sails, to avoid breaking through too
soon. The essential element of this starting technique is total control
of the windward boat.

When the leeward boat emerges, she should be ten to twenty
feet to weather of the boat next to leeward. During her transition
through the weather boat's lee, the time and distance remaining
should be called aloud. If the windward boat is not up on the line,
the leeward boat must carry on toward the line beyond the bow of
the boat to weather. Awareness of other neighboring boats is essential; if others to windward or to leeward are starting to move faster,
to push their boats farther ahead, their pace must be matched. No
other boat's bow should be farther ahead than one's own when the
gun fires. If a general recall results, one will merely be part of it; if
none results, one will have a start as good as one's neighbors'. When
the gun fires, the boat to windward should be completely stopped
and the boat next to leeward should be at least ten feet away. If a

significant gap to leeward has been acquired, one should crack off with sails full and well twisted. If the gap to leeward is minimal, it will be necessary to maintain the luff for a few seconds after the gun fires. Under these circumstances the boat to weather must be completely stopped so that during the crucial moments ahead she will be unable to override. This solution, even though it further delays the acquisition of speed, is preferable to bearing away close aboard the boat to leeward. In no circumstances should one bear away until the boat to leeward has done so. Once you are in her backwind, boats to weather are certain to override. After speed has been acquired it may be necessary to shift into "pointing gear" to work out to windward.

The purpose of this starting technique is to separate the boat from the boats to leeward *and* prevent any boats to windward from overriding. Once this position has been acquired, a capability reasonably comparable to that of the remainder of the fleet will permit it to be maintained. From this position the fleet as a whole can be observed. And this, after the start itself, is the most important determinant of success on the first beat. One must get out where the boats on the same tack to leeward, on the same tack to windward, and on the opposite tack can be observed. Only then can a rational decision concerning the first (or second) tack be made. Only then can significant shifts be recognized. Only then can a gain be recognized which can be consolidated by a covering tack. Being overridden or forced to tack after a poor start not only causes slowing and the loss of the neighboring boats, but, far worse, buries the boat in a melee from which detection of subsequent shifts and their effect upon the fleet becomes impossible.

Many techniques are available that will insure starting in clear air; various circumstances necessitate differing modifications. In large fleets, fancy gambits are unlikely to be successful. A standard technique that will guarantee clear air every time should be practiced and perfected. Such disastrous losses in distance result from failure to obtain clear air that position on the line, and heading direction, become insignificant by comparison. Once clear air has been acquired there will be an opportunity to tack in the right direction, to overcome the leads of boats that may have escaped from the melee at the favored end of the line. It is not essential to have the best start— only to have clear air, in race after race. And the way to get clear air is to stick to the plan, the technique, which has been proven by experience.

20. The Timed Start

I have assumed for many years that timed starts were for J-boats and similar dinosaurs. A segment of the starting area sufficiently free of other boats to permit a timed reach away from the line and a beat back has yet to appear in my racing career. I was surprised, therefore, when both Andy MacGowan and Graham Hall during their sailing-symposium lectures emphasized the importance of timed starts. Andy described how Bill Ficker, taking charge of *Charisma* for the SORC, practiced timed starts to the desired point on the line repeatedly, before each race. Small-boat sailors may pass this method by, regarding it as a technique for offshore racers. However, Graham, formerly coach of New York State Maritime College's top-rated sailing team, claimed that he trained his intercollegiate dinghy sailors in timed starts—hour after hour.

Although Harold Vanderbilt's broad reach away and beat back along the lay line to the desired point on the line may be inapplicable to crowded small-boat starts, accurate timing is as important now as it was then. And practice can perfect timing. What is needed is the ability to judge how long it will take to sail from here to there. The basis of this understanding is an accurate assessment of speed.

Practice provides a feel for the distances involved; and once speed can be estimated, timing becomes accurate. The port-end mark is forty feet ahead and there are fifteen second to go. Shall I sheet in and drive for it? ease sheets and luff? continue at my present speed? Only practice and many starts will provide the accuracy necessary for hitting the optimal point on the line at full speed as the gun fires. But there are a number of shortcuts, a number of basic principles, whose application will make it possible to get close to this goal, usually closer than the competition.

Since the speed range of the average sailboat is relatively narrow, learning to assess the speed is not difficult. The maximum speed to windward for boats between twelve and thirty feet long is about 6 knots, while a minimum of 1 knot can be expected in even very light air. The range can be further narrowed by the use of standard slowing techniques—luffing the jib, easing the main—which limit the maximum speed to 4 knots. Maneuvers integral to starting, such as tacking and luffing, can easily reduce this speed by 50 percent, to 2 knots. Thus the range of starting speeds for small boats is generally 2–4 knots (with an occasional 1 knot or less in very light air). The particular range for any individual boat can easily be ascertained by testing. What the racing sailor needs to know is how far his boat will travel, at these speeds, in certain critical time periods.

Table 2 shows the distances traveled at various speeds during the time intervals that are most important in starting. Five seconds is the usual time needed for a very light boat to get up to speed; ten seconds is more appropriate for longer, heavier boats. How far should one be from the desired point on the starting line when the effort to attain speed is initiated? How far should one be from this desired point when the approach tack is assumed with twenty seconds to go? thirty seconds? a minute? Practice is required to assess distance, but with practice, if the boat's speed is at least approximately known, one can tell not only how far away the line markers are but how long it will take to reach them.

The most important speed–distance relationships are those associated with a speed of 3 knots. This is average for moderate air—between the 2 knots achieved at the completion of an average tack and the full speed (4 knots) attained by most boats with their sails partially luffing. Furthermore, 3 knots is a speed easily attained in various wind strengths—by careful trimming in light air, by luffing in heavy air. It provides complete maneuverability and permits the ready acquisition of full speed in a very short time. It is a control-

TABLE 2
DISTANCE TRAVELED IN FEET AT SPEEDS
BETWEEN 1 AND 6 KNOTS

	TIME REMAINING IN SECONDS							
	5	10	15	20	25	30	45	60
6	50	100	150	200	250	300	450	600
5	42	84	125	167	208	250	375	500
4	33	66	100	133	167	200	300	400
3	25	50	75	100	125	150	225	300
2	16	33	50	66	84	100	150	200
1	8	16	25	33	42	50	75	100

SPEED IN KNOTS

lable speed, capable of modification upward by better sheeting, downward by a variety of slowing techniques. Most important, the distances sailed at 3 knots are easily remembered—25 feet in five seconds, 50 feet in ten seconds, 150 feet in thirty seconds. A feel for this speed (or one close to it) should be cultivated. Once this speed becomes recognizable and reproducible, distances to go to the desired point on the line become meaningful. At 50 feet from the desired point with ten seconds to go, a 3-knot speed can be continued. At 70 feet, speed must be increased to 4 knots. At 35 feet, speed must be decreased to 2 knots.

Prior to the start, a good speed is desirable, for adapting to neighboring boats, for passing boats ahead, and to prevent being overtaken from astern. Therefore, approaches to the line should be planned at speeds of 3 knots or greater. Control modifications and adjustments can then be made by slowing. An increase in speed may not be attainable in a crowded starting area but slowing is always possible. The timing of windward-end starts is simple because slowing can easily be accomplished by luffing—while retaining control over nearby boats and without the danger of being forced over the line. Leeward-end starts, which require reaching down the line, provide no such option and therefore demand a more accurate control of speed.

Variations in the position and technique of tacking at the initiation of the approach tack determines the speed on the approach (Figure 19). When reaching into the planned approach position, the tack (from port tack) or the luff (from starboard tack) onto the approach course can be made a little closer or a little farther away from the line, so that the boat will be at the distance which is opti-

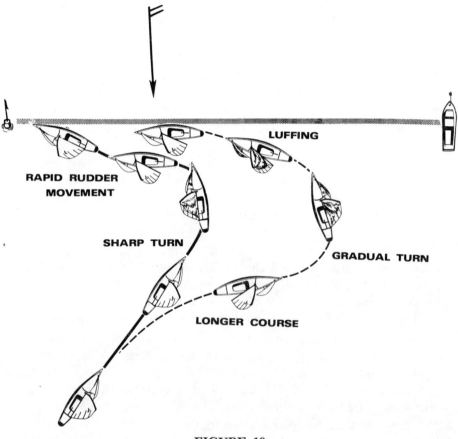

FIGURE 19

mum for the amount of time remaining. If other boats interfere, the tack or luff itself can be modified to adjust speed—an abrupt turn will slow the boat and a smooth gradual turn will preserve speed. One should, of course, know the time consumed by such maneuvers and the variations achieved by altering their management. (Most small boats take about ten seconds to complete a tack from reaching to close-hauled.)

Once on the approach, with the seconds ticking away and the

desired point on the line drawing near, speed must be continually adjusted to maintain a distance from the line which will permit the acquisition of top speed in the final five to ten seconds. If few boats are nearby, sharp changes in course—made by luffing and bearing away sequentially—can reduce speed by one-third. More drastic reductions, to a near stop, can be achieved by repeated violent tiller motions which alter the course very little. This technique is particularly useful when the port-end mark is coming up too soon and many boats are crowding nearby.

The jib is the sail that determines speed. The crew member who trims the jib should keep it unstalled (with a slight luff perhaps) unless specifically ordered otherwise, so that speed can be readily reacquired when needed. Maximum slowing is achieved by overtrimming and stalling the jib, not by allowing it to luff, but unfortunately, this technique will usually result in forcing the bow to leeward. A luffing main and a tightly sheeted jib cause maximum slowing but marked leeway. A luffing jib and a closely sheeted main cause less slowing but preserve pointing and are therefore appropriate to windward-end starts. In light air, neither main nor jib should be allowed to stall—slowing should be achieved by luffing— since speed is difficult to reacquire after stalling. Coordination between the jib trimmer and the helmsman is essential; the former must be acutely alert to orders for the split-second adjustments that may win the start.

Timing—a feel for the time required to sail a given distance— and techniques of speed control must be acquired. These are among the few elements of racing skill that can be attained by practice without a competitor. Any buoy can be used for the rehearsal of both leeward- and windward-end starts. And this practice is of genuine relevance, since starts at the ends are chiefly dependent upon timing. Full-speed approaches help develop the judgment of distance. When these have been mastered, progressively shorter approaches should be undertaken, involving various degrees and methods of reducing speed. Windward-end starts (passing the buoy to leeward) should be controlled chiefly by luffing, as is customary in an actual race. Leeward-end starts (passing the buoy to windward) should be controlled chiefly by changing direction—alternatively luffing and bearing away. Both starts should be modified by variations in the rapidity of the tack or luff to the approach position, variations in sail trim, and variations in the rapidity of rudder movement.

21. *Starting at the Windward End*

Since most boats cross the starting line on starboard tack, only the one farthest to leeward and those that started on port have clear air immediately after the start. All others are (to varying degrees) in the backwind of their neighbors to leeward. Thus, if the line is square to the wind or if the port end is farther to windward, the best start is on the lee bow of the fleet (providing starboard tack is to be continued). When the starboard end is upwind, a larger portion of the fleet is more nearly bow to bow (rather than bow to transom) and therefore in clearer air. Hence, a start within the fleet is more likely to be successful when the starboard end is favored than when the port end is favored. Only if freedom to tack is essential (because the wind is oscillating or very light or the right side of the course is advantageous) is it necessary to start at the extreme end of the line. If the left side of the course is advantageous and starboard tack is to be continued, a start farther down the line, where there is less congestion, is usually successful.

A start at the weather end must be on starboard tack, so the only choices concern the location of the approach tack and the base leg, the sailing angle for reaching the approach-tack position, and the speed of the approach tack. These choices are determined by the data collected—the size of the fleet, the angle of the line, the velocity of the wind and of the current. The exact position on the line depends on whether starboard tack will be continued or a tack to port attempted immediately after the start. The approach may be made from above the lay line, on the lay line, or below the lay line and may be reached from a base leg on port or starboard.

Standard Approach

The standard weather-end start is made on an approach course parallel to and just below the lay line (Figure 20). If freedom to

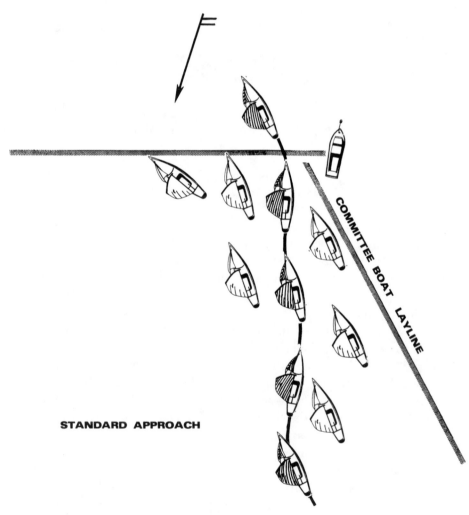

STANDARD APPROACH

FIGURE 20

tack is essential, the approach must be made close to the lay line; if it is not, a less congested track farther to leeward may be selected. The base leg can be on port tack regardless of the approach course. A boat making a starboard approach will be in heavy traffic two or more minutes prior to the gun while the boat coming in on port will have clear air as late as forty-five seconds before the start. However, if the starboard approach is made in a long swooping curve from slightly above the lay line, and from a position a hundred yards or more from the starting line, speed and maneuverability can be preserved. In small fleets, coming in on port permits an accurate assessment of the timing of the starboard tackers and provides an opportunity to select the rank most likely to arrive at the line on time. If the leaders are holding back, those to leeward can be crossed and a tack made on the lee bow of a boat just below the lay line. If they are early, the first few can be allowed to pass ahead and a tack made where an opening appears in the second or third rank. The larger the fleet and the more heavily favored the weather end, the more difficult it will be to tack into the desired position late in the starting sequence. Under these circumstances it is better to come in on port early or to make the entire approach on starboard. If a start right at the end of the line is contemplated, early entry into the starboard-tack fleet is essential.

Once on starboard tack, two considerations become paramount: arriving at the front row before the gun, and not being forced to windward of the lay line. For boats within the amassed fleet, speed is minimal. Instead of the twenty-five feet in five seconds (at 3 knots) that could be expected in the middle of the line, twenty-five feet in fifteen seconds (at 1 knot) may be all that is possible. With one minute remaining, one should never be more than two hundred feet from the desired point on the line, and if already slowed and in heavy traffic, one should probably not be more than a hundred feet away. Once slowed and too far back to make the front row, escape will be impossible. Little of the basic wind flow will penetrate that mass of flapping Dacron, and what does will be so disturbed by nearby boats that speed will not be attainable for minutes after the start—by which time the boats in clear air will have developed insurmountable leads. It is far better to reach the front line too early than too late, so one must keep pressing up as the seconds tick away.

To maintain the control necessary for working through the fleet (from a position astern on starboard or after tacking into the second or third rank), one must enter the heavy traffic well below the lay line. Control of boats to weather, which threaten to drive over, as well as escape from boats to leeward, which periodically luff, requires room to luff. The approach therefore consists of a series of luffs to stop the boat to weather, escapes from the luffs of boats to leeward, and returns to the close-hauled course. The result is a progressive movement to weather of the original close-hauled course. This movement must be allowed for, since once the lay line is reached, the boat to leeward takes command; the weather boat has no choice but to stop and let her through when she luffs, and is then forced either to limp across the line in the second or third rank or to luff to the wrong side of the committee boat, for a restart. If the sea is smooth and the wind moderate, one can expect to make an approach to the windward end on a course halfway between close-hauled and dead to windward. If the air is light or heavy, leeway will be greater and one can safely begin the approach closer to the lay line. If the current is running down the line, the approach may be initiated close to, on, or above the lay line (depending upon its strength). If the current is running up the line, the approach must be made farther to leeward and in some cases from a position dead to leeward of the end of the line.

Precise control of speed is essential. Early on the approach, speed between 1 and 2 knots can be expected—fifty to a hundred feet in thirty seconds. Near the line, speed may have to be reduced to half a knot (twenty-five feet in thirty seconds) or less. Both main and jib should be luffing continuously—completely when above close-hauled, perhaps 50 percent when close-hauled. (If full sail is required in the last minute of the approach, the boat is too far from the line.) Speed can be further reduced by turning the boat more into the wind, increased by a modest improvement in sail trim. The jib is the greatest determinant of speed and its trim (between full luff and "soft") should be directed by the helmsman. The sails must never be allowed to stall, since the reacquisition of speed is then extremely difficult.

The ultimate purpose of the approach is to arrive, barely moving, within a few feet of the line at the desired location with but a few seconds to go. Boats ahead on the latter part of the approach must be encouraged to peel off down the line. A threat to establish a leeward overlap will induce them to move ahead, and when the line is near, a luff across their sterns will provide them room to make the escape they so desperately desire. When a boat ahead and to windward bears away across your bow, do nothing to hinder her passage.

Give her all the room she needs; you don't want her ahead and to windward when the gun sounds. Boats abeam or astern to windward must be given periodic luffs to induce them to fall astern as the lay line is approached. Success is finally determined by the proper management of the last boat to windward as the gun is about to sound. If enough time remains and she appears fearful of being forced over the line, feint toward her lee quarter and then wave her across your bow to a leeward escape. If insufficient time remains, sheet in and go through her to leeward so as to bring your bow even with or ahead of hers as the gun fires. If you have commenced the approach sufficiently far to leeward of the lay line, boats farther to leeward can be essentially ignored during the approach.

Once you have arrived close to the line in the front rank, you must stay there. In moderate air, a small centerboarder can be kept in position with both sails luffing and almost no forward way for a minute or more. The same technique can be utilized in racing keel boats, the only disadvantage being a greater difficulty in reacquiring speed. For the boat luffing on the line, there is no danger that one farther back will be able to acquire sufficient speed to charge through the dense mass astern. Even though the reacquisition of speed is difficult, it is easier for the boat in the front rank than for any other. Being in the first rank early therefore entails little risk. A variant on this approach is the "hurry up and wait" technique of setting up in the first rank before the fleet arrives and just staying there. When the time to start finally comes, the sails must be sheeted in gradually and synchronously while, if possible, the boat is borne away to slightly below the close-hauled course and speed is reacquired in "starting gear."

Success at emerging in clear air requires precise understanding of the position of the line and of the time remaining. A slight luff a few seconds before the gun may hold back the boat to weather and allow just a bit more room for bearing away at the start itself. If a weather boat begins to drive in advance, an instantaneous decision must be made—to go with her if she is approximately on time or to let her go if she is obviously early. When in doubt, it is better to go with her, to prevent her emerging ahead of bow to bow. After the start boats to leeward become dangerous; once in a safe leeward position they are in control until you tack away. Unless you are certain the boat to leeward will be over early, you must sheet in with her and go. The calling of the time and of the distance to the intended position on the line becomes crucial. To be farther than a foot or two behind the line when the gun goes is to have wasted all the effort that was required to get there.

Variant Approaches

In the vast majority of circumstances, the standard approach is the most likely to be successful, but unique conditions may justify a weather-end start by a variant technique.

Very Light Air:	Swoop down to leeward
	Late barging
	Port-tack base leg
Very Heavy Air:	Swoop down to leeward
Current Down the Line:	Barging
Current Up the Line:	Port-tack base leg
Right Side Heavily Favored:	Late barging
Left Side Heavily Favored:	Port-tack base leg

SWOOP DOWN TO LEEWARD

In very light or heavy air, if competitors tend to bunch at the windward end, luffing close to the line, an excellent windward-end start may be made by a boat reaching astern and to leeward of them with the intention of breaking through at high speed a few boat lengths farther down the line. The essential element is the maintenance of speed. The technique must be applied at the last possible moment, after all the rest have committed themselves to a luffing position close to the line. Unfortunately, this method (like many others) becomes increasing less desirable as more competitors attempt it. The presence of boats that are on or near the lay line and coming in late will necessitate a slower swing, which limits the possibility of breaking through to leeward. If it becomes evident that the mass of the fleet is arriving at the line late or that one or two boats are hanging back and that circumnavigating them will be costly, the plan should be canceled in favor of a late start right at the buoy (or committee boat). This resort is always available if the helmsman is willing to make a quick port-tack escape before he commits himself. I am surprised at how infrequently such an escape is utilized, for it permits the recovery of clear air and free maneuverability to weather of the fleet at a crucial time.

BARGING AND LATE BARGING

In large fleets, a barging start will be successful only when the current is running down the line, setting boats to leeward of the lay line as they make a standard approach. In these conditions Gardner Cox was able to make a series of successful starts from above the lay line to win the 1968 Olympic trials in the 5.5-meter class. Boats luffing along the lay line, and particularly those that initiated their approach to leeward of the lay line, were swept to leeward, leaving a large hole between the most windward boat on the line and the committee boat. Cox managed his pre-tested starts by sailing away from the committee boat on a fixed broad reach, jibing toward the lay line, and emerging at the committee boat under nearly full speed. A tack away to the strongly favored right side of the course provided two firsts and two seconds in the first four races.

When the need to tack away is clearly present (in oscillating winds, very light air, a persistent veer, or the like), a late barging start may be successful in the absence of a current down the line. For the individual willing to wait until the fleet has cleared out, an arrival timed so that the boat is just astern of the last boat to cross the line at its weather end can provide freedom to tack and ultimate major advantage (Figure 21). When this technique is used, if only one or two boats are able to tack before you cross the line, the result may be a third place at the weather mark. Speed must be maintained and a swoop down from above the lay line accurately timed

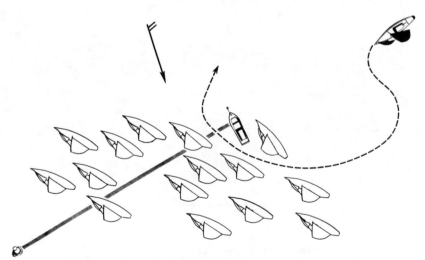

FIGURE 21

(by variation in the radius of the swoop) to result in arrival just astern of the last boat. If she escapes ahead, she (and others) may be able to tack first and may then be directly on your wind during the prospective long port tack. (See Chapter 25, "Starting in Light Air.") Late barging is obviously a useful technique if another weather-end pattern has been attempted but fails.

PORT-TACK BASE LEG

The standard approach can be accomplished readily from a port-tack base leg in small fleets. If, particularly in very light air, the left side of the course is strongly favored or the current is setting up the line, a standard start at the weather end will be hazardous. The greater risks associated with the congestion at the end of the line, and the necessity of continuing within the disturbed air of the fleet for a prolonged period, can be avoided by selection of a start nearer the middle of the line on the lee bow of the fleet (Figure 22). Be-

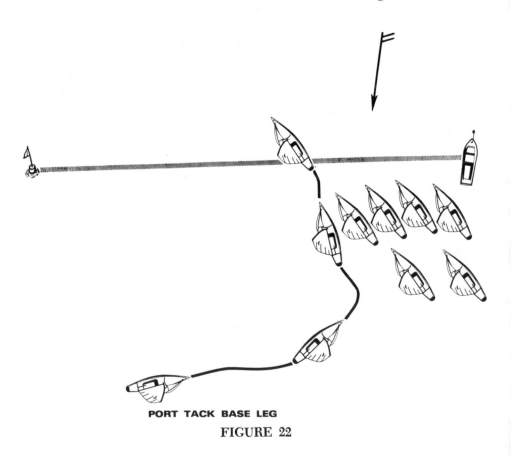

PORT TACK BASE LEG

FIGURE 22

cause few, if any, boats will be farther to leeward, backwind will be diminished and the general disturbance due to the fleet minimized. It is essential to avoid being driven over to windward, since there is then no possibility of escape through a tack to port. Once free on the fleet's lee bow, the leeward boat will find herself working progressively ahead as the boats to windward fall in astern in the disturbed air which surrounds them. As the fleet carries its umbrella of disturbed air along with it, most of them will continue to be adversely affected until they tack to port.

The base leg on port should be undertaken late in the starting sequence—yours should be the last boat returning on port—to insure that all boats have been committed and that you will in fact end up on the lee bow of the fleet. The base leg should begin well below the starting line, so that speed can be maintained through a course high on the wind and time–distance relationships can be controlled by modifications in direction. It should be timed toward a tack under the most leeward starboard tacker with approximately twenty to thirty seconds remaining. The tack should be made close aboard and from a position that will result in the boats remaining overlapped after its completion. The windward boat must then be luffed to a standstill so that she will not be able to drive over to windward or to slip astern and come through to leeward before the gun. The luff should not be relinquished until it is time to bear away to charge down and across the line. After the gun the danger is to windward. With clear air to leeward the boat should be driven off to attain maximum speed as quickly as possible. It will be easy enough to work back up later, once speed has been acquired.

22. Starting at the Leeward End

Peter Barrett, who—like me—prefers to make a leeward-end start after a base leg on port, has written that he is able to tack beneath the first starboard tacker coming down the line and make the ideal start at the pin nine times out of ten. Although I was routinely successful in this approach five or six years ago, I find that I rarely am nowadays. (Either he is a far better starter than I, or his competition is considerably less sophisticated.) In large, competent fleets this approach must be made in the teeth of six or eight boats, several of whom will be early and will be forced to re-round the mark and several of whom approach from well to leeward with a good head of steam and will drive past to weather. Bruce Goldsmith claims that he prefers to "set up" on starboard early—in part because he does not wish to antagonize his neighbors, who—he says—are more likely to act aggressively if irritated by a boat tacking beneath them. Neither extreme is necessary, of course, but each helmsman should acquire facility in one particular technique by practicing it regularly.

Although an approach that provides entry into the starboard-tack fleet thirty or more seconds before the gun and behind the leaders is usually more appropriate, going for the pin is occasionally justified. The port-tack base leg from beyond the line provides an opportunity to judge the likelihood of congestion at the leeward end. If the fleet does not appear to be pressing, tacking on the lee bow of the leader is sensible. If a current is setting to windward, with boats luffing along the line likely to be swept over, a late approach on the lee bow of the entire group is the conservative technique. An opportunity to go for the pin is likely to develop after a general recall, when boats are reluctant to risk disqualification by being over the line early. However, even in the presence of these enticements, if the fleet is large the most leeward start should be attempted only if the wind is moderate and the sea smooth. When the situation is right, the lay line should be accurately determined in advance and the final approach made just to windward of it, to assure being to leeward and in control of all neighboring boats (Figure 23). An approach at full speed (or at as high a speed as possible) is necessary if the boat is to break through the blanketing of the boats to weather. This means that the last twenty seconds of the approach, at least, should be sailed at 3 knots or faster. Since a speed of 3 knots takes the boat a hundred feet in twenty seconds, the approach tack should be completed approximately a hundred feet down the lay line and approximately twenty seconds before the gun. The base leg can be made on a close reach from beyond the leeward end, with speed and sailing angle adjusted as necessary to result in arrival at the lay line with the desired time and distance remaining. A smooth, speed-saving tack should initiate the approach just above the lay line, and the line should be charged. If speed can be maintained and timing is accurate, the boats massed to windward near the line will have no choice but to luff out of the way. Because a boat approaching on the lay line establishes an overlap from a considerable distance to leeward, she need not modify her approach in order to grant boats on the line "ample room and opportunity" to keep clear (rule 37).

If you approach, luffing, with adequate time to reach the line, boats ahead and to windward will be forced either to luff or to peel away to leeward. In the final moments they will be either stopped to weather or sailing free and away from you to leeward. It is the boats astern and to leeward that are dangerous. If, with little time remaining, another boat approaches from astern, your lee bow must be protected. If possible, bear away in front of her before she comes too close. Once she is overlapped to weather, she is under control; a sharp luff at your convenience will keep her in her place. If she

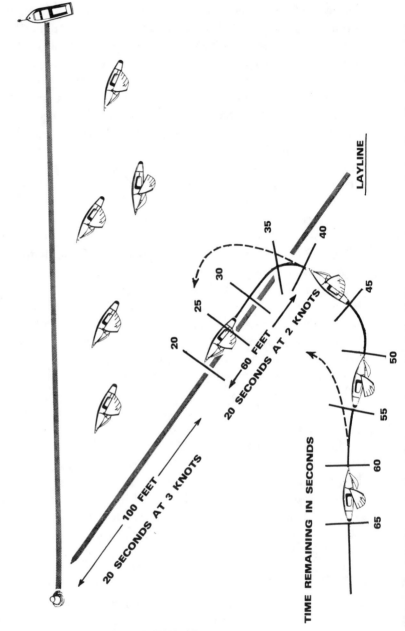

FIGURE 23

seems determined to break through to leeward (and it is impossible to cross ahead so as to trap her to windward), then a choice must be made between luffing sharply and letting her go (so as to be as far to weather of her as possible after the gun) and driving ahead with her (so as to keep your lee bow clear). The former is usually the better technique until the final few seconds. Then it is essential to drive ahead and to reach the line as the gun goes, in order to maintain clear air above and below. Usually a sharp (but not too sharp!— rule 40) luff followed by a bearing away to pick up speed just before the gun fires takes the boat far enough to weather to be free of competitors to leeward.

The major danger, and the one most misunderstood, is involved in bearing away in front of a boat approaching from astern or to leeward. There is no proper course before the start and no prohibition of bearing away to prevent an overtaking boat from passing to leeward. Indeed, an overtaking boat is required to keep clear of any gyrations that the boat clear ahead may undertake—until—until that critical moment when suddenly a perpendicular extension from the leading boat's transom would pass behind the bow of the follower (rule 40). Then, abruptly, the following boat becomes the right-of-way yacht, and the leader must keep clear. The latter is left with two recourses: (1) to continue on, bearing across the follower's bow, on the assumption that though she is at risk, she is far enough ahead to get away with it, or (2) to luff, breaking the overlap but leaving the follower the option of coming through to leeward. If the follower is forced to alter course or a collision occurs in instance (1), the leader is disqualified (rule 37). However if the overlap is broken, as in (2), the follower must keep clear and if a collision occurs prior to giving the windward yacht "room and opportunity to keep clear," the follower is disqualified (rule 40).

If an overlap is established and not broken by a luff, the leeward (overtaking) boat may hold her initial course (or bear away), or she may begin to luff and under certain circumstances disqualify the windward boat by subsequently running into her boom (Figure 24). The new rules have considerably altered the tactics available to the leeward boat: they permit her to luff (*slowly*) as soon as she has acquired an overlap (bow just ahead of transom—rule 40). The windward boat does not have to anticipate this maneuver by the leeward boat; she need not take any action to keep clear until the overlap has been established. Thereafter, she must be given "room and opportunity" to keep clear and cannot be forced to luff except

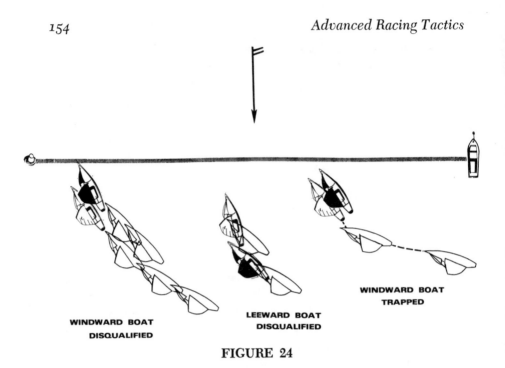

WINDWARD BOAT
TRAPPED

LEEWARD BOAT
DISQUALIFIED

WINDWARD BOAT
DISQUALIFIED

FIGURE 24

slowly. If the overtaking boat establishes the leeward overlap so rapidly and so close aboard (bow within a few inches of leeward quarter) that the windward boat is unable to keep clear, the leeward boat will be disqualified (rule 37). The best recourse of a windward boat to the sudden establishment of a close leeward overlap is an immediate luff (as sharp as is permissible relative to windward boats) to break away. If a collision occurs, the leeward boat will be disqualified for establishing the overlap too close aboard. On the other hand, a windward boat must begin to keep clear as soon as an overlap has been established. If, after the overlap has existed for a few seconds, she fails to make any effort to break away and a collision occurs or the leeward boat is prevented from luffing, the windward boat will be disqualified. The leeward boat may not luff above close-hauled, however, until she has acquired luffing rights by virtue of passing ahead of the mast-abeam position (rule 40).

One effective technique which meets these limitations is as follows (Figure 25): Two minutes, or less, before the start (depending on the length of the line), approach the port end of the line on port tack, on a close reach toward it or sailing parallel to and below it. Plan to arrive at the desired position below the line—near the leeward end or in the middle, but well to windward of the leeward-

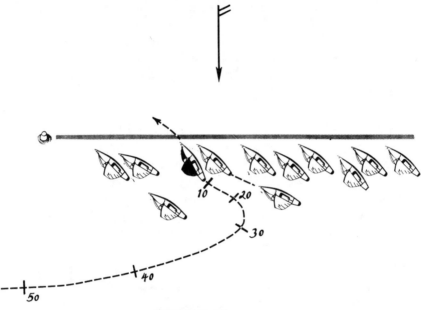

FIGURE 25

end lay line—with approximately thirty to sixty seconds remaining. Cruise along at nearly maximum speed approximately a hundred feet below the line, passing well to leeward of approaching starboard-tack boats. As the time remaining decreases, the approach course can be angled closer to the line, to reduce the distance to go after the tack. When approximately thirty to fifty seconds remain, be ready to tack to starboard as soon as the opportunity appears. No boat should be to leeward; there should have been a significant interval since the passing of the last starboard tacker (a pigeon if at all possible); and the next starboard tacker should be far enough to windward so that, after completion of your tack, she can be trapped. When the bow of the approaching starboard tacker is about 1½ to 2 boat lengths away, tack gradually (allowing ten seconds), in such a manner that upon completion of the tack you are just ahead of her (your bow ahead of her bow) but *overlapped*. The precise placement of the tack will, of course vary with the speed of the approaching boat(s); the windward boat must not be tempted to bear away beneath you in any case. The tack should be preceded by a gradual speed-increasing luff and should be followed by a period of speed-regaining optimal sail trim.

The use of this approach technique should result in your being ahead and to leeward of all nearby boats (those within two or three boat lengths), moving rapidly with clear air about fifty feet below the line with twenty to forty seconds remaining. Thereafter, you must (1) maintain speed, (2) avoid falling down into the backwind of boats ahead and to leeward, and (3) arrive at the line on time. Here is where the avoidance of stalling is so important and where telltales on both sails (the luff of the jib and the leech of the main) are so valuable. If you bear away so far at the completion of the tack that either sail stalls, you will be unable to regain the speed necessary for a good start. Watch the telltales (preferably, have your crew watch the telltales) and ease the sails whenever the boat bears away; luff them, if necessary, but don't stall them. The average speed shortly after a tack is about 3 knots, and the length of the close-hauled course to the line from a position 40 to 60 feet below it is about 75 to 100 feet. The distance traveled at 3 knots is 25 feet in five seconds, or 150 feet in thirty seconds. Thus if but twenty seconds remain, the boat may be brought to a close-hauled course, and after only a modest luff or a slight shivering of the jib, she may charge the line. If forty seconds remain, a proportionate lengthening of the course and/or reduction in speed is necessary. Both can be largely accomplished by luffing closely under the boats to weather, for as you luff above close-hauled, speed drops and the course is lengthened. At the same time the hole to leeward is further enlarged, and when you do bear away (without stalling the sails) in the last ten to fifteen seconds, there will be plenty of room to gather speed without falling into the backwind of boats to leeward. As the gun goes you are rounding up, trimming in both main and jib sheets, but retaining an open leech (plenty of twist) and draft forward until nearly full speed is attained. Other boats, committed earlier, are usually moving very slowly, and in most instances are already trapped. Only you have the speed which leaves open the various options: bearing away beneath a boat to leeward to get farther down the line, shooting up to stop a boat to weather, or charging for the line.

23. Middle-of-the-Line Starts

I have recently noted that many of my competitors are making starts from the middle of the line. I have always felt that since no line is even—since one end is always favored—I should start at an end. But getting a good start at the favored end is not easy when everyone else it trying to be in that same place at the same time. Even when I do get the best start at the favored end, I often spend the next five minutes trying to break away from the boats that surround me, unable to tack away when I need to do so. Meanwhile, boats starting in the middle of the line are surging along unimpeded by close neighbors; they are often in a commanding position by the time I have a chance to look around. When it is clearly evident that one side of the course is favored, a start at the end of the line nearest that side is essential. However, when the strategy of the beat is in doubt, or when, as so often happens, the opposite side of the course turns out to be favored, the start at the supposedly favored end may be the worst start of all.

At the first SPORT regatta, the second race was conducted in a strong 20- to 30-knot northwesterly. The weather end of the line was slightly upwind, and we elected to start there. I was surprised to find that when the gun sounded most of the fleet was well down the line, and subsequently I was dismayed to note that they were working out on my lee bow. As we approached the shore, there was a progressive heading shift, and less sea. The farther we continued, the more the advantage of the boats that had started down the line increased. The boats in the middle were bound to gain in relation to boats at the initially favored (more upwind) end. In Bermuda a few weeks later, I elected to start on port as an oscillating westerly shifted to provide a port-tack lift. I had to go under the first six or seven boats but emerged from the middle of the line with clear air, going in the right direction. A short way up the weather leg, it was evident that my competitors for the lead were the boats that had started with me in the middle of the line and had been able to tack to port soon after the gun. In a similar situation in a later race, instead of starting on port, I tacked under the leading group of boats reaching down the line on starboard. I made a fine start at the favored port end but found that I couldn't tack to the lifted port tack, and by the time the starboard-tack lift reappeared, I was far down to leeward. We were tenth at the first weather mark and finished seventh; it was our worst race. (We had won the race in which we started on port near the middle of the line.)

The start in the middle of the line is advantageous in the following situations:

> The air is very light.
> Freedom to tack is essential (in oscillating winds).
> The air is very heavy.
> A persistent shift is probable but its timing and direction are uncertain.

The advantage of starting in the middle of the line is commonly recognized in the first two situations. In very light air it is essential to remain near the line prior to the start (can one get nearer than its middle?) to retain boat speed and clear air and to be free to tack toward whichever side of the course subsequently appears to be favored. All these advantages are obtained by hovering near the middle of the line (and usually slightly to windward of it). If (as so often happens) a new wind fills in from one or the other side of the course as the gun fires or shortly thereafter, the boat in the middle is best able to maneuver in either direction. In an oscillating wind, when port tack is lifted, a port-tack start is preferable. The knowledgeable realize that it will pay to pass behind many transoms for the privilege. When the leeward end of the line is favored (more upwind), the port-tack starter will usually have to reach down to the middle of the line before she can break through.

Less often recognized is the advantage of the middle of the line in heavy air. The essential element of a good start in heavy air is the preservation of boat speed; the worst start is one that results in the presence of a competitor close on the lee bow. Slowing—whether to deal with many boats at the favored end, to achieve accurate timing, or to keep clear of a competitor close to leeward—results in marked leeway and marked delay in reestablishing boat speed (because of inadequate hydrodynamic side force in the presence of excessive aerodynamic side force). Boats romping down the line at full speed and charging across its middle in clear air will be far ahead by the time slowed boats establish normal progress to windward. If the wind is oscillating and/or a persistent shift subsequently appears, the start in the middle of the line provides even greater advantage.

The persistent shift is the major cause of disaster, and occasionally of dramatic success, in series racing. The prevention of disaster requires staying near the rhumb line early in the first beat. Starting in the middle of the line reduces the risk initially and more readily permits a tack toward the rhumb line early in the leg. Subsequently, the boat that started in the middle of the line is in a position that enables her to tack away from the rhumb line inside and to windward of the mass of the fleet and to tack back toward the rhumb line inside and to leeward of the mass of the fleet. And the boat in this position suffers the least possible loss if a persistent shift from an unexpected direction appears.

The middle of the line provides a location where competitors are less aggressive, where the front rank is likely to be well back from the actual line, and where individual boats are unlikely to be recognized. The outstanding East German Solings regularly start from this position. They are able to emerge consistently in clear air with freedom to tack, unimpeded by the less competent competitors they find about them. When the "around the end" rule is in effect, competitors are particularly hesitant about approaching the middle of the line, and the location accordingly becomes all the more attractive to the aggressive helmsman. What is required is a keen sense of the position of the line. The first considerations must be the distance of the helmsman from the bow of his boat and the distance of the white flag from the bow of the committee boat. Observations from a position at an appropriate distance back from a long line of cars in a car park can provide some understanding of the relationships involved. The bow of an imaginary committee boat is readily obscured by cars close at hand but not by those far away. Dramatic changes in perspective occur consequent to slight alterations in position when close to the committee boat, minimal changes when far away. From the middle of a long line in a large fleet, the bow of the committee boat can usually be seen across the bows of the intervening boats (unless they are very close aboard) *before* one crosses the line—even if the intervening boats are on the line. If they are not—and this should be expected—most of the committee boat may be visible (Figure 26). (A useful technique to

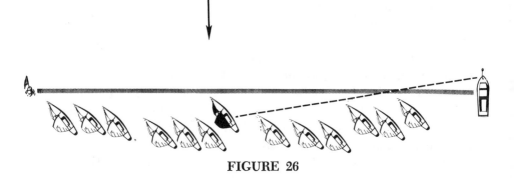

FIGURE 26

practice is to estimate position while approaching close-hauled in advance of the start and then to turn parallel to the line to check the relationship to the range between the ends.) If a range is available between the end of the line and a distinctive feature on the shore beyond, these other means of estimation are unnecessary, of course. But whatever the means, when starting in the middle of the line one can expect to be ahead of the fleet but behind the line as the gun fires.

24. Off on Port

From the committee boat, I watched Argyle Campbell make the most dramatic start of the 1966 O'Day Single-Handed Championship series. I had set a near perfect line, square to the wind, and boats were starting on starboard all along it when Argyle appeared on port at the port end. He narrowly passed ahead of the first starboard tacker and then successively crossed, by steadily increasing margins, boat after boat of the starboard-tack fleet. I presume he finally breathed an exhausted sigh of relief, slumped in the bilge, and gratefully abdicated the lead, because at the end of the round, he was far astern. His accomplishment was none the less significant. It demonstrated that of boats starting equally far to windward along a line set square to the wind, the one on port has the advantage. Argyle, in clear air, had been moving progressively faster than his competitors, each in some measure backwinded by his neighbor to leeward.

The massing of sailboats in the starting area causes the lower levels of the wind stream to rise above them and eddy about them. Even boats on the windward edge of the fleet receive a disturbed flow. Boats that assume a tack opposite to that of the majority find

themselves moving, as they separate, into a progressively cleaner
wind flow. Hence, a port-tack start, which is always opposite to
that of the majority, provides not only freedom from the backwind
and blanketing of neighboring boats but also a stronger and less
disturbed air flow. Argyle Campbell demonstrated that even without separation from the fleet freedom from backwind is advantageous. When port tack takes the boat away from the fleet as well,
a far more dramatic gain results. When the starboard end of the
line is favored, the advantages of a port-tack start may be obtained
by crossing the line on starboard and tacking to port immediately
thereafter. It is difficult, often impossible, to tack after starting on
starboard when the port end is favored. Therefore, when the leeward end of the line is favored, port tack must usually be attained
by crossing the line on port.

The advantages of port tack immediately after the start are so
great that starting on port or tacking to port should be attempted
whenever there is no clear advantage to continuing on starboard.
Unfortunately, the risks of an early tack to port often prevent
utilization of its probable advantages. In some conditions, however,
port tack is so important that the start should be planned with its
selection as the prime consideration. Starting on port tack should
normally be undertaken only when the port end of the line is upwind or when, in very light air, the line is square. The risks of a
port-tack are justified if

The air is light.

The wind is oscillating and a backing shift has appeared.

The right side of the beat is preferred.

When the air is light my first thought is to consider a port
tack. At Ottawa in a recent Soling regatta, what little air existed
was inshore and to the right, where the unfavorable current was
also much decreased. I wanted to go to the right immediately, and
I didn't want to have to tack in that light air to do so. Even though
the line slightly favored the starboard end, I decided to start on
port. We close-reached along the line, bore off slightly behind three
starboard tackers, while the remainder limped up to the line in
each other's backwind, and were soon romping off alone to a huge
lead at the weather mark. In our best race at CORK in 1973 we
started on port tack in a dying northerly by taking the sterns of
about forty-five starboard tackers, massed bow to stern on the line.
Although we had given away a hundred yards or more, we were
soon close to the lead. At the weather mark our only competitors
were the few other boats that had been able to escape on port. The

rest, pinned down by neighbors close astern and to weather, unable to tack, were forced to remain on starboard within the general zone of air disturbed by the fleet and a local zone of backwind from neighbors ahead and to leeward. They continued within this disturbed air for many minutes and ultimately tacked within it, while we, unimpeded by neighbors and separated farther and farther from the fleet, slipped away with increasing speed.

In the race at Cowes for the Weymouth Town Trophy during the 1967 P.O.W. Week, I sought a leeward-end start, found that starboard tack was so headed that I could scarcely lay the leeward-line mark, looked astern and found the nearest boat dead astern rather than on my weather quarter, drove ahead a few yards, and then flipped to port as the gun fired. I was soon all alone, far in the lead, as the remainder of the ninety-boat fleet floundered in each other's dirty air, unable to make progress on starboard or to tack to the suddenly lifted port tack. In a similar situation at the start of the fourth race of the 1967 U.S. Nationals, I found myself pinned down by a boat on my weather quarter, was forced to continue on starboard, and experienced a prolonged struggle to drive over a boat on my lee bow. When the boat to windward had finally been forced about and I had clear air to leeward, I looked around. The boats that had taken the port tack from the weather end of the line were sailing in a port-tack header or were coming about in a starboard-tack lift on a course that would cross far ahead of mine. I had missed their shift and was now out of the running.

When the wind is oscillating, careful observation of its direction during the last few minutes before the start can snatch success from the jaws of disaster. Because of the oscillation, each end of the line may be alternately favored. When the leeward end is favored, port tack is almost always the lifted tack. Continuance of starboard tack beyond the line takes the boat not only on a poor angle to the median wind but away from the subsequent oscillation in the opposite direction. When the veer arrives, the starboard tackers are far astern of the boats which escaped on port, and they may never catch up. A start in an oscillating air flow must always be managed in a manner that at least permits an early tack. It should be made preferably on the lifted tack—and ideally at the upwind end of the line. The only way this can be achieved in a backing oscillation is to cross the line on port. Under such circumstances, if a port tack has not been planned and a tack to port is blocked, a jibe away to cross on port is warranted.

A port tack from the port end of the line covers the fleet. It is a tack back toward the rhumb line from a position to port of that line. In the same manner, continuing on starboard from the starboard end of the line is a tack toward the rhumb line from a position to starboard of that line. The opposite possibilities—continuing on starboard from the port end of the line and tacking to port from the starboard end of the line—are risky, as they take the boat away from the fleet. When a persistent shift is probable but its direction is uncertain, staying close to the rhumb line until the situation clarifies is wise. When the right side of the course is clearly favored but the leeward end is upwind, many helmsmen prefer to start back on the line to assure an early tack to port. The initial disadvantage is soon negated by a major persistent shift or a more favorable current.

Starting on port is not risky if two simple rules are observed (Figure 27). First, when in doubt, go astern; a hole will always appear. The more the leeward end is favored, the more the starboard tackers will be lined up bow to stern, the more each will be slowed by the boat ahead, and the more readily the port-tack boat can slip through. Don't expect to cross the entire fleet or even to cross astern of the first few boats. Be willing to bear away again and again, waiting for a safe slot. Second, keep going. If you are trying to start on port, you want to get to the opposite side of the fleet, into clear air, beyond the last starboard tacker. Never tack back before you are completely in the clear. Tacking back results in being pinned down by the boat that forced you about, far less able to escape on port than you were originally. And then you are in the midst of the fleet, buried in bad air, conducted willy-nilly away

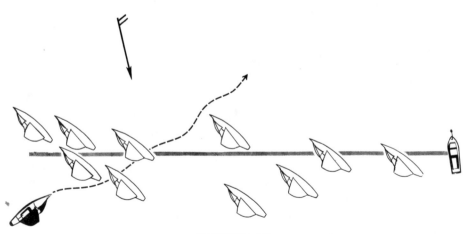

FIGURE 27

from where you wanted to go. Always go astern, again and again; if port tack was worth trying in the first place, the ultimate gain will fully compensate for the initial loss in distance. Once on the far side of the starboard tackers, you have all the advantages: clear air, freedom to tack, and control over the competitors when they come back to you on port.

25. Starting in Light Air

In light air, successful starting demands the refinement of all starting skills. Minor errors tolerable in moderate air now become disasters. The ability to sail toward the advantageous side of the
course, always of first importance, becomes even more crucial. The
second essential, almost as urgent, is getting clear air, and this
requires separation from boats on the lee bow. Every starting plan
must focus upon methods of acquiring these two ingredients. In
light air, five major techniques are available, two for use when the
port end of the line is farther upwind, and three for use when the
starboard end of the line is favored. Each is designed for obtaining
clear air while progressing in the desired direction.

Port-End Starts

(1) If the advantageous side of the course is to the left, then
starboard tack is the preferred tack from the line. Unless it is possible to obtain the ideal position at the pin as the gun fires, the
only way to obtain clear air while sailing in the right direction is
to proceed from a position to leeward of the fleet (Figure 28). In a

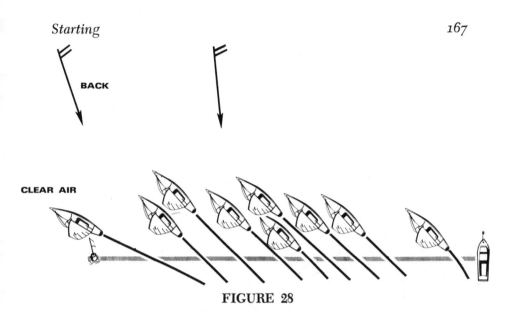

FIGURE 28

race of the 1969 Great Lakes Soling Championship series, I found myself trapped by a fleet of boats on my lee bow. I bore off across their sterns at 60° to the wind and slipped away just to weather of the port-end mark. I was going so much faster than the opposition that I soon had clear air to port of the fleet. I then sailed into better air from a backed direction and went on to win. In a recent Soling Midwinter Regatta, Ti Hack developed a dramatic lead by "footing to the header" (the backed upper air flow brought to the surface near Key Biscayne) after slipping past the port-end starting mark and making for the shore at top speed. He had dropped nearly a hundred yards to leeward by the time he reached the shift, but had a lead greater than that when he rounded the weather mark. Speed is what counts in light air. Pointing is ineffective; attempts to sail close to the wind merely reduce speed and speed made good to windward. Sails must be trimmed well off the center line and the boat borne away from the close-hauled course. This situation is only attainable to leeward of neighboring boats.

(2) If the right side of the beat is favored but the port end of the line is farther to windward, the ideal start is on port tack. In light air, the entire air flow is lifted above and deviated around the massed fleet at the line. Boats starting on starboard tack will be additionally slowed by other boats ahead and to leeward. Only boats on the periphery of the fleet have reasonably clear air. A boat on port tack approaching the line of starboard tackers at

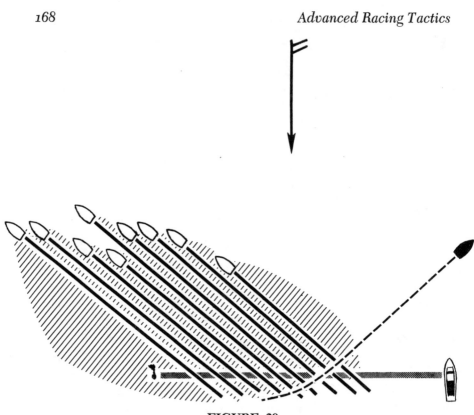

FIGURE 29

good speed can usually slip through the chain (Figure 29). Many
sterns must be crossed and much distance sacrificed to attain clear
air. But once attained, it will more than compensate for the earlier
loss. If the port-end mark must be re-rounded, port tack is the best
route to recovery. A boat trapped by a competitor close on the lee
bow must arrange an escape tack to port as soon as possible. It may
be necessary to luff to force a boat astern to tack, or to bear away to
obtain sufficient room to clear a boat to windward before tacking.
Such immediate sacrifices will be more than counterbalanced by the
clear air acquired on port. If there is to be an escape on port it
should be done immediately—before the rest of the fleet gets the
same idea and causes port tack to be as disturbed as starboard.

Starboard-End Starts

(1) The standard starting technique for the windward end is to
luff close to the mark or committee boat just beneath the starboard-
tack lay line and acquire speed only as the gun is fired. In light air

a boat in this position is at the mercy of competitors to leeward, some of whom will start at greater speed and will subsequently backwind boats to weather. If the left side of the beat is advantageous and starboard tack is to be continued, it is wiser to attempt a start to leeward of the luffing group at the weather end. This position can be acquired either by reaching down through the luffing boats, well before the starting signal, or by approaching on port and tacking ahead and to leeward of the competition. Both techniques have serious hazards, and success in employing them requires a willingness to sail well down the line, giving up distance to windward, in order to preserve speed and obtain clear air. If the reach down astern of boats luffing near the line is attempted late, the gun will fire while the boat is still in the second rank, with almost no possibility of escape. Nothing disturbs the wind more, or slows the boat astern and to leeward more, than a boat (or boats) luffing ahead. One must reach through early and not give up speed by luffing until completely free of boats with the potential of acquiring a lee bow position. The better technique is to approach on port tack and then tack to starboard beneath the approaching fleet. Again the danger is that one will be blanketed initially and backwinded later. The tack must be completed far enough from approaching starboard tackers so that speed may be reacquired and clear air maintained until the gun fires.

(2) The techniques just described should generally be utilized if the fleet is characterized by bargers who completely seal off the windward corner, if the current is setting to starboard, or if the left side of the course is strongly favored. However, if the fleet tends to spread out, if the current is setting to port, or if the right side of the course is favored, a barging start may be preferable. This should be attempted from a reaching position well to windward of the lay line, a position that permits an evaluation of the timing and intent of competitors to leeward. If most or all appear to be making an early approach, a swoop down astern of them may be made in the final ten to twenty seconds and a hole sought to leeward of the most windward boats (Figure 30) (which may be completely stopped awaiting the gun) or right at the mark as the most upwind boat bears away for the start. Do not attempt to join, a few feet to windward, a line of boats approaching on the lay line, and do not be deceived into thinking the boats in such a line are not laying the mark. They always are, unless the current is setting down the line to port.

(3) When in doubt—particularly in very large fleets and in

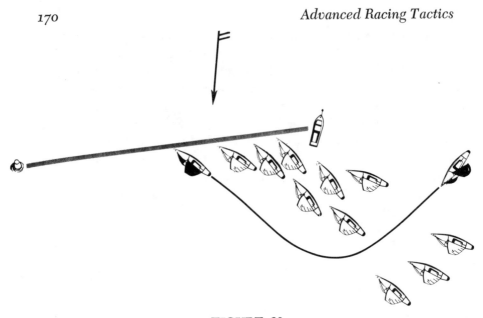

FIGURE 30

light air, and certainly if the current is setting to starboard—the barging start should be timed for a late arrival. The last boat across at the weather end of the line is often the only boat that can tack to port. If that is the advantageous direction, being late is more than worth the sacrifice. If the starboard end of the line is strongly favored, a late barging start may be useful even if a tack to port is not contemplated. The essence of success is patience. Don't commit yourself until the fleet has cleared away. Keep speed up by reaching about above the lay line, but don't get too far away—timing is difficult in light air. Jibe away toward the line to preserve speed. A swooping, broad-reach approach from above the lay line permits accurate timing. For an earlier arrival, the swoop can be reduced; for a later arrival, it can be extended. From a position on an extension of the starting line and 150 feet from the mark, a start can be made in thirty seconds (if an opening unexpectedly appears) or in ninety seconds (if the fleet jams up in the corner) with speed fully preserved. Charge in right on the transom of the last boat, *but don't get there too soon.*

Always watch out for other boats behaving in a similar manner. Nothing ruins a good start or makes a complicated start more dangerous than other boats following precisely the same plan.

26. Starting in Oscillating Winds

After winning three successive races in a recent Soling Winter Series regatta by large margins, we were pulled up short by starting disasters in the next three. It had been blowing 18–20 knots out of the northwest, but late in the day the wind velocity dropped and the oscillations were larger and less frequent. A big back appeared about ten minutes before the start of the fourth race, and since the line had not been shifted, we elected to start on port, near the port end (Figure 31). As we approached the line, we reckoned that we could easily clear all but the first of the starboard tackers. However, when we bore away, it became evident that the next two boats were lifting and we'd have to pass astern of them as well. By the time we emerged in clear air, a full-fledged veer had developed. We had sailed the headed tack through the entire fleet. The subsequent shift, another back, soon appeared, and we found ourselves far to leeward, with half the fleet a hundred yards ahead. We should have tacked beneath the starboard tackers at the line when we recognized that they were lifting.

At the start of the fifth race, the wind was again backed, and had been so for about five minutes. To avoid the sequence that had

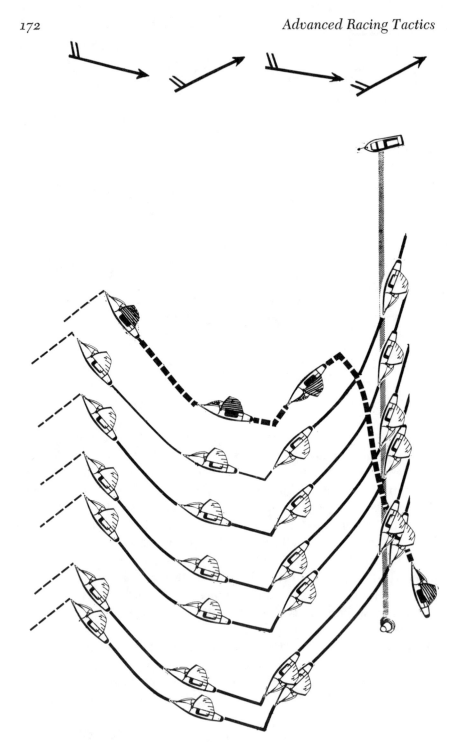

FIGURE 31

followed our port-tack start in the previous race, we started on star-board, at the strongly favored port end. The start was perfectly timed, but as we congratulated ourselves, the fleet began to lift away from us. A big veer was developing and there was far more of it to windward. In a few minutes we appeared to be behind half the fleet. When the back reappeared, we were almost to the lay line. Two boats crossed us as we returned on port, and we had to settle for third at the weather mark.

In the sixth race (on the following day, in similar conditions), we determined to start at the weather end in an oscillating veer. This technique should have permitted us to tack in concert with any subsequent shift. Unfortunately, our timing and position were a little off, and when the gun fired, we were a boat length below the committee boat, with several boats ahead. We had to tack to port to clear our air. We emerged on the headed tack, but immediately thereafter the wind began to back; and as we lifted, the entire fleet, now to our left, tacked to port and lifted inside of us. We held on, but the veer did not return until we had reached the lay line. When we tacked back, the one boat we had to beat crossed and tacked ahead and to weather.

Before the start, the boat should be so set up and the crew so trained that during the race the helmsman need pay little or no attention to either. He must be able to look around continuously as the line is approached—not only so as to arrive at the desired posi-tion on the line on time but so as to detect the occurrence of any shift at the moment of the race's start. In oscillating winds, readi-ness for the shift is the essential determinant of successful starting. A starting plan must be developed that is consistent with the wind direction prior to the start, but also allows for adaptation to a shift occurring as the line is crossed or immediately thereafter.

The formulation of an effective plan requires an adequate survey of wind variations prior to the start. Sufficient time should be allowed to determine the complete range of compass headings on each tack (or at least the complete range on one tack, with an estimate of the range on the other). From this data can be calculated the median headings (midway between the extremes) for each tack. Since these are the headings that determine the need to tack, they should be ac-curate—and the degree of accuracy depends upon the extent of the observation. Although the occurrence of oscillations is subject to random variation, their approximate frequency should be estimated. (The heavier the air, the more frequent the oscillations will be.) If a shift occurs within a few minutes of the start, it can be reasonably expected to continue for several minutes thereafter. However, if the wind has persisted from one direction for nearly the interval expected, a shift in the opposite direction must be anticipated in the immediate future. The plan in the first instance may merely provide for a good start in the existing wind. In the latter instance, it must in addition provide for an immediate tack.

The worst possible starting course in oscillating winds is the one from which a tack cannot be made. Thus a start on starboard tack at the port end of the line—or to leeward of the mass of the fleet at any point on the line—must be avoided. A start on starboard at the port end, even when the port end is heavily favored in a back, is a start on the headed tack (carrying the boat away from the next shift), and will not permit a tack to the lifted tack. If a veer appears, the entire fleet will be inside and to weather. If a backing shift has just begun and the port end of the line is to windward, a start on port tack is the only reasonable solution. This takes the boat on the lifted tack toward the next shift. However, if the backing shift has been present for a period approximating the interval between shifts, the port-tack start must be made with the expectation of a veer during the approach or during passage through the starboard tackers. An immediate tack to starboard should be made if a veer is indicated by lifting of the starboard tackers. A safer start if a back is about to terminate is on starboard tack on the windward edge of the fleet. The boat will then be lifted into a major advantage by the imminent veer.

When the starboard end of the line is to windward in an oscillating veer, a start there is always appropriate (Figure 32). If the veer has just occurred (and may be expected to continue for a few minutes), a start on the leeward border of the fleet takes the boat on the lifted tack farther toward the next expected shift, a back. However, this technique risks control by boats to windward, which may prevent a tack to port when the back appears. If the veer has been present for several minutes, a start at the windward end is essential; an immediate tack to port in the imminent back will then be possible.

Starting Patterns in Oscillating Winds

Beginning of Veer: Starboard tack
                         Leeward border of fleet (but in a position
                            permitting an early tack)

End of Veer:	Starboard tack
	Windward border of fleet
Beginning of Back:	Port tack
End of Back:	Starboard tack
	Windward border of fleet

If for some reason these ideal starting patterns are not attainable, one must be prepared to make the best of the shifts that appear during the start or immediately thereafter. The basic rule is stick to the lifted tack regardless of the bad air. A tack away from the lift anytime on the leg, but particularly just after the start, may result in an irremediable loss. The compass headings must be called as soon as the boat is on the close-hauled course, and someone must be looking around to evaluate the orientation of the other boats to

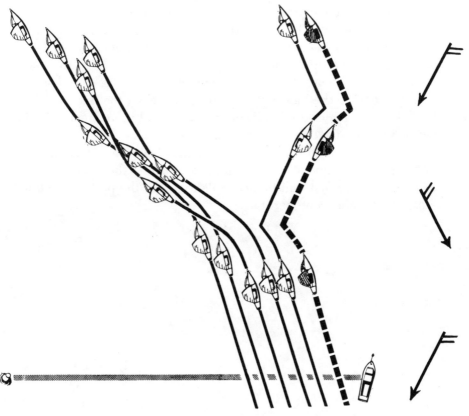

FIGURE 32

the line and to each other. As is true elsewhere on the leg, boats on the weather quarter and boats that are being crossed should be watched particularly. If a further lift occurs, the tack should be continued. A tack to port to escape disturbed air should be made only in a backed oscillation or early in a veer. To make one late in a veer is disastrous. If a header appears, a tack should be made immediately. This is an obvious response when, on starboard tack, a backing shift appears after a veer. The port tack must be discontinued as soon as it becomes evident that a boat or boats which one expected to cross will be impossible to cross. (This is the one exception to the usual dictum for port-tack starts—*Keep going.*)

In summary, plan an approach that will permit the acquisition of the lifted tack immediately after the start. Determine the median wind for each tack and the average interval between shifts. Keep to leeward of the fleet but close to the line. A late modification of the plan will be possible only if you are free of control by neighboring boats and close enough to the line to opt for a new position upon it in the final minute. The orientation of other boats to the line, and the luffing of other boats on the line, are useful indicators of late-occuring shifts. Late in the starting sequence, a luff head to wind, the ideal test of wind direction, is impracticable, but a close-hauled course is not. If the base leg is made from below the line, a close-hauled course may be periodically assumed and the compass heading noted. The boat that is best able to determine the wind direction in the last minute will be able to make the best start. If late in the starting sequence a sudden back appears, the boat that detects the change first will be best able to go for the port end and to cross the entire fleet on port tack.

27. Match-Race Starts, I: Meeting and Circling

Maneuvering against a single competing boat with the intention of controlling her is match racing. It matters not whether the two boats involved are the only ones in the race or but two of fifty-seven. Opportunities for control are greatest before the start, since escape is prevented by the necessity of crossing the starting line after the gun. It is possible to so control another boat before the start that she is forced to start very late or in a very disadvantageous position, or she may subsequently be placed under such control that she cannot escape. Late in a series in which a large fleet is contending, a number of pairings often occur, in which the ultimate standing of one boat depends almost entirely on whether or not she defeats the other. Where a throw-out race exists, a boat may be able to beat her rival in the series only if the latter is forced far down in the fleet in the final race. With or without a throw-out race, two boats may reach the final race essentially tied, with no others in close contention for their prospective places. In this situation, if other conditions prevail which are clearly advantageous, control need not be sought, but where doubt exists concerning the outcome, the techniques of match racing should be applied to assure success.

Before the start control is accomplished when, after a meeting between two boats, one acquires a position either close astern or close to leeward of the other. Thereafter, the boat ahead finds it difficult to do anything except continue to sail ahead; the boat to windward is similarly restricted to continuing to sail to windward (even though she is able to tack). The outcome of this confrontation—maintenance of control, or escape—is determined by which of the opponents is the more competent helmsman, able to maneuver his boat more effectively. The two essentials of starting success in a match race are an ability to escape any control achieved by the opponent and an ability to maintain maneuverability despite major variations in speed (including stopping).

In match racing, certain of the racing rules seem inverted. In open racing, freedom and advantage seem to belong to the right-of-way yacht; she is normally able to maintain her desired course. In match racing, because of the customary proximity of the two competitors, the right-of-way yacht seems restricted and disadvantaged; she may not so alter course that the non-right-of-way yacht is obstructed. This means that in match-race starts, the non-right-of-way yacht—the yacht astern, for instance—is in control. She may alter course at will, forcing the right-of-way yacht into a disadvantageous position as desired. A port-tack yacht approaching a starboard-tack yacht may alter course at will; a starboard-tack yacht must maintain her initial course when she reaches the proximity of the port-tack yacht. Of the major control techniques available to the match-racing helmsman, only luffing requires acquisition of the right of way.

Strategic considerations are as important in planning a match-race start as in planning a fleet-race start. Recognizing the preferred side of the course is essential, so that you can place yourself between the opponent and the advantageous side after the start, or induce the opponent to sail toward the disadvantageous side. The favored end of the line should be determined in advance and the ultimate starting position planned accordingly. Timing is the single most important factor. Which turn of the circle to peel away from, when to release the boat forced ahead beyond the line, whether to attempt to drive through to leeward or to force her beyond the port-end mark—all these desicions, and others, depend upon an accurate awareness of the time remaining before the start.

Meeting

The timing and location of the initial meeting are extremely important. Racing does not commence until the preparatory signal (in NAYRU match racing, the warning signal). It is desirable to keep away from the opponent until after racing commences, to avoid the possibility of a deliberate foul at the gun. Once the boats meet, aggressive activity is likely to be constant. For the sake of avoiding prolonged emotional tension, the initial meeting may on occasion be beneficially postponed. However, since most opponents are impressed and some are intimidated by aggressive behavior, that first encounter should be deliberately arranged, not avoided. Deliberate, confident maneuvers are essential to success and disturbing to the opposition. Delay the meeting if desired, but arrange it on your terms—not the opponent's.

If the boats are to meet on opposite tacks (as they do when the NAYRU match technique of separating them at each end of the starting line is utilized), the desired location of the meeting and the relative position of the boats at the time of passing should be decided in advance. Initial meetings above or near the line should be avoided unless gaining control is assured. The farther to leeward of the line the first encounter occurs, the more space will be available for escape (if things go wrong) before the boat is pushed over the line. Ordinarily, for the sake of prolonging the final approach, the controlling maneuver should be initiated at the farthest possible distance from the favored end of the line. For example, if the far end of the line is favored, the opponent should be permitted to come to or beyond the near end. If you plan to attack by pouncing upon the tail of the opposing boat as she passes, you should approach from to weather or pass initially to weather so as to peel off and jibe into position astern. A frequently successful technique is to sail well to weather of the line before the preparatory signal and then approach the opponent on a broad reach (Figure 33). A swoop up or a jibe into a close-astern position can then be made regardless of the opponent's maneuver. Since jibing can be accomplished more smoothly and with less loss of speed than tacking, it should be used for aggressive maneuvers wherever possible. If you wish to pass and postpone the initial maneuvering, you should pass to leeward— well to leeward—to avoid being caught by the opponent, who might otherwise gain an astern or leeward controlling position.

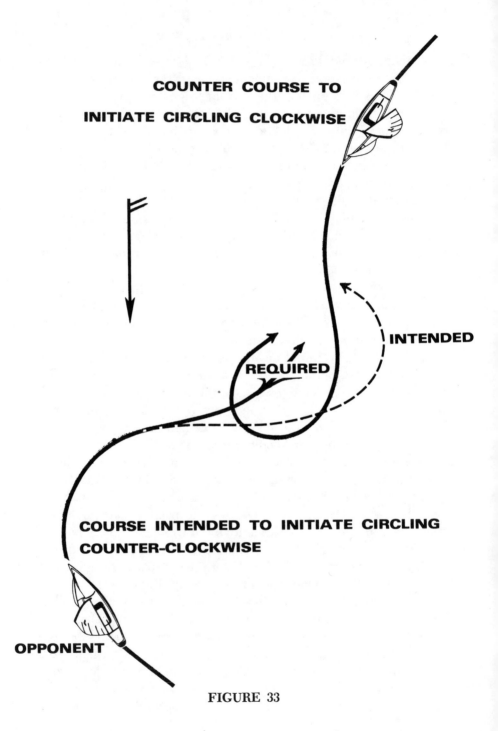

COUNTER COURSE TO
INITIATE CIRCLING CLOCKWISE

INTENDED

REQUIRED

COURSE INTENDED TO INITIATE CIRCLING
COUNTER–CLOCKWISE

OPPONENT

FIGURE 33

An aggressive meeting should result in one of the following out-comes (unless both boats elect to cross and separate again):

1. Boats circling—utilizing an escape technique which postpones or prevents control by either one
2. Boats in line—opponent ahead
3. Boats overlapped—opponent to windward

The meeting may, of course, be unsuccessful and result in one of the following:

1. Boats in line—opponent astern
2. Boats overlapped—opponent to leeward

Circling

Circling is a means by which the boat ahead obtains a draw, preventing the boat astern from gaining control. Failure to circle immediately after an opponent acquires a position close astern will usually result in being trapped ahead. An immediate tack or jibe, before the opponent gathers full away, is safe. Once the opponent is up to full speed, neither may be possible. The boat being attacked should always seek to initiate the circle clockwise, as this permits escaping from the circle, if necessary, by jibing to starboard. She should counter the initial close-aboard attack with a gradual, speed-preserving bearing away to jibe. Circling can usually be continued indefinitely, since neither boat can gather sufficient way while turn-ing to interfere with the other. And as long as it is continued, circling is an escape for the boat ahead. Since speed is proportional to the radius of the turn, it is usually easy to maintain position, increasing speed by lengthening the turning radius or reducing speed by reducing it.

Successful circling depends upon skill in boat handling. Speed must be preserved by attention to sail trim. As the boat bears away, the sails must be eased synchronously; as the boat comes on the wind, the sails must be trimmed. The need for changes in sail trim is reduced by the fact that the apparent wind, affected by the turn itself, moves forward when the boat bears away and aft when the boat comes on the wind. The sails should be trimmed either side of a wind-abeam position but never full out and never close-hauled. As tacking results in a greater degree of slowing than jibing, circling is best done in a triangular pattern, closer to the circle's center on the jibe side and farther out on the tack side. The helmsman must refrain from turning faster than his sail trimmers permit. To bear away before the main is eased or tack before it is fully trimmed is to slow the boat by rudder drag. Each boat has an optimal circling radius, which must be learned.

Unless one of the boats is poorly handled, circling is unlikely to lead to a controlling situation. Aggressive, skillful circling can intimidate the opponent, however, keeping him off guard as he barely escapes being caught while tacking on each round. A helmsman preoccupied with escape is less likely to select the right moment for the breakaway. Rarely, it may be possible to catch him when he is on the verge of a tack or jibe to port, and thus to acquire the controlling boats-in-line, opponent-ahead position.

In circling, the limitations on the right-of-way yacht become evident. Whenever the boat ahead is tacking or jibing, the boat astern becomes the right-of-way yacht and may not alter course so as to obstruct the boat ahead in her attempt to keep clear (rule 34). In practice, this means that the boat astern must hold her course without variation as soon as the boat ahead passes head to wind while tacking and as soon as her boom crosses her center line while jibing (Figure 34). If after such a maneuver the boats are on opposite tacks and the boat astern is on starboard, she must continue to hold her unvarying course until the boat ahead is clear (or until a collision must be avoided or actually occurs). If, while the right-of-way yacht, she alters course so as to obstruct and the boat ahead is unable to keep clear, she is disqualified. Only when the boat astern is freed of her right-of-way "privileges"—when she is on port and the other boat is on starboard, or when she is astern on the same tack—may she continue her turning and pursue the attack. Thus circling is actually a series of maneuvers—a turn, a straight course, another turn, another straight course, and so on and on. Only if the boat astern assumes a controlling course before the boat ahead commences her jibe or tack can the latter be forced to abandon the circle.

There are four ways to terminate the circling:
1. Executing a breakaway timed appropriately for the start-approach pattern (Figure 35)
2. Forcing the opponent out of the circle ahead in advance of the start-approach time

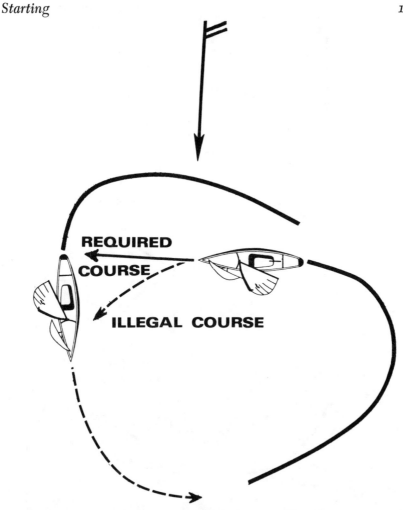

REQUIRED COURSE

ILLEGAL COURSE

FIGURE 34

3. Undertaking a breakaway early, with the opponent astern and final resolution postponed
4. Adopting a figure-eight pattern to break away or regain control (Figure 35)

The latter two methods constitute returns to the basic patterns of boats in line and are temporary rather than final resolutions of the situation. If a breakaway is attempted when the opponent has dropped back, a subsequent turn may be made in the opposite direction, away from the circle. Although the opponent will follow

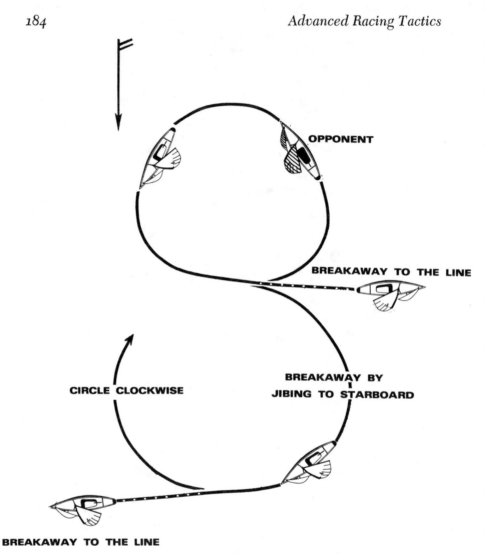

OPPONENT

BREAKAWAY TO THE LINE

CIRCLE CLOCKWISE

BREAKAWAY BY
JIBING TO STARBOARD

BREAKAWAY TO THE LINE

FIGURE 35

this maneuver if he is clever, he often does not, or does so belatedly. If he fails to follow, the boat ahead is temporarily free and may turn again onto the tail of her opponent. The breakaway into the starting pattern is a final solution, and each boat will attempt to achieve it successfully. If the site of circling has been satisfactorily chosen, it will be at a significant distance from the preferred point on the starting line. The safest plan is to break away before the opponent, so as to reach the line in the ahead (preferably ahead to windward) position. However, if the circle is abandoned prematurely, the boat astern may go through to leeward and luff, forcing the boat ahead beyond the line or over the line early. Since the boat ahead may modify the speed of boats in line, some delay should be possible, and the boat astern may then be caught astern and to leeward as the gun fires. Obviously, accurate timing of the breakaway is essential. If the opponent breaks away first, an immediate decision must be made to attack by overtaking to leeward and luffing the opponent across the line (desirable if adequate time remains) or to accept astern and to windward preparatory to an early tack after starting. Strong pressure on the opponent while circling may well induce him to break away too early. This is the most desirable outcome of circling, since the opponent can then be forced over the line early and into a very late start.

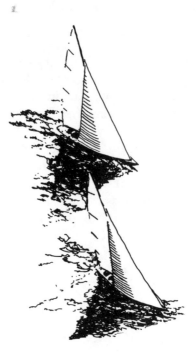

28. Match-Race Starts, II: Control Techniques

Aggressive maneuvers at the start are intended to provide a large lead at the commencement of the race, and may have the added advantage of intimidating the opponent. A successful match-race start requires more than merely beating the opposing boat to the line or to the favored site on the line. If she can tack into clear air, the start must be considered unsuccessful. When fully successful, the leading boat starts far ahead, with the opponent controlled dead astern or astern and to leeward. Subjected to this control at the commencement of the beat, the opponent will be unable to escape from either blanket or backwind thereafter. As was indicated in the preceding chapter, this result can be achieved before the gun by the imposition either of control from astern, forcing the opponent away from the line; or of control from to leeward, forcing the opponent to windward of the line.

The cool confidence which determines aggressive success depends in part upon an assurance that any control by the opponent may be evaded. Hence, the technique of escape must be learned first of all. Mastery of this technique is the best insurance against really needing it. Particularly in breaking away from circling, it may often be useful to deliberately permit the opponent to acquire a controlling position astern. If escape is certain, the tables can be turned; the opponent, off guard, may be more than usually susceptible to a reversal of the situation.

Boats in Line—Opponent Astern

This is the classic controlling condition from which escape must be achieved. The dependable techniques (Figure 36) are:

1. Luffing head to wind
2. Stopping abruptly
3. Jibing to starboard
4. Circling the committee boat

Sailing close-hauled at maximum speed is rarely an effective defensive technique, for it requires considerable time and carries the boats to windward of the line. However, it is useful in small centerboarders, where full speed is rapidly acquired and the boat astern is

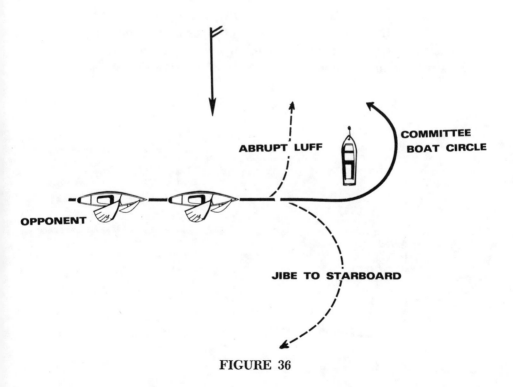

FIGURE 36

markedly affected by backwind. In International 14's a lead sufficient to permit a tack away may be attained in approximately one
minute, since the opponent falls progressively astern and to leeward.
In keel boats, many minutes may be required, and when the tack is
finally attempted, the opponent will probably be able to tack synchronously into a control-to-leeward position. Jibing away is then
virtually impossible, and therefore the only escape is another tack.
The result may be capture, wiith the opponent overlapped to leeward and no alternative remaining except to make a series of fruit-
less tacks.

The successful employment of luffing head to wind as a means of
escape requires proper timing and also skill in managing the slowed
or stopped boat and in controlling the boat when it is moving in reverse (Figure 37). If the unwary opponent allows himself to tail to
leeward of dead astern or can be induced to attempt a very close
leeward controlling position, a luff may fix him in an overlapped,
leeward position. The boat ahead should be free to tack away after
luffing. This is a particularly useful maneuver on the approach if
the ideal position on the line has been passed and the opponent is
attempting to establish a leeward overlap to force the leader over
the line early. Rule 34 requires that any alteration in course by the
boat ahead, the right-of-way yacht, not obstruct the following boat
while she is keeping clear. If the following boat is clear astern or to
leeward, the luffing-before-starting rule (rule 40) probably does not

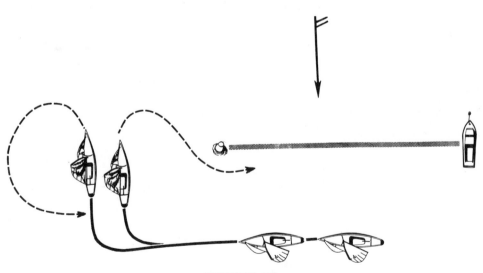

FIGURE 37

apply, since there is no "windward yacht" to be given room and opportunity. Therefore, although the luff must not obstruct or prevent the following boat from keeping clear, it can be performed rapidly (and thus more effectively). Should a collision result, the luffing boat would have to prove that the follower could have escaped to leeward.

The clever helmsman astern will not be misled by a luff, however. He will remain far enough astern so that he can deviate to windward or to leeward, keeping between his opponent and the line or the preferred site on the line. This usually means that he will have to luff sharply with the boat ahead and that the boats will end up side by side, head to wind. How this situation is resolved will depend upon the skill of each crew in recovering speed and maneuverability. The boat initially ahead may escape if she can stop her opponent head to wind, bear away and gain speed more quickly than her opponent, and subsequently jibe in the desired direction. The boat astern to windward must keep clear and if overlapped cannot prevent her opponent from jibing away. Again the major limitation is time; it may take a full minute to resolve a luff head to wind and then to jibe away.

An abrupt stop is a rarely utilized but extremely effective means of escaping control by a boat astern. Although the boat ahead, the right-of-way yacht, may not so alter course as to obstruct the following boat, she is allowed to alter her speed at will. Abrupt and marked variations in speed will at least cause the boat astern to keep a respectful distance from the transom of the boat ahead, since a bow-to-stern collision would, of course, disqualify the boat astern. If she does not keep this respectful distance astern (which would facilitate other escape maneuvers), an abrupt stop by the boat ahead will force the follower to pass to windward or to leeward to escape collision. Once the following boat has overlapped the boat ahead, close aboard, the latter can escape by either tacking or jibing. But the boat ahead must stop without altering course. In light air both main and jib can be abruptly backed; in heavy air they must be let go "by the run." These maneuvers require careful coordination of helmsman, jib tender, and mainsail tender to prevent an inadvertent alteration of course.

Because jibing is an almost instantaneous procedure, with the jibe completed as soon as the sail fills, jibing from port to starboard from a controlled position ahead is almost always possible. However, jibing onto port can usually be blocked; therefore, maneuvers to escape from circling and other meeting situations should, if possible, be on port, to prepare for a subsequent jibe to starboard in the escape from the boats-in-line, opponent-astern position. A rapid bearing away and jibe to starboard may obstruct the opponent, so it is better to make a gradual turn and to throw the boom across abruptly. If the opposing boat jibes inside, she may be trapped to windward, with the boats overlapped. To avoid this position, she may pass astern and jibe outside the turn of the boat ahead.

The committee boat provides protection for the inside of a turn, so the boat ahead can tack or jibe toward it without interference from a boat astern. The defender cannot expect complete escape, but can usually maintain a circling draw until ready to separate for the start. Since a committee-boat circle is much safer than a circle in open water, it may be sensibly substituted when the latter is deteriorating. The committee-boat circle may be resolved if the boat astern gains sufficiently to interpose herself between her opponent and the committee boat (Figure 38). She may acquire a windward overlap as the boat ahead hardens on the wind after passing the committee boat's stern. A position slightly to windward but clear

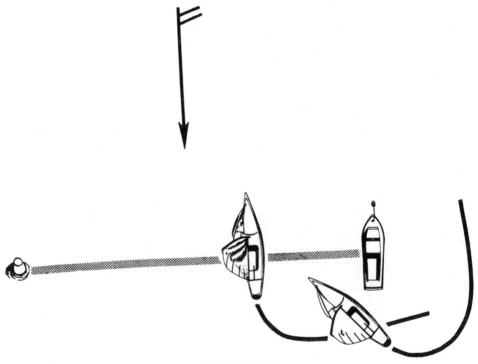

FIGURE 38

astern may be sufficient if the boats are circling clockwise as then the leader will be tacking to port. If the boat ahead is prevented from continuing the circle, the boats may end up luffing head to wind, side by side. If (and only if) the circle is counterclockwise, the following boat may, when the boat ahead approaches the committee boat's bow, reverse her circle to meet the opponent on port at the committee boat's transom. The port-tack boat must then hastily jibe or tack away and will usually end up controlled, with her opponent astern or to leeward. Despite this danger, if in the boats-in-line, opponent-astern position, because the tack will be made to starboard, it is best to initiate committee-boat circling counterclockwise.

Boats in Line—Opponent Ahead

The purpose of initial maneuvering is to gain, ultimately, a control position—boats in line, opponent ahead. This is accomplished by jibing (or tacking) into a tailing position at the time of a crossing by aggressive resolution of circling, or by proper management of the escape from a controlled opponent-astern situation. Once a position close astern has been achieved with both boats moving at reasonable speed, the boat ahead is trapped, at least temporarily. To hold her advantage, the boat astern must stay close astern, constantly threatening to establish an overlap to leeward. Accordingly, her speed must be kept exactly the same as that of the boat ahead, which must be constantly observed. If the boat ahead stops suddenly, the boat astern must stop as abruptly; if she increases speed rapidly, the boat astern must do so as quickly. Control will be lost if an overlap is established close aboard to windward or to leeward, since this will permit the boat ahead to tack or jibe away inside the turning radius of the outside boat. If the boat ahead luffs or bears away, the boat astern must keep a respectful distance. She should be aimed on a course that (unaltered after the opponent initiates her tack or jibe) could carry her directly into her opponent if the latter tacked or jibed. A few judicious warning hails—e.g., "Don't try it!"—may then prevent the boat ahead from taking rash chances. If the opponent luffs, the follower must luff immediately, far enough away to permit her to bear away again and block a subsequent jibe (and, of course, far enough away to avoid any danger of contact). Since a committee-boat circle can be established by the boat ahead without interference, tailing should be initiated in a direction which carries the opponent away from the committee boat. Whenever possible the tailing position should be established on starboard tack. The boat ahead may be able to escape successfully by jibing onto starboard, but she will find it virtually impossible to jibe away onto port.

Boats Overlapped—Opponent to Windward or to Leeward

The position of ultimate advantage in match racing is boats overlapped, with the opponent to windward. It is achieved when the boat ahead is so desperate to avoid her opponent that she permits herself to be driven away from the line in the boats-in-line position. Once a leeward overlap is established, the boat to windward may be luffed across the line or its extension and carried progressively farther to windward of the line. The leeward boat should not be brought too close. If the intimidation is carried out from a distance (which is usually possible) she will be able to tack whenever the opponent tacks, reacquiring an overlap after each tack and preventing the opponent from escaping to leeward. If response to the initial luff is delayed until the leeward boat is close alongside, then a tack away will provide an escape. If the leeward boat urges the windward boat on from about half a boat length to leeward, she will be able to keep constantly between her and the line. With each tack the windward boat will be carried farther and farther to windward of the line. A false tack or a sharp luff without tacking may provide a means of escape, particularly if the leeward boat is thereby induced to come up close to leeward. The windward boat must attempt escape before being carried significantly to weather of the line. This situation is, however, much more difficult to escape from than the boats-in-line, opponent-astern position and should therefore be avoided whenever possible.

Approach Situations

The boat ahead forced away from the line by a boat astern or to leeward must constantly seek escape. Since some escape techniques take a considerable amount of time, they are likely to be initiated as soon as a controlled position is recognized. The boat astern must be alert to successive escape attempts and must be prepared to thwart them. The timing of the relinquishment of control should be coordinated with the opponent's escape attempts. Unless one is convinced that control will be lost imminently, it should be continued until after the starting gun. If control is about to be lost, it should be yielded early, before the opponent initiates his escape maneuver; there may then still be an opportunity to reacquire control, by a different means. The opponent may expect to be released immediately after the gun fires; he often seems quite disappointed if pressure to drive him away from the line is continued. Therefore, the helmsman of the boat astern should maintain control until the helmsman ahead despairs of mercy and seeks a new effort at escape. While the opponent is preoccupied and slowed by an abrupt luff, or caught and forced up again after an unsuccessful attempt to jibe, the boat astern should peel off the jibe (preferably) back to the line. It is most important to utilize the full advantage of the control by relinquishing it when the opponent least expects it, preferably when his boat has been abruptly slowed and one's own is at peak speed. If, instead, the opposing helmsman is alert and breaks back synchronously, he may be a mere boat's length astern at the line and may easily tack into clear air. A successful start provides a lead of several boat lengths at the line, which permits the boat ahead to tack ahead and to keep to windward of any subsequent maneuver of the boat astern.

When the boats approach the line close together after breaking out of a circle or after an inadequate resolution of a boats-in-line or boats-overlapped situation, the use of additional control techniques may be possible. If the boat ahead is close to the line and a significant interval remains before the gun, the follower should attempt to go through to leeward so as to force the boat ahead over the line early. If the latter races ahead to avoid the leeward overlap, she may be forced beyond the end of the line before the gun and held there. If she luffs, the follower gains the ahead-to-leeward position for the start. However, too easy acquisition of this position may be risky, since the boat to windward may still have time to turn the tables and break through to leeward herself. When very little time remains, the follower is best advised to work up to weather and to tack away as the gun goes. Indeed, if the opponent is unaggressive and permits it, an excellent start may be made by a final approach on port, crossing close astern of the opponent, undoubtedly on starboard, into clear air.

When the opponent is close astern and the line is near, the boat ahead should attempt to control the boat astern instead of giving her the option of going through to leeward and/or acquiring luffing rights. If the end of the line away from which the boats are headed is favored, the follower should, of course, be encouraged to break through to leeward. The windward boat is then free to tack away toward the favored end just before the gun. If the opposite end is favored, the boat ahead should slow up and bear away to catch the opponent overlapped to windward. A progressive, slow luff head to wind can then stop the opponent completely, leaving the leeward boat the option of deciding when to peel off for the favored end of the line. Luffing before the starting signal, unless the leeward boat is forward of mast abeam, may be to close-hauled only (rule 40). However, a previous hail of "Mast abeam" cannot be used to limit the subsequently acquired right of a leeward boat to luff beyond close-hauled after she has reached the mast-abeam position. "Obstructing" by luffing is exempted only after the start (rule 38); before the start the leeward yacht must not luff in such a manner that the windward boat is unable to keep clear. Luffing before the start is a technique to be used to control the opponent, not abused to disqualify him.

A start nearer the starboard end of the line provides subsequent control, since the opponent starting to leeward must eventually tack back toward the weather boat. The latter may then counter by tacking on her lee bow or ahead and to weather. Thus, if an option exists, unless the leeward end of the line is greatly advantaged, a start to weather should always be attempted.

If control has indeed been acquired at the start, it must not subsequently be relinquished through failure to cover. In a race with only one other boat, the risks of separating on the beat, unless advantage is sure to result, outweigh any possible gain. It is better to continue in a backwinded weather-quarter position, staying with the opponent, than to tack away and allow him to continue into a 15° header a hundred yards beyond. The opponent should never be allowed to continue for more than a few boat lengths on a tack which is carrying the boats apart. If *he* does not tack back, the suspicion must arise that he is heading for something highly beneficial and that *you* had better get over there with him.

IV. *Beating*

29. Recognizing the Persistent Shift

Persistent Shift: A shift that, following its occurrence, persists for the remainder of the leg, and that is anticipated in advance of its arrival.

Progressive Persistent Shift: A shift that, following its occurrence, continues to change in the same direction and persists for the remainder of the leg, and that is detected during its development.

Completed Persistent Shift: A shift that would, if detected earlier, have qualified as a persistent shift, but that is not detected unil after it has been completed (prior to or during a particular leg).

I become increasingly convinced that the most important preparation for racing is the determination of close-hauled compass headings before the start. Acquiring a "feel" for the wind—its velocity and its directional variations—sets the stage for the successful race. Compass headings obtained over a period of twenty to thirty minutes before the start indicate whether the wind is stable and subject to minimal variation, stable and subject to progressive variation in a single direction, or unstable and subject to periodic oscillations. Sufficient time must be taken to permit distinguishing between a prolonged oscillation (which even in light air rarely lasts more than fifteen minutes) and a persistent shift, and to detect the full range of oscillations. It is for this reason that up to thirty minutes may be required. If only a short time is available for observation, it is usu-ally best to take continuous readings on a single tack. Then, a lift or header will be recognized when it appears, and after an immediate tack, the complementary heading on the opposite tack, header, or lift can be obtained. This technique may permit the detection of the full range of oscillations by observation of only half the cycle—and makes possible the identification of the compass heading for a lift and for a header on each tack. If a continuous shift in one direction is evident over a long enough period of observation (twenty or more minutes), a progressive persistent shift may be presumed. Occasion-ally, however, oscillations due to the recurrent appearance of two winds which are present simultaneously in the area may persist for longer periods and be very difficult to distinguish from persistent shifts (which have, by definition, a duration longer than that of the beat).

The second element in the preparation for detecting persistent shifts is observation of one's surroundings. Burying one's head in the bilge to watch the compass is no more appropriate before the start than afterward. One of the major reasons for having a member of the crew call the compass headings (both before and after the start) is to free the helmsman to look around. Sailboats on the horizon, smoke from a stack ashore, dark lines appearing on the water, a change in the texture of the water surface—if detected—may pro-vide clues to the subsequent appearance of a persistent shift. The best wind indicators of all are other boats racing. Particularly use-ful are boats in fleets starting earlier on the same course. These must be watched carefully as they proceed up the beat, for their behavior may indicate the appearance of new winds, local variations in di-rection, and the frequency and extent of oscillations. One's expecta-tions of persistent shifts may be confirmed, and more important, their timing may be revealed. An understanding of how winds are generated enables one to know when a persistent shift is likely, but only observation can indicate whether it will appear during the beat to come. The activities of boats in a fleet ahead may provide evi-dence of continuing oscillations. When approaching the lay line in a lift that threatens to persist, this recognition of the true character of the wind can be extremely reassuring—and justify continuing the tack instead of "bailing out."

Although the time-honored principle of tacking on headers is ap-propriate only to oscillating-shift conditions, the practice has become so ingrained that most sailors tack instinctively when they detect a header. The logical converse of this principle is not to tack on a lift, and few sailors have the guts to violate this "rule." But these principles are the direct opposite of those appropriate to the management of a persistent shift. If a persistent shift (or a progressive shift or a series of shifts in the same direction) will occur during the beat, the proper course is not to continue in the lift but to tack toward the shift—to sail on into a header—until close to the new lay line (Figure 39). In a progressive shift a lift is carrying the boat away from the shift into a progressively longer circular route to the mark, outside of all the competitors that sail the shorter course inside. Thus, all the instinctive reactions are wrong when a persistent shift occurs. And the handling of a persistent shift often determines the outcome of the race. Missing a header during a period of oscillating shifts merely permits the boat to get farther to the side of the course where an even greater advantage will be obtained in the subsequent header (a cycle ahead). Missing a header—continuing in a lift—during a progressive persistent shift means irremediable disaster. Significant oscillating shifts occur only in certain special conditions —particularly in unstable air flows (cold over warm), such as the offshore outflow from high pressure. Persistent shifts, however, occur at some time on most days in most sailing areas, both with oscillating shifts and in their absence. A more generally appropriate principle, therefore, may be to sail on in headers and to tack in lifts!

It is important to distinguish between a single, instantaneous, completed persistent shift and a progressive persistent shift. A persistent shift may or may not progress in the same direction. If a variation in direction is accompanied by a variation in velocity of not more than a few knots from the mean (particularly in light air), the shift should be presumed to be completed (and may be followed by a shift back). The usual cause of a persistent shift is a new wind (replacing an old wind or a calm), which must develop and then mature. It may arise as one of the ODSSSIC factors—a sea breeze, an upper-level air flow appearing at the surface after an inversion breakthrough, a squall—or a movement of the weather system itself. A squall and a weather-system movement are, by definition, moving, and therefore progress, i.e., the wind in question is constantly changing in direction—either backing or veering—but its overall movement is always in the same direction. The initial direction of a sea breeze or of an upper-level air flow following an inversion breakthrough is modified by the direction of the preexisting air flow (weather-system wind or sea breeze) and by the velocity of the

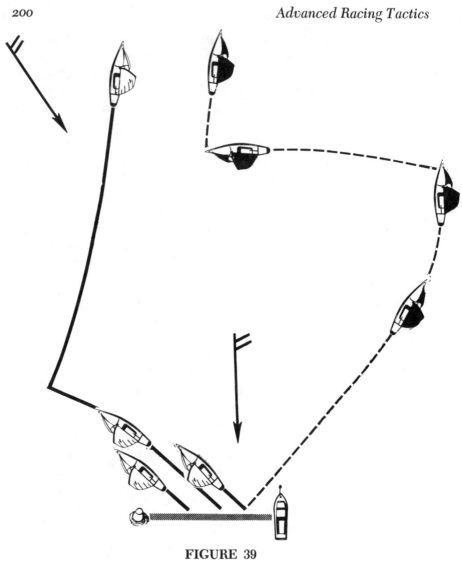

FIGURE 39

new flow. The shift will progressively back or veer from the direction of the preexisting wind toward the gradient flow characteristic of the new wind *and* will progressively veer as the new wind increases in velocity. An increase or decrease in velocity will cause a progressive alteration in wind direction as long as the velocity continues to change.

Although all persistent shifts tend to progress at least briefly, the early cessation of this progression is likely in three types: (1) a shift due to a change in velocity, (2) a shift due to the superimposition upon the old wind of a new wind with a geographically fixed gradient, such as a sea breeze, and (3) a shift due to the presence of a shoreline.

When a strong, new wind or a wind with a significant velocity variation is first recognized, its accompanying change in direction should be assumed to be a progressive persistent shift. This means that if one is sailing toward it (into a header) on a beat or away from it on a run, one's position will improve, whereas if one is sailing away from it (into a lift) on a beat or toward it on a run, one's position will deteriorate, and an immediate tack or jibe is in order. If the shift does not progress, if it has been completed, such a tack or jibe is useless; the shift has already had its effect for good or bad (depending upon one's position relative to other boats), and no subsequent action can change the result. Indeed, if the progression has ended, a retrogression is likely, with the wind swinging back once it has completed its movement in the initial direction. This is why it is important to be familiar with the compass headings of the standard sea breeze and the geographical influences in a particular area—to have local knowledge. If the compass indicates that a persistent shift has progressed beyond the direction expected, retrogression (oscillation) rather than progression should be expected. The extent of a velocity shift is even more difficult to assess. It is hard to decide whether an increasing wind will continue to increase or a dying wind continue to decrease. Again an understanding (gained through local knowledge) of the peak velocity expected for a given air flow at a particular time of day at a particular season of the year is invaluable.

Racing at CORK illustrates the problem. Most races are conducted in weather-system winds in the southerly and westerly quadrants which amalgamate with varying success with the local lake (sea) breeze. As the heating of the land increases during the afternoon, a progressive shift from the early weather-system flow toward the standard lake breeze (200°–220°) is to be expected. Usually in cP air the weather-system gradient prevents complete domination by the lake breeze, so a progressive shift toward the standard lake breeze ceases short of fulfillment. In maritime tropic gulf (mTg) air the shift is more likely to be complete. Superimposed upon the progressive shift toward the lake-breeze sector are persistent shifts due to velocity changes. As the lake breeze increases in velocity it veers, as it dies it backs, but such velocity changes may be obscured by, or merely accentuate, a shift from the weather-system to the local lake-breeze gradient. The immediate question on a particular beat or run at CORK is, Will a detected shift progress or has it already reached its furthest deviation? Once the wind direction swings within 20° of the standard lake breeze, it may cease to progress and thereafter oscillate as velocity varies.

At CORK, 1974, we found that after a shift was detected the wind usually oscillated back before it progressed farther. Generally, as the race was started the developing lake breeze was increasing in velocity (that was why they had started the race!) However, if the earlier weather-system wind had been in the west, the velocity increase was associated with a back to the standard southwesterly lake breeze rather than with a veer. Even when the weather-system wind had been in the south, the expected veer, evident just before the start, often failed to progress because the wind did not continue to increase in velocity (Figure 40). An early tack to port in a veering, increasing wind would turn out to be a disaster if, as frequently happened, the wind died and backed. A round or two later it would strengthen and veer (and there was excellent correlation between velocity increases and veers, velocity decreases and backs), but just how much it would strengthen during a particular leg was impossible to predict. A progressive 10° veer associated with an increase in velocity from 8 to 12 knots permitted us to pick up a number of boats on one run. We reasoned that the increasing wind would veer further as we started up the beat and decided to hold off to the right. A slight additional increase in velocity and in veer did occur, but the wind stabilized at 14 knots and backed (5°–8°) progressively thereafter. We lost a boat that had tacked off to the left. What was needed was a more accurate understanding of how great a change in velocity would occur during a single leg—or of the extent to which the amalgamation of the lake breeze with the weather-system wind would progress during a single beat. If further progression was expected, a tack toward the shift was indicated (Figure

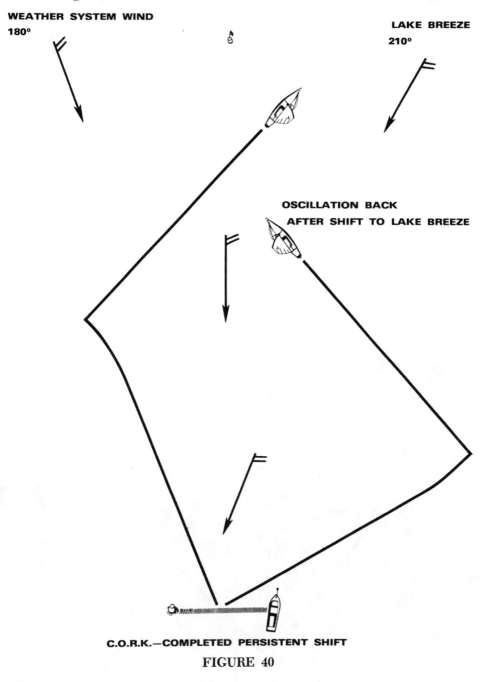

WEATHER SYSTEM WIND
180°

LAKE BREEZE
210°

OSCILLATION BACK
AFTER SHIFT TO LAKE BREEZE

C.O.R.K.—COMPLETED PERSISTENT SHIFT

FIGURE 40

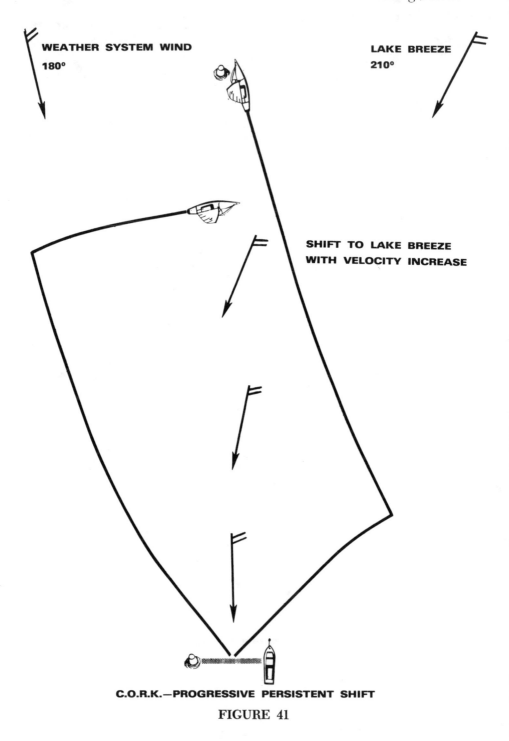

WEATHER SYSTEM WIND
180°

LAKE BREEZE
210°

SHIFT TO LAKE BREEZE
WITH VELOCITY INCREASE

C.O.R.K.—PROGRESSIVE PERSISTENT SHIFT

FIGURE 41

41); if the progression had been completed, a tack away from the shift was indicated. At CORK, at least, once the progression had ceased, an oscillation back in the original direction was usual.

Prior to the initiation of a beat or run the question that must be asked is not, Will a persistent shift appear? but, Will a persistent shift appear and progress or has a detected shift already been completed, to be followed by an oscillation in the opposite direction?

Classification of Persistent Shifts

1. A persistent shift is a shift anticipated in advance of its arrival and is
   a) Explainable by an ODSSSIC factor,
   b) Often associated with vertical stability (warm air flow over a cold surface), as in easterly weather-system winds along the East Coast of the U.S.,
   c) Usually not associated with vertical instability or with the prior appearance of oscillating shifts,
   d) Going to persist for the duration of the leg.

2. A progressive persistent shift is a persistent shift detected during its development and is
   a) Associated with a continuing change in velocity, dying or increasing (because of a squall, sea breeze, inversion) or with the presence of a shoreline,
   b) Going to persist for the duration of the leg.

3. A completed persistent shift is a persistent shift that is detected after its completion, that has ceased to progress and is
   a) Associated with a cessation of any change in velocity or with the presence of a shoreline,
   b) Associated with light air and particularly with *light air induced by the presence of two winds opposed approximately 90° to each other* (a sea breeze and a weather-system wind for example) when neither wind establishes a major increase or decrease in velocity.
   c) Likely to be followed by a shift back toward the original direction.

Management of Persistent Shifts

The management of a persistent shift depends upon when it is detected—prior to its development, during its development, or after its completion.

1. A persistent shift (a shift anticipated *in advance* of its presence) should be managed as follows:
   a) If the leg will remain a beat or become a beat, sail toward it. When the expected header is perceived, the tack should be continued until near the new lay line (or nearer than most of the competitors).
   b) If the leg will remain a reach or run or become a reach or run, sail away from it so as to attain the best possible sailing angle after it arrives.

2. A progressive persistent shift (a shift detected during its development) should be managed as follows (Figure 41):
   a) If the leg will remain a beat or become a beat, sail toward it (tack in a lift, continue in a header) until near the new lay line (or nearer than most of the competitors).
   b) If the leg will remain a reach or run or become a reach or run, sail away from it so as to attain the best possible sailing angle after its completion.

3. A completed persistent shift (a shift detected after its completion) should be managed as follows:
   Once a shift has been completed, no alteration in position can be of use until and unless another shift occurs. The most common subsequent shift (particularly in light air and particularly when two winds are acting together) is a shift back toward the original direction. Sail toward the next shift— away from the completed shift, as if it were an oscillating shift (Figure 40).

30. Sail Away from the New Wind?

Sailboat racing is not an exact science; no principle always applies, not even, Sail toward the new wind. If a developing sea breeze will result in a 20° veer during a windward leg, one must take off on port toward it. But if the same sea breeze results in the same veer on a run, one must initially take starboard jibe away from it. And if the same sea breeze results in a 40° veer at the beginning of the second windward leg, one had better take starboard tack away from it in order to obtain a position ahead and to leeward on a one-leg beat. (Never "sail toward the new wind" if the resultant shift will position the boat beyond the new lay line!) If two winds are blowing simultaneously, the boat must be sailed so as to acquire the best approach position in the wind that is blowing at the mark. There are obviously plenty of exceptions. A more fundamental restatement of the principle would be, Sail toward the new wind if (upon reaching it) the mark will be to windward; otherwise sail so as to approach the mark in the new wind at the fastest possible sailing angle (usually a close reach).

A light southwesterly was blowing at the start of the fourth race of the 1969 Great Lakes Soling Championship series, but immediately after the gun a new wind, a 15-knot northwesterly, appeared. We were off on starboard tack at the initially favored port end, but alerted to the beginning of the new wind by the lifting boats to weather, we tacked immediately—to "sail toward the new wind!" It would be better to throw away a little at first, we felt, than to go down the drain on the outside of a progressive persistent shift. We tacked back on the weather quarter of the fleet and for a moment thought ourselves to be in the ideal position, inside and to weather in a big lift. Shortly thereafter, however, as the shift progressed and the lift increased, we recognized that we were astern and to weather on a one-leg beat—in the worst possible position. And then it became evident that the boats to leeward were laying the mark!—that if we had stayed where we were, we'd have been in the lead.

Recently we raced the Soling in a club race in Annapolis harbor. The wind had been fluctuating between a weather-system westerly and a southwesterly sea breeze, with the latter predominant. On the third leg of the second race (a reach) the westerly showed signs of returning (Figure 42). It seemed obvious that we should keep to the west of the fleet on the upcoming beat. Our major competitor had an inside overlap at the leeward mark, but we were first off on port toward the new wind. Later the opponent on port chose to make his last covering tack close aboard to windward, and as he tacked, we charged through his lee—fortunately, since we were nearly to the lay line in the new wind, and ahead and to leeward was where we wanted to be. Thereafter, as the westerly shift progressed, we realized that we were overstanding and that a third boat, which had held starboard from the mark (except for one short tack), was laying the mark on our lee bow! We had gone for the new wind and lost the leg.

When a major persistent shift appears, two of the most important tactical principles of windward sailing are in direct conflict. If the position "inside and to windward of the fleet" is sought and is achieved on the lay line, it is impossible to adhere simultaneously to the principle of keeping "to leeward near the lay line." If the shift is large or the layline is near, boats "ahead and to leeward" have the greater advantage.

The principle applicable on a particular leg is determined by the position of the new lay line at the termination of the leg. If the tack toward the new wind results in overstanding, then the attempt to sail toward the new wind has been carried to excess and boats on

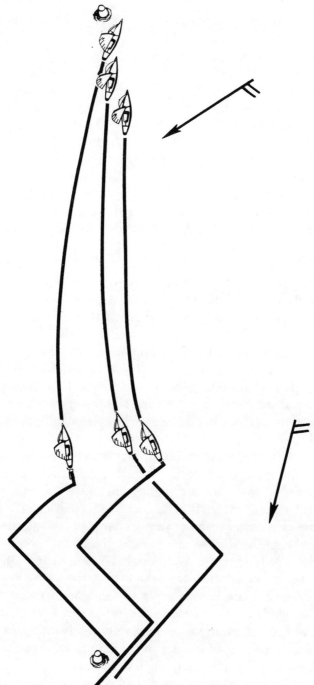

FIGURE 42

the lay line to leeward ("ahead and to leeward") have gained more. If the tack toward the new wind is terminated short of the lay line, boats nearer the layline ("inside and to windward") have gained more. The boat that tacks precisely on the new lay line gains the most. However, as this position is difficult to gauge from afar and there is never any means of recouping the loss resulting from the windward overstanding position, the tack should be made to leeward of the lay line. From this position a further lift (and persistent shifts are likely to progress) will bring the boat up to the lay line, while a header will bring all the boats that were to weather down in line astern (Figure 43).

At the start of a beat, before the fleet has spread out to opposite sides of the course, a marked shift of 30°–45° should be managed by assuming the lifted tack, the position "ahead and to leeward" of the fleet. The lifted tack is the major tack and offers the greatest likelihood of gain whether the lift progresses or the old wind (a header) returns. Boats that initially tack toward a persistent shift may be close to the new lay line when they reach that new wind (or the new wind appears). If so they should tack immediately, so as to be ahead and to leeward on the long-approach tack. Boats which initially tack away from a persistent shift will be far from the lay line when the shift appears. They should tack toward the shift immediately, in compliance with the standard recommendation to "sail toward the new wind," so that if the shift progresses their loss will be minimized.

If a 90° shift appears after boats are spread laterally across the beat, some will be approaching the "weather mark" on a close reach, some on a run. Those that are highest on the wind (up to close-hauled) will reach the mark first, far ahead (particularly in light air) of those on a broad reach or run. Under these circumstances, an early tack toward the shift results in a progressively poorer ultimate sailing angle the farther it is continued. The initial tack should be away from the expected shift; then the farther the tack is continued, the higher the ultimate sailing angle to the mark will be. Getting between the wind and the mark results in the worst possible sailing angle, a run. Indeed, sailing so as to maintain advantage in the old wind as it recedes ahead of the new wind may provide the best position, to leeward, in the new wind when it arrives.

When a new wind appears while the fleet is on a reach, all boats enter it at approximately the same angle. If, however, the new wind will cause the leg to become a beat, one should work to windward

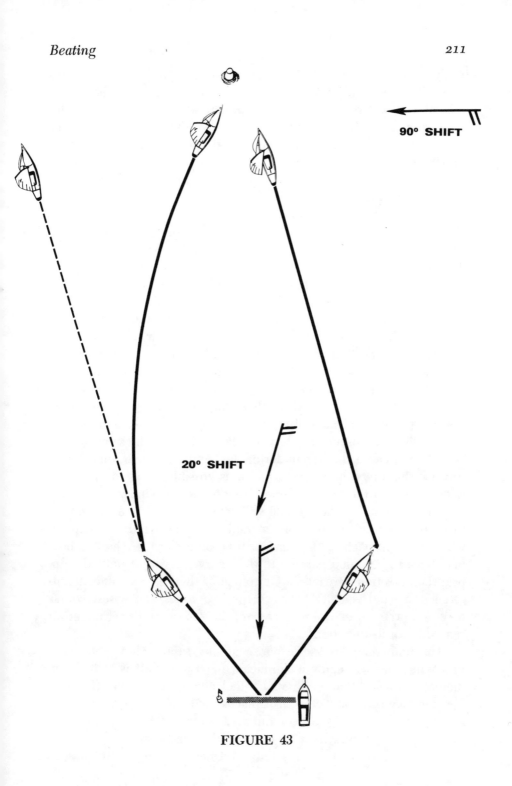

90° SHIFT

20° SHIFT

FIGURE 43

on the reach so as to be farther upwind, nearer to the new lay line, when the new wind arrives. If the new wind will cause the leg to become a broad reach or run, one should work to leeward on the reach so as to be farther downwind, "ahead and to leeward," when the new wind arrives. When a new wind appears while the fleet is on a run, boats may be spread across the course on opposite jibes. If (with a shift of 10°–20°) the leg will remain a run, the standard technique is to take the lifted jibe away from it initially—so as to be "ahead and to leeward" after the new wind arrives. However, if the shift is expected to be so great (20° to 135°) that the mark can be laid at a good sailing angle on the initially headed jibe, that jibe should be assumed (or continued). If the run will become a beat, the headed jibe toward the wind should be assumed, so the boat will be closer to the lay line ("inside and to windward") after the new wind arrives. (See the chapters in Part VI, on running.)

When a new wind fails to obliterate the old wind but instead invades only a portion of the course—the typical result of the meeting of an offshore weather-system wind and an onshore sea breeze of approximately equal temperature—one must sail so as to achieve a preferable position in the wind that will be operative at the mark. Reaching that wind may often require traversing the intermediate zone of light to absent, highly variable air flow. If the wind on the far side will cause the remainder of the leg to be a beat, one should traverse the intervening zone as soon as possible, so as to move upwind, closer to the new lay line, "inside and to windward" of the fleet. If the wind on the far side will cause the remainder of the leg to become a reach or run, one should enter the wind at the point where the approach to the mark will be on a close reach. The boat may have to be sailed parallel to the intervening zone until the appropriate position is reached. Of course, if there is a significant difference in wind velocity between the two zones, the wisest course may be to remain in, or cross over to, the zone with the stronger air regardless of its direction.

The immediate, reflex response of any sailor who perceives a new wind that will cause a significant persistent shift is to tack immediately toward that wind. Such a tack achieved ahead of the competition may provide victory if it places the boat in a position inside and to windward of the fleet but to leeward of the lay line—the ideal position from which to manage the sea-breeze "fan" or the bend in the river or the refracted wind near the shore. But if such a tack positions the boat on or beyond the lay line, or if the shift so progresses that at the termination of the leg the boat is above the lay line, then all boats to leeward will gain and those ahead and to leeward will win. Go for the new wind—but don't go too far!

31. The First (or Second) Tack

Nowhere in a race is a deliberate attitude more essential than immediately after the start, when the first tack is contemplated. If every tack is critical—either correct or incorrect, taking the boat either toward or away from the advantageous side of the course—the first tack is the most critical of all. It provides the opportunity to recover from a poor start or to capitalize on a good one. It must not be hurried. An impulsive response to a boat on the lee bow or to what appears to be an opportunity to consolidate an initial gain may throw away the race. On the other hand, how often does an inability to tack result in the boat's continuing in what turns out to be the right direction—for which thanks are given later?

The advantageous side of the course for the windward leg and the preferred tack for the start will be determined ahead of time. If the initial tack across the line takes the boat in the desired direction, the plan will demand that it be continued. If starting on the tack toward the advantageous side of the course is not possible, the initial tack will take the boat away from that side and, particularly if assumed from the opposite end of the line, will do so while other boats are tacking toward the advantageous side. The plan will then be to undertake the desired tack "as soon as possible." However, even if there is convincing evidence that one side of the course is distinctly advantageous, it is essential to look around before becoming deeply committed—to reconsider before tacking to comply with the plan, and to reconsider before continuing the tack in accordance with the plan.

When doubt exists about whether there is a distinctly advantageous side or about which side is advantageous, it is even more essential to reconsider before making the first tack or continuing the initial tack far from the line. If the doubt continues, a tack back to a position directly to windward of the line may provide the best vantage point from which to make a final decision. However, such a tack should be undertaken only in moderate to heavy air, when an additional tack and the absence of early commitment cannot result in major loss. In light air, particularly when the wind strength is variable and dead spots are present, it is important to keep going. Excessive tacking to "get a good view" under such circumstances can be nothing but disastrous.

When oscillating-shift conditions are detected before the start, early tacking must be to the lifted tack no matter which side of the course is thought to be advantageous. It pays to get ahead—farther to windward in the median wind—first. Later, if a persistent shift or a current difference exists, the boat can be worked to the advantageous side. In stable wind flows, as the line is crossed, all attention is focused on the time and place of the next tack; in unstable air, the next header is merely awaited.

The first (or second) tack is a tack for position—to consolidate an initial advantage or to compensate for an initial deficit. It is determined by relationships to other boats, to the competition, rather than by strategic requirements. What is needed is position, ahead of the fleet, between them and the mark. The timing of this tack therefore depends upon the recognition of gain which can be solidified by a tack. This is the occasion for looking around—and the place to look is the weather quarter. (No advantage can be attained relative to the fleet to leeward except by continuing the present tack.) A prolonged evaluation should be made of the relative progress of the weather-quarter boats. The ability to recognize your own position in relation to these boats, and to detect subsequent variations in that position, is essential. The first (or second) tack must be made on a pragmatic basis—"take what you've got when you've got it." The problem, of course, is to determine when, with respect to the boats on the weather quarter, you have made the greatest gain or the least loss. Tacking too soon or too late, before a heading shift has reached its maximum or after it has ceased and the lift has begun again, will reduce the gain. If you continue to gain as you cross the boats previously to weather, the tack should be continued. If you begin to lose, at some point, dependent upon strategic considerations (is there an oscillating or a persistent shift?), you should tack back.

If boats on the weather quarter are obtaining a progressive advantage—sailing into a progressive persistent shift to their side of the course (Figure 44), sailing into more wind, sailing into more favorable current—your relative position will never improve. Tack as soon as their advantage is recognized. If boats on the weather quarter are alternately gaining and losing—sailing in a wind whose direction is oscillating, sailing in a wind whose velocity is fluctuating—your relative position will periodically improve. Tack when your advantage seems to be maximal. If boats on the weather quarter are steadily losing—sailing into a persistent shift to your side of the course, sailing into less wind, sailing into less favorable current—tack when you have attained the advantage you need. Don't be greedy; the advantage may not continue.

In a recent multiclass regatta on the Olympic Circle at Annapolis, the first classes experienced a 20° veer as they progressed up the first weather leg. The easterly weather-system wind was apparently being replaced by the southerly sea breeze. When we started (in the International 14's), the sea breeze was far from its fully veered position; I assumed that the veer would continue. For this reason, and because the light wind seemed stronger and the current less adverse to the right, we elected to start at the weather corner and tack immediately. We were able to do so, but there was almost no wind at the line; what little existed was out to windward, and it still seemed stronger to the right. As we entered the 3-to-4-knot air, I looked at the boats on the opposite tack on my weather quarter. They were all markedly headed—apparently receiving a backed wind different from ours. I should have tacked, but the wind ahead looked stronger and I was still convinced that the veer would progress. I continued and *my* wind began to back. If the back continued, I'd be in deep trouble; I might never be in a better position relative to the competition. I tacked. Most of the fleet (on starboard tack) was still moving, and although we were lifted in relation to them, we were running out of air. The wind veered a little

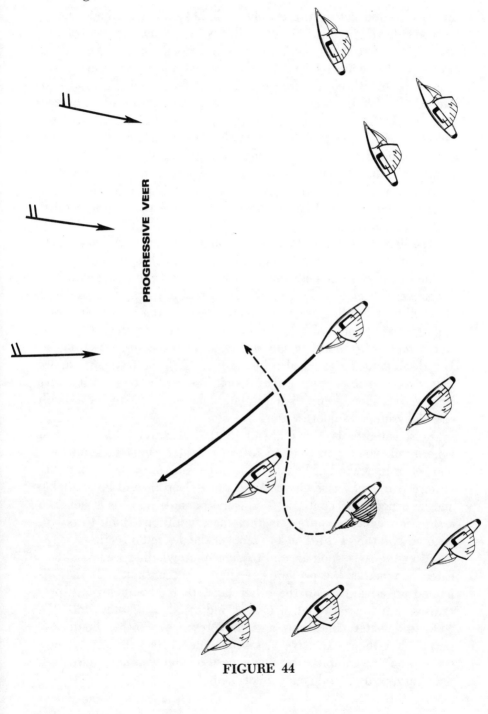

FIGURE 44

and still looked better to the right. I should have continued; doing so would have given me a gain with respect to the majority of the fleet. But my strategic delusion was still dominating. I tacked to port—and the wind backed. By the time we reached the mark, we were seventh—three hundred yards out of first—and the wind had backed 20°. We had been dealing not with a progressive sea-breeze veer; but with a completed shift; the weather-system wind had returned. I had failed to make, did make, and then unmade, the second tack on the basis of strategic considerations—and lost disastrously. If I had tacked in accordance with tactical considerations, as soon as I detected the major back revealed by the headed boats on the opposite tack, I would have been in the race, a close third at the weather mark.

The first (or second) tack should be postponed if the conditions ahead on the initial tack improve. In light air, the presumably desirable tack should be postponed until a patch of increased wind appears. *Never tack in a dead spot!* The sign of a letup, of course, will be an abrupt heading shift; the momentum of the boat swings the apparent wind forward when a decrease occurs in the true wind. *Never tack in a header when the wind is decreasing in strength.* The desired tack should also be postponed if there are unusually large waves or motorboat wakes. Don't lose by the tack itself; don't let it reduce speed more than absolutely necessary. Wait for a patch of good wind and smooth water.

Most important—think ahead to the situation after the tack. Where will you be in relation to other boats? Don't tack into the blanket or backwind of boats on the other tack or of boats that may be forced to tack close ahead. Wait until clear air will be available and be expected to continue. The worst possible move is a tack into a situation which requires an immediate additional tack to obtain clear air and then a third tack to recover the desired direction.

After the start, look around to determine whether a tack is indicated or whether the present one should be continued. If there is indeed an advantage to the other tack, that advantage may progressively increase. When a tack is indicated, wait only until the wind and water conditions and the presence of other boats will permit it without excessive loss. And when a tack is clearly indicated, don't be inhibited by boats close on the weather quarter—if necessary, bear off and go astern of them.

32. Watch the Competition

Races are frequently won or lost in the first quarter of the first leg. At this stage of a race, sailing a few hundred yards in the wrong direction may cause an irrevocable loss, a loss so disastrous that it offsets an entire sequence of top finishes. The usual cause of such a disaster is a failure or inability to look around to see how the race is developing. If a persistent shift occurs, or some boats receive an oscillating or geographic shift which others do not, recovery or disaster depends upon how soon the change is detected and how soon the leaders are followed. To continue a tack away from a progressive persistent shift is to increase the loss; an immediate response is essential. Alertness is the secret of success. Just after the start, the helmsman must get his head out of the bilge and his eyes off the compass to watch the boats going off on the opposite tack. A developing shift is easy to see after the fleet has spread out, but difficult to detect in the melee of the start and the confusion of involvement with neighboring boats. The theme of the first part of the initial weather leg (a theme that justifies starting at an uncontested position on the line) must be, Get out where you can see and cover.

In a Barnegat Bay Bowl Regatta there was one boat we had to beat—to win the regatta and clinch the season International 14 championship. In the first race we made an excellent start at the leeward end but were pinned down by boats on our weather quarter while the dangerous boat tacked to port. We were able to tack at last and drove off, sacrificing pointing for speed, to get between our opponent and the apparently favored starboard shore. We overrode him, forced him to tack, and continued on in the desired direction. I told my crew to keep an eye on the opposition and concentrated on "full speed ahead." "He's lifting on us!" I glanced astern and indeed he *was* beginning to lift out on our weather quarter. But the wind was stronger a hundred yards ahead, the compass was steady, and the boats on our lee bow seemed to be headed. Why tack now, when things were so much more favorable ahead? We continued. Fifty yards later I glanced astern again. Our opponent was in a major lift which had nearly eliminated our lead. We knew we should tack—but we were in a light patch, this was hardly the ideal time. We continued. I glanced astern again. It was now too late; not one but three boats were nearly abeam to windward in a lift we had never received. We rounded the mark sixth, having lost five boats while waiting for that last hundred yards.

A mere two weeks before, we had found ourselves in a similar situation, in the fourth race of the Chesapeake Soling Bowl. We had had a good start and were creeping out on starboard toward the beginning sea breeze which seemed to be developing ahead. Two other boats accompanied us on starboard as the bulk of the fleet tacked away on port. The wind was obviously increasing ahead and we were moving away quickly as the remainder of the fleet wallowed near the line. Should we tack and cover? We began to lift gradually, and the wind looked better and better. (If we didn't win this time, we never would!) The port-tack boats appeared to be headed slightly—and we lifted further. For the first time we began to worry. Despite our tremendous lead, if this shift to the south continued, we could be in trouble. We knew we should tack—but a hundred yards ahead the wind was obviously stronger; its dark fingers played along the water's surface. We continued, and lifted further. We reached the stronger wind—a big lift, up 30° from its initial position—and at last we tacked. The shift continued, another 10°—and the entire fleet which had gone out on port crossed ahead!

It is very easy to wait, very difficult to tack at the first indication of trouble, the first indication of a persistent shift to the opposite side of the course. So many excuses are available: the wind looks better ahead; there'll be a header ahead; the waves are wrong for a tack just now; we don't want to tack in this flat patch. The hope is, in fact, that if the problem is ignored, it will go away.

Most high-performance boats require close attention to steering. This is particularly true just after the start, when other boats are clustered nearby. Nevertheless, if no one else sufficiently competent is available, the helmsman must force himself to look about—and particularly, to look over his shoulder. No amount of boat speed, no tactical advantage over one nearby boat, can make up for a failure to detect a major change in wind direction. Ideally, a member of the crew should be responsible for watching all boats on the other tack and those on the weather quarter on the same tack. This observation must be continuous, but is particularly important as the race begins. When the observer detects a significant change, the helmsman must take a look.

A shift revealed by boats on the opposite tack demands interpretation. This is where data previously collected—compass headings obtained before the start, indications of the appearance of ODSSSIC factors, previous experience in the same waters—is so valuable. Is the lift or header that is affecting the competition an indication of a persistent shift or merely of an oscillation? Is it within the range of oscillating shifts detected in pre-race observation, or is it outside that range? Is it apparently confined to the vicinity of the other boats, or does the compass indicate that it is beginning nearby as well?

Three general possibilities exist, each requiring a different response:

(1) The detected shift is within the range of oscillations expected (whether due to the fluctuations of a truly oscillating wind or due to the long variations induced by the mixing of two wind flows) and is affecting you in the same manner as it affects the other boats.

Obey the compass—continue in a lift, tack in a header. This is the usual response, and is consistent with the recommendation to "take what you've got when you've got it". If your position with respect to the fleet improves, tack to consolidate; if your position deteriorates, continue. When boats on the same tack are headed or boats on the opposite tack are lifted, tack; otherwise, continue.

(2) The detected shift is within the range of oscillations expected but is affecting other boats without affecting you.

Proper Response: Utilize the difference in wind distribution for positional advantage. Assume the tack which improves your position relative to the fleet. When boats on the same tack are lifted or boats on the opposite tack are headed (but you are not), tack; otherwise, continue.

(3) The detected shift is outside the range of oscillations expected; you may or may not also be affected (Figure 45).

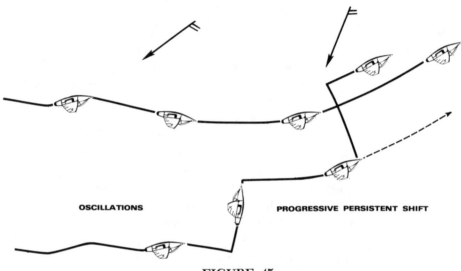

OSCILLATIONS   PROGRESSIVE PERSISTENT SHIFT

FIGURE 45

Proper Response: Assume that a progressive persistent shift is developing and that you must sail toward it. When boats on the same tack are lifted or boats on the opposite tack are headed, tack; otherwise, continue.

The compass, if called continuously, is extremely useful in evaluating the significance of changes in the direction of the wind, both where the boat is sailing and in relation to other boats, at a distance. It indicates whether or not a shift is outside the range of previous observations—whether or not it is a persistent shift. Because it shows the wind direction, it indicates the advisability of a tack for tactical control at the time of a meeting with other boats. It is essential to the evaluation of boat speed, since gains and losses may be mistakenly attributed to boat-speed variations if changes in wind direction are not detected. And, of course, it is essential to the management of a truly oscillating wind. However, the major tacks of the weather leg in most winds must be made for the sake of position with respect to the other boats, not at the dictates of the compass. The compass cannot detect a shift operative only on the opposite side of the course.

Preoccupation with the compass facilitates self-deception. With the compass, you sail a race alone, concerned only with the wind at hand, ignoring the changes in the wind at a distance—as if a shift not in the immediate vicinity were meaningless, as if the winds received by other boats did not affect the race results as much as the winds received by your own. And, of course, the other treachery of the compass is that it does not distinguish at first between those good little lifts which indicate the oscillations you seek and those disastrous big lifts which spell disaster. In the heat of battle, when you want everything to be an advantage, it is so easy to read a benefit into every compass heading. If your own compass doesn't show the lift obtained by boats on your weather quarter, you decide the lift won't last; and if it doesn't show the header experienced by boats on the opposite tack half a mile away, then they'll tack back into your wind, not you into theirs!

I sometimes long to throw away the compass and go back to sail with Peter Barrett in simple splendor, spurning its aid. Peter says he's now taken one aboard; I hope that he will disregard it ruthlessly (at times), and so get even with it for me, and that he will see through its treachery when it seems to flatter him with intimation of benefits ahead.

The compass is not a diabolical instrument, of course. It can be used most successfully, by those able to maintain control over it and themselves. A proper amount of suspicion is all that is necessary. Look around whenever the heading is what you'd hoped for. And look around when it's not. Most important, look around. Remember that you are trying to beat the other boats and that you may have to beat them in their wind, not in yours. When the boats on your weather quarter are lifted beyond the expected range, don't give them another hundred yards (perhaps ten?)—tack! Things can't always go your way—regardless of what you believe your compass is indicating. Expect the worst, and cover what you've already got.

33. Tacking

My crews have often told me that I tack too often. And they have often been right. Until recently, however, I thought that they were telling me that I often tacked at the wrong time or in the wrong place (which was probably true). I hadn't been aware (or been willing to admit) that the tacking itself might be doing me more harm than good. There always seems to be a good reason for tacking. The question that needs to be asked is whether the reason is good enough—whether the distance lost in the tack will be compensated for by the advantage gained. Every tack in every boat in every condition results in some loss—more or less, depending on the boat and the conditions. My experience in International 14's has been poor training for moderation in tacking, since there is probably no boat that loses less per tack. Adaptation to the Soling, which frequently loses a lot, has been difficult for me. The heavier the boat and the smaller its sail area, the greater will be the loss per tack. The lighter the air and the larger the waves, the greater will be the loss per tack. Circumstances which justify a tack in a heavy, undercanvased boat in moderate air and smooth water may not justify one in light air and a lumpy sea even in a light, overcanvassed boat.

The first requirement in tacking is that it be accomplished in the most efficient manner. All racing boats that are affected by crew weight benefit from roll tacking. As the boat is brought into the wind, the crew should hike (or maintain the hike) on the initially windward side. As the boat rolls to windward, the apparent wind shifts aft, permitting the sails to remain functional until the boat is almost head to wind. As the boat passes head to wind, the crew should shift rapidly to a hiking position on the new windward side. By this means the boat is rolled in the opposite direction. The apparent wind is again shifted aft, so the sails begin to function as soon as the boat passes head to wind. The boat should be turned smoothly, with minimal rudder action at first and more later, as required. A gradual turn preserves speed; a rapid turn dissipates it. The operation of tacking should be so perfected that it can be carried out as efficiently when other boats are close aboard as it is in practice. If another boat is near, the tack should be made so as to control her, if that is intended, or to avoid being overridden, if that is a risk. If control is desired, the tack should be completed no more than a few feet to leeward (or dead ahead or slightly to windward, if possible) of the opposing boat's course. Otherwise, she may be able to luff and subsequently drive over. If it is impossible to control the opponent, the tack should be made so far ahead and to leeward that she will be unable to drive over.

In a recent Atlantic Coast Soling Championship series, the Chesapeake behaved like Long Island Sound. By the last race of the series, I was convinced that frequent tacking was a major reason for our poor showing. I had won the Great Lakes Soling Championship a few weeks before, so I knew that boat speed was not the problem. Tacking to reach an area of better wind or to profit from the oscillating shifts had been extremely effective in that series. But the wind had been considerably stronger and the water considerably smoother at Rochester. In the Atlantic Coast races, instead of tacking deliberately with the expectation of gain, we found ourselves tacking out of necessity, with only the hope of minimizing our losses. And with every tack we seemed to drop farther back in the fleet, into more disturbed air, among more boats capable of forcing us about.

In the final race of the series, in a 2-to-3-knot easterly, we took off from the port end of the line and with good speed were soon leading the starboard-tack fleet strung out astern on our weather quarter (Figure 46). We wanted to get to the opposite side of the course, however, since we were sailing out into the stronger northerly

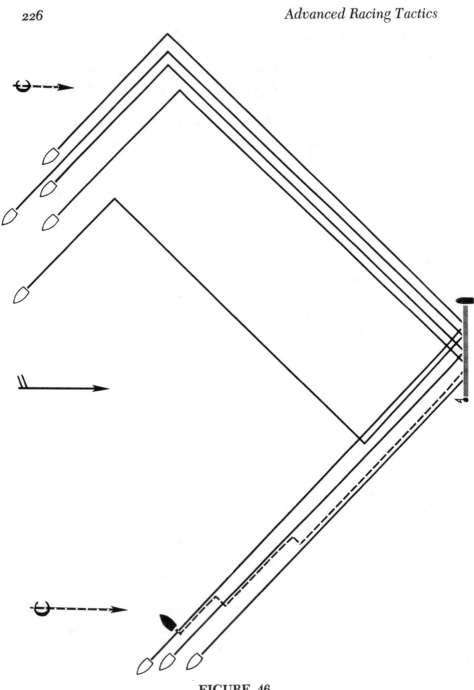

FIGURE 46

current offshore. We tacked as soon as we felt we could clear all the boats on our quarter. Unfortunately, we didn't get going after the tack, and we recognized, when it was too late to go astern, that we would be forced to tack back ahead of the first crossing boat. By the time we were able to tack again, the entire starboard-tack fleet had moved up, and we were then in no better than third. We tacked again, again just missed a crossing, and again had to tack back. When we looked around after that, we were sixth or seventh and the port-tack boats had escaped completely. Obviously, we should have made but one tack and, properly prepared, passed astern of the first boat. The consequence of our failure to do that was impressive—from the lead, or a good chance at it, we had dropped to twentieth or worse by the time we reached the weather mark.

In light air or in a lumpy sea, and particularly in a heavy boat, it is necessary to look far ahead to eliminate occasions which would call for excessive tacking. First, situations involving close crossings should be avoided, since they may abruptly deteriorate and require an unintended tack. When on port tack, watch boats to leeward that may create a risk of collision when they tack. Be prepared to bear away beneath them if you are convinced of an advantage beyond. Tack to leeward of them if nearing the lay line, so as to maintain clear air on the long tack toward the mark. When tacking to port, check the boats on your weather quarter in advance and determine how you will deal with them. In light air and a lumpy sea, always go astern when in doubt about your ability to pass clear ahead. The distance lost in going astern rather than crossing close ahead is approximately 2¼ boat lengths. This will be increased if the boat is slowed by an abrupt, last-minute decision to bear away, but can be reduced by the increased speed acquired in a controlled, close reach to the crossing astern. Proper adjustment of main and jib is essential; stalling will markedly reduce speed and postpone the time of its reacquisition. A tack may lose three boat lengths in light air, and if the starboard-tack boat overrides to windward, the loss may be increased to five or more boat lengths. Then if a tack back is necessary to continue the original plan, the loss is doubled.

Second, situations should be avoided in which disturbed air from a boat ahead, or—particularly—ahead and to leeward, will necessitate a tack. Assuming a reasonable start, the greatest congestion in a large fleet is likely to be near the lay line and in the middle. When you are on the presumably correct tack, sail through a group of crossing boats on the opposite tack and tack on their weather quarter. When in doubt or nearing the lay line, tack to leeward of a group of crossing boats. Continue beyond only if certain of advantages at the lay line. When on the weather quarter of a group of boats, keep your eye on them. If the majority of the group tacks (which is likely near the lay line), be prepared to tack on their lee bows. Don't be caught off guard; if the first boat appears crossing ahead, you may not be able to find a clear spot to tack until you are at the lay line—or beyond. Never tack close on the weather quarter of a boat which has just passed astern. Even when tacking to starboard check boats on your weather quarter before tacking, as it may be disastrous to force an unsuspecting port tacker to tack on your lee bow. If at all possible, wave close crossing port tackers across. It is far better to give a little than to find them camped on your lee bow, forcing you to tack a short while later. If you are in bad air, look around before you tack; things could get worse—and you would only have to tack back again. Be willing to accept some interference (unless the interfering boat is close aboard to leeward). The harmful consequences of tacking twice and going the wrong way would probably be far more disadvantageous.

The basic principle—and an overriding consideration in light air, lumpy seas and heavy boats—is, Don't allow yourself to be forced into tacking. Look around—or better, have your crew look around—so that you can adjust well in advance to boats which may subsequently cross or interfere. Weigh carefully the risks of tacking and of not tacking. And when in doubt, don't.

Here is a general plan for the first weather leg, after the first (or second) tack. (See Chapter 31, "The First (or Second) Tack.") The helmsman following this plan will obtain reasonably clear air while sailing in the proper direction in a large fleet.

A. Continue the selected tack toward what is believed to be the advantageous side of the course. Thereafter,
   1. If the air is light and the wind is merely variable in strength and direction (without a major and obvious increase, generally or locally), continue the initial tack. Unless a new wind with a significant increase in strength appears—a progressive persistent shift—assume that any shift is an oscillation.
   2. If a major advantage has been obtained, tack.
   3. If the air is changing significantly in strength (from light

to moderate, or moderate to light), assume a progressive persistent shift. Tack toward it.

4. If the majority of the fleet is on the other tack, tack no later than halfway to the lay line.

B. When many boats are ahead on the same tack and there will be a large group crossing ahead short of the lay line, tack back before (on the lee bow of) the majority (approximately three-quarters of the way to the lay line).

C. When there is an obvious and major advantage in continuing,
1. Tack back late (but always short of the lay line).
2. Tack back last if neighboring boats tack early.

D. When in or near the lead, tack back when the group tacks,
1. If initially to windward of the group, tack on the lee bow of the closest crossing boats.
2. If to leeward of the group, tack earlier, when the first of the leaders tacks.

E. Tack back again before the opposite lay line is reached, on the lee bow of the majority of the crossing boats and at a time when no other boats will be close ahead and to leeward.

F. Continue starboard tack or tack from port to starboard beneath the starboard-tack parade (on the lay line) until close to the weather mark. Tack to enter the parade on the lay line within a hundred yards of the weather mark.

G. It is always better to tack short of the lay line (unless the mark is close); the loss from two additional tacks is usually less than the loss from overstanding. Once on the lay line or near it, the leg becomes a one-leg beat, and the proper tactical position for a one-leg beat is ahead and to leeward. The position ahead and to leeward provides a gain in either a lift or a header and makes possible control of a boat close on the weather quarter.

H. Continued control by the leading boat approaching the lay line depends upon her position with respect to her closest opponent on the lay line approach tack (Figure 47).
1. If the leading boat is ahead or ahead and to windward, she arrives at the lay line first and may easily overstand. If the mark is a long way off and she is well ahead, she should

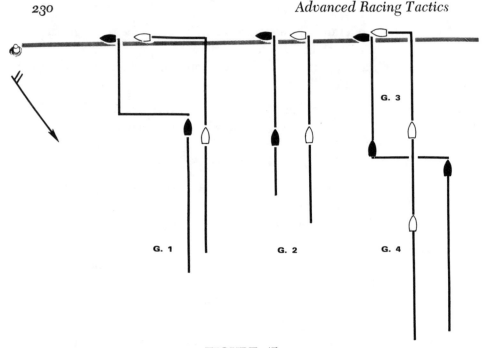

FIGURE 47

tack well below the expected lay line to take full advantage
of any subsequent shift. If her lead is slight, she should
tack back and tack again into a close lee-bow position after
her opponent tacks.

2. If the leading boat is abeam to windward, she should tack
   when she is certain that she has reached the lay line, or as
   soon as the opponent initiates her tack. If the opponent
   induces the leader to carry on beyond the lay line before
   tacking, the opponent may slip off to leeward in clear air
   and still lay the mark.

3. If the leading boat is to windward and astern, she should
   wait for her opponent to tack and tack on her lee bow.
   She should cross ahead or cross astern and tack to windward only if the mark is close and she is *certain* that it cannot be laid from a lee-bow tack (or if, in light air, many
   boats are close aboard).

4. If the leading boat is to leeward, she risks having her opponent in the favored lee-bow position on the mark-ap-
   proach tack. She should tack early, crossing ahead or possibly, if on port, astern, so as to acquire the lee-bow position

herself. If the cross tack is successful—i.e., not covered by the opponent's tack on the lee bow—the cover should be reestablished by a second tack to weather abeam or astern of the opponent. From this position, a third tack on the lee bow will, of course, be possible whenever the opponent tacks for the mark.

34. The Tack Away

Impulsiveness, almost always detrimental to racing success, is particularly harmful when it occasions a quick tack. During the summer of 1968, while on a racing tour of the West Coast, I was struck by the frequency with which the impulsive tack away lost the race—and often the regatta. The instinctive response to the appearance of a boat on the lee bow is to tack away for clear air. Subsequent recognition that both boats have been on the preferred tack may come too late to permit recovery. A little dirty air in the right direction may be far more advantageous than a sea full of clean air in the wrong.

In the West Coast Championship series at Marina del Rey, I took a 4½-point lead into the final race. When I was halfway up the weather leg, with my two closest competitors tucked safely away astern and to leeward, Dick Rose of Seattle tacked a boat length ahead of me. I immediately took a short starboard hitch. By the time I tacked back, a minute (?) later, I had dropped from second to sixth and had lost both of the boats I needed to cover. I had tacked from the port tack (up-current, up-westerly, oblique to the waves), which is almost always the preferable tack off the southern

California coast, to the starboard tack (crosscurrent, away from the westerly, head on to the waves). Variations in wind strength may have contributed to my disaster, but it was the tack away to the so obviously wrong tack that was fatal.

Two weeks later in Seattle, after winning the first race, I started poorly in the second and required most of the beat to work back into contention (Figure 48). The wind was highly variable in strength and direction but shifted distinctly off the land (a breakwater) and was strongest close to shore. I was laying the weather mark on port paralleling the breakwater when a violent header appeared. I tacked, as did Jeff Ingman, who had been abeam to weather, and found myself in the lead but so close to windward of Jeff that I was in danger of being luffed out of the race. I tacked again—and allowed Jeff to continue alone toward the persistent near-shore shift and the stronger breeze. Moments later, the wind shifted back, and Jeff tacked into a port-tack lift that permitted him, but not me, to lay the mark. As the wind gradually disintegrated, he rounded the weather mark second and went on to win the regatta. I rounded tenth and finished fourth in the series.

In the final race of the 5.5-meter Olympic trials, we had a 4.4-point lead over Ernie Fay in *Sundance*. Victory depended upon staying ahead of him or close astern, and under Olympic scoring would be insured by positions down in the fleet for each of us. We started on starboard at the weather end of the line, with Ernie dead to leeward. He tacked to port and we tacked to cover, recognizing that the port tack was greatly to be preferred in the light air. It led inshore, out of the current and toward the expected westerly shift. Unfortunately, another boat tacked ahead and slightly to weather, on our wind. We tacked out on starboard, looking for clear air, but were forced to pass astern of boat after boat before we obtained it. By the time we tacked back to port, *Sundance* was far off on our lee bow, well on her way to the beach. She was two hundred yards ahead at the weather mark, with three boats between us.

In these instances it would have been wiser to accept a defective relationship to one boat in order to preserve a desirable relationship to the fleet. An excellent series position was jeopardized or lost for the questionable and temporary benefit of relief from interference. Although the significance of the tack away is most obvious for the leading boat in a series, its hazards are similar for any boat in any race. The difference between second and tenth may be the right tack in the right direction. The abrupt appearance of a boat ahead

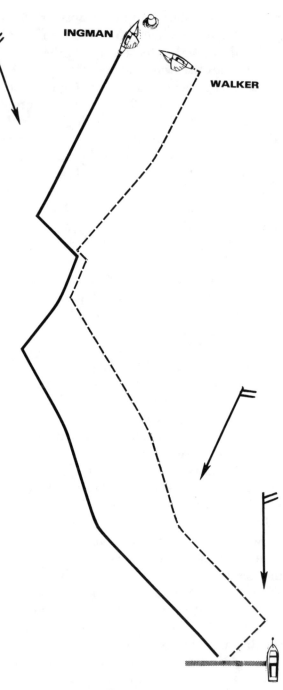

FIGURE 48

or on the lee bow should cause an instinctive reaction—not to tack away, but to hold on. If the opposing helmsman is attempting to force a tack away, why comply to his advantage?

Several decisions are needed. Will more be lost by not tacking than by tacking? Will more be gained by tacking than by not tacking? There is usually little time available for consideration of these question—although that time can be extended by an alertness to boats which are capable of tacking to lee bow or ahead positions. But the time must be taken. As a boat tacks ahead or to leeward, an evaluation of her expected position must be made. Decision 1: If she will complete her tack more than six or eight feet to leeward and/or no farther forward than a half-overlapped position, the weather boat should attempt to drive over. In smooth water this attempt should be initiated by a luff to obtain clear air farther to weather (Figure 49). In a significant chop, particularly in light air, luffing will be harmful; then the correct procedure is to crack sheets, bear away (to the extent that is safe), and drive. The attempt to pass to weather should not be made unless there is reasonable assurance of success. Decision 2: On rare occasions it may be possible or desirable (sensible to try) to break through to leeward. A decision to do so should be made only in the following situations: (a) in an oscillating wind flow when on an obviously lifted tack (breaking through to leeward will result in an advantageous position ahead and to leeward in the subsequent header); (b) in heavy air and in

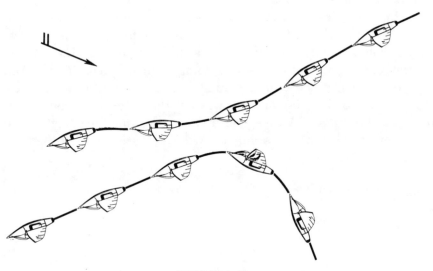

FIGURE 49

a planing boat, particularly when the opponent makes a bad tack; (c) or in very light air, when tacking itself is harmful and the best way to keep moving is to leeward of the fleet. I can think of no other circumstances in which an attempt to break through to leeward will result in a loss of less than four to five lengths.

Decision 3: When, as is so often the case, it will be impossible to drive over or to break through to leeward, a choice must be made between tacking and just hanging in there. The first consideration is the possibility of a major advantage in continuing the initial tack. If the advantage is imminent and large—sailing out of an adverse current, sailing into a persistent shoreline shift, sailing toward a major oscillating shift—the tack should be continued. The adverse effects of sailing in dirty air will rarely cause a loss of more than four lengths; sailing away from the advantages listed for even a few lengths may result in far greater losses. Decision 4: In the absence of a major advantage in continuing, the best response to the appearance of a competitor ahead or on the lee-bow is usually to tack. The tack should be made with the specific intention of tacking back *as soon as* clear air is obtainable and sufficient time has elapsed for the full recovery of speed. Two good tacks should result in a loss of no more than two boat lengths (except in light air and a choppy sea), half the loss to be expected from continuing in dirty air. This response is the only possible one if the original tack must be continued for a long period in the absence of a significant advantage ahead— a circumstance typical of the starboard-tack lay line.

In all of these decisions, the essential is awareness of the opponent's intent. He wishes to slow you and/or to cause you to tack. You should comply with his wishes as little as possible. Do not tack away unless you will lose less by doing so than by continuing. And if you do tack, proceed in the wrong direction no farther than necessary. (If the tack you were on was not the better one, you should not have been on it.) Give your opponent his due for being able to tack on your lee bow; give him a few boat lengths, but not the race.

35. *The Management of Oscillating Shifts*

All winds oscillate—shift to and fro between alternate sides of some median direction—but only cold air flows coming off warm land (unstable winds) are truly oscillating winds. Most winds must be utilized according to the principles described in the preceding chapters, with (1) a constant alertness for a persistent shift, (2) long tacks made while observing the behavior of boats on the weather quarter, and (3) tacking determined by considerations of position with respect to major segments of the fleet. Tacking on the minor oscillations of most winds is usually inappropriate. Major oscillations indicated by the lifting out or falling in astern of the fleet on the weather quarter must be utilized, but shifts of this type usually occur but two or three times per beat on a two-mile leg. Truly oscillating winds are managed differently; they present the one situation in racing when all the usual rules are disregarded, when a unique technique specific to the circumstances is required. This situation must be recognized, since failure to apply the appropiate technique is disastrous. It should be suspected in the presence of northerly weather-system winds and sea breezes coming off an intervening shore. Its presence can be confirmed by the observation of compass headings while sailing close-hauled before the start. In general, the greater the wind velocity, the greater the range (up to 20°) and the frequency (as often as every two minutes) of the oscillations.

The management of oscillating shifts to windward (Figure 8) requires paying constant attention to the compass and, with few exceptions, ignoring the competition. Gains and losses from a single shift can be on the order of ten to twenty boat lengths (or more), so covering is impossible, and the attempt, if it entails a shift, may be disastrous. (A boat covering from dead to windward, already as far ahead as she can be, will lose with every shift.) This is simple sailing with few surprises; if you obey the simple rules, you should come out on top. Even if you get behind, there are ways of recouping. (For a detailed discussion, see Chapter 13, "The Utilization of Wind Shifts.") The basic requirements are these:

1. Determine the range of oscillations and for each tack calculate the median heading (halfway between the extremes). Record the extremes before the start and during each beat, and revise the determination of the median heading accordingly.

2. Keep to the tack lifted to the median heading—sailing toward an expected header.

3. Keep ahead and to leeward of competitors.

4. When in doubt as to whether a shift has reached its full extent (and the boat's heading is close to the median), don't tack.

5. Sail toward a persistent shift (developing or expected) in addition to tacking on the oscillating shifts (Figure 45).

When the wind is oscillating, the short course to the weather mark is on the tacks lifted by the successive oscillations. If the tack away from the starting line is the lifted one, a major lead is immediately gained upon boats on the headed tack. Boats on the initially headed tack not only lose at the instant of the next oscillating shift but enter into subsequent shifts astern and to leeward of the fleet. When port tack is the lifted tack or becomes the lifted tack at the start, smart sailors start on port or start so that they can readily tack to port. If they are caught at the leeward end on starboard in a sudden back, they jibe away and cross the line on port. When starboard is the lifted tack most boats are on it, advertently or otherwise. If a heading back appears, it is easily recognized and dealt with by a tack to port. If an abrupt veer appears, the planned start on starboard has only to be continued. The risk is that the lifting veer will not be recognized and an early tack to port will carry the boat away from the next shift on the headed tack.

The winds of Bermuda are characterized by oscillating shifts. As they approach Bermuda almost all winds, but particularly those from the north, are unstable (as a result of cool air flowing over the warm Gulf Stream). In two successive races in International Race Week one spring, we were forced into an early port tack during an oscillating veer. In the first of these we had an excellent start on starboard at the starboard end of the line, but found a boat close to our lee bow and were soon forced to tack away. When the northerly oscillated back to the west and the starboard tackers tacked to port, we found ourselves far to leeward of the leaders. We clung to port through a series of oscillations, however, and eventually, when far to the right of the fleet, tacked to starboard in a veer and crossed all but the leading boat. We were not so fortunate in the second instance. This time the port end of the line was upwind in an oscillating back and we elected to start there on starboard. The wind oscillated to its veered position as we crossed the line at the pin—half a second early. We jibed around the mark and crossed every stern in the fleet on port. We tacked back to starboard when we finally had clear air and were met with an oscillating back-headed again! We couldn't tack immediately because of the proximity of other boats and—well, the story is well known from here. We didn't obtain clear air on the right side of a shift until we were two-thirds of the way to the mark. We were lucky to round in tenth place.

Now, it's simple enough to recognize retrospectively that a leeward-end start on starboard in an oscillating wind is hazardous. Even if you don't start early and aren't forced to a headed port tack, you may be pinned down on starboard by all the boats on your weather quarter in a backed oscillation. Clearly the sensible start in a frequently oscillating wind is from a position that will provide freedom to continue or to tack as required by subsequent conditions, i.e., from an uncrowded area of the line. But we all get caught occasionally, and the question is what to do when you discover that you're on or have just been on (remember the half worm in the apple?) the headed tack. Perhaps, as soon as you recognize the situation, you should tack to the lifted tack—no matter how dirty the air is. It is certainly unreasonable to be sailing away from the next shift when you know it's coming. But if, as soon as the initial mistake is recognized, you try to recoup your losses by getting back into phase with the shifts, you spend the rest of the leg sailing in bad air or making frequent tacks to avoid your neighbors or both. There is another solution—and in a big fleet it is the better one.

For any given shift, the farther a boat is to the side of the course from which the shift emanates, and the more she is separated from her competitors, the more that boat gains. Many sailors deliberately seek such a position in oscillating winds, sailing through successive heading shifts to reach the side of the course. They intend to utilize one final shift to recoup the losses they have incurred en route. If only one shift to their side of the course occurs (it is then a persistent shift), this is clearly the strategy of choice. However, if there are oscillating shifts (that is—by definition—if each oscillation lasts significantly less than the time it takes to sail half the weather leg), it is extremely unlikely that a boat which has sailed far to one side of the course will be able to make it all the way back to the mark in a single shift which comes her way. The wiser course is certainly to tack on each shift as it comes, keeping continually to the tack lifted to the median wind. But if the first shift of a series has been missed and keeping to the lifted tack requires sailing in dirty air and making frequent avoidance tacks, a second-best solution is to sail on through the first header, the second lift, the second header, the third lift, and finally to tack in the third header (or the fourth or fifth—*but well short of the new lay line*) so as to trade off the deficit of continuously bad sailing conditions for the risky advantage of being far to the side of the course. Most of the rest of the fleet will have been missing a shift now and then, sailing in bad air or being forced to tack out of a lift, and many will have stayed near the rhumb line, where gains from individual shifts will have been slight. It is possible to recover these boats and to get back far more than is deserved—as we did in the first of the two races described.

Ultimately, what is needed should be sought. If a large number of boats have been lost through an early mistake, it is worth taking a gamble that presents a significant possibility of getting most or all of them back. Of course, they should not have been lost in the first place, but once the damage has been done, there's little use in following in their wakes.

36. Oscillating Wind Angles

In oscillating winds the compass, by indicating the relationship of the course being sailed to the median wind, determines the strategy of the windward leg. However, it only shows the direction of the wind where the boat is sailing, not the direction of the wind where the competition is sailing. And it does not distinguish between a shift which will be followed by another in the opposite direction (an oscillating shift) and a shift which will continue for the remainder of the leg (a persistent shift). Hence it is important to look around, beyond the rim of the compass, to detect the presence of shifts elsewhere on the course. Early in the leg (in an oscillating wind), a shift in one direction is likely to be followed by a shift in the opposite direction. Later in the leg, a shift is increasingly less likely to be followed by a shift in the opposite direction (until after the windward mark has been rounded). The final shift of the windward leg is by definition a persistent shift and therefore requires a different, an essentially opposite, management than the previous oscillating shifts. In oscillating conditions much of the windward leg can be accomplished almost automatically, merely by tacking on headers at the dictate of the compass. However, one must be alert to critical shifts in which a leg-winning tack must be made (or not made) contrary to the implication of the compass.

An understanding of certain principles underlying oscillating-wind strategy is necessary. First, the farther two boats are from each other, the greater the effect of a given shift will be. It may be desirable at times (particularly when only one other boat is in contention) to avoid the risks of separation. Second, gains and losses (assuming that there will be a return shift) occur only when the competing boats tack (or fail to tack) in a manner opposite to each other or experience different shifts. (If both boats experience the same shifts and tack simultaneously as the shifts appear, each gain or loss in one shift will be canceled by an equal loss or gain in the next shift.) Third, a tack away from a prospective shift results in a major loss; failing to tack, sailing through a header, brings little or no net loss, since it results in a better position, farther to the side of the course, in the next header. A decision on whether to tack may depend not only upon the compass but upon the tack of the opponent and upon his experience with shifts. The assumption of a tack opposite to the opponent's will consolidate a gain or a loss; maintenance of the same tack as the opponent's will diminish the likelihood of any gain or loss.

The following rules for beating in oscillating winds derive from these principles:

(1) Obey the dictates of the compass (tack when headed below the median wind direction) whenever a return oscillation can be reasonably expected, i.e., early in the leg. As long as a shift can be assumed to be an oscillating one, it must be acted upon regardless of its effect upon an opponent. What matters is the shift you experience; if the opponent does not receive the shift, he cannot profit from it and will lose. Early in the leg, ignore the competition; obey the indications of the compass.

(2) Whenever a shift may reasonably be expected to be persistent, late in the leg, consider your position with respect to the opponent (Figure 50). In some circumstances (detailed later in this chapter) this means ignoring the compass. The last shift of the windward leg is a persistent shift, and its effects will fix the positions of the boats affected by it. You must sail toward the shift, so as to be farther upwind than the opponent when it arrives, that is, you must continue in a header rather than tack—if it is regarded as persistent and progressive. Thus, late in the leg the decision on whether to comply with the implications of the compass must be

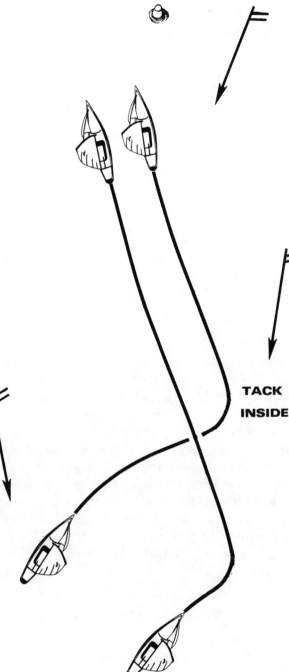

TACK DELAYED TO BE
INSIDE IN FINAL VEER

FIGURE 50

based upon an analysis of the gain or loss possible in relation to the opponent. This decision is most readily made with reference to only one other boat, but the principles suggested can be applied even when a number of boats are in contention.

When to Accept the Indications of the Compass

(1) When both you and your opponent are affected by the same shift, following the dictates of the compass is appropriate even late in the leg. However, if you are both on the same tack and your opponent does not tack, it is not necessary for you to do so, since you cannot be adversely affected if it is an oscillating shift and if neither boat tacks. If the opponent tacks appropriately, you must, of course, tack with him.

(2) When you and your opponent are on opposite tacks and experience the same shift late in the leg, you must comply with the dictates of the compass. One of you has been on the wrong tack. If you are headed, you must tack to consolidate your gain. If you are lifted, you must continue the tack with the expectation that he will tack to your tack.

(3) When you receive a shift but your opponent does not, compliance with the compass is usually appropriate. Any shift beyond the median wind direction should shorten the course to the weather mark. It should be welcomed and acted upon—even late in the leg. However, when you are nearing the weather mark, a little restraint may be appropriate. If a slight header heralds what may be the last shift of the leg—and your opponent does not tack (as he will not, until he receives the shift)—you should delay your tack and continue toward the persistent shift. Do not tack until the opponent does—or until the header reaches its maximum. By the same token, if you begin to be lifted (when presumably already sailing a lifted tack), you should tack immediately toward the new lay line so as to avoid continuing a tack away from a persistent shift.

When to Ignore the Indications of the Compass

(1) If an opponent receives a shift and you do not, his response may be utilized as an indicator of what is to come. If the opponent is on the same tack and receives a header, this can be taken to indicate that you are sailing (correctly) toward the next shift. You

should not tack until you receive the header (early or late), and late in the race should delay your tack until the opponent tacks. If the opponent is on the same tack and receives a lift, this can be taken to indicate that you are sailing (incorrectly) away from the next shift. (Receiving a lift while sailing in oscillating winds is always a bad sign, of course. Since you should always be sailing the lifted tack, you should never receive an additional lift. Receipt of a significant lift can only mean that your initial compass readings were in error—that you've been sailing in a header without knowing it—or that a persistent shift has appeared.) Late in the leg, sailing away from a shift may be disastrous. If it is the last shift of the leg, you must sail as far toward it as possible (without overstanding) before it arrives. Tack when your opponent on the same tack is lifted and you are not—particularly late in the leg (Figure 51). Even if the shift turns out to be an oscillating one, you will have gained more (or lost less) by tacking than by continuing, with respect to the opponent, in a relative header.

(2) If an opponent on the opposite tack receives a shift and you do not, the same considerations apply. He may be receiving a shift which will later reach you. Late in the leg, it must be managed as a persistent shift. If the opponent is headed, you, on the opposite tack, are sailing away from the shift—you should tack immediately. If the opponent is lifted, you, on the opposite tack, are sailing toward the shift— you should not tack, at least not until the shift (a header) arrives.

(3) In light air particularly, but in oscillating wind flows of any strength, tacking should be avoided unless a significant gain will result. Do not tack to cover—especially, do not tack to cover because you are losing. If one shift causes a gain over boats on the lee bow and a loss over boats on the weather quarter, the next will have the opposite effect. In short races and on crowded first legs, tacking should be dependent upon position first and compass heading second:

Continue the present tack when you lift above boats on the lee bow and boats on the weather quarter lift above you.

Tack when you fall down upon boats on the lee bow and boats on the weather quarter fall in line astern.

In light air, where speed pays, it is best to crack off a bit in the lifts so as to drive over the boats to leeward. Then, when the header comes, they will no longer be threatening on your lee bow and you can elect to tack rather than be forced about.

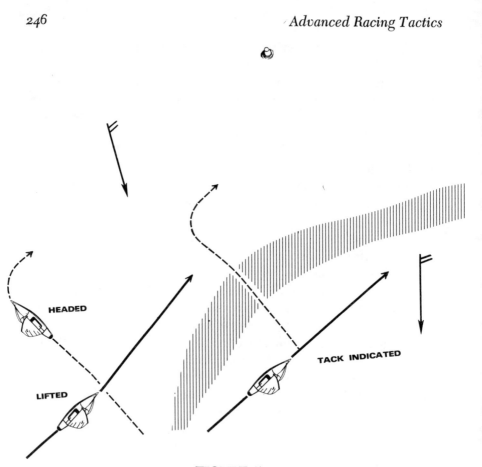

FIGURE 51

When you decide to tack because of a gain with respect to boats on the weather quarter, a particular boat in that position should be selected as a reference. One member of the crew should estimate the expected relationship upon meeting, and after the tack should constantly observe the reference boat to determine whether the relationship is improving or deteriorating. "We should cross her by about two boat lengths." "OK. Let's tack." "Two hundred and forty degrees." "We may be closer than I thought." "Two forty-three." "Now it looks like we'll barely cross her." "Two forty-eight." "We won't cross her." "Two fifty." "OK. Lets tack back. We have a reverse oscillation." Don't merely decide to tack, in response to a detected shift and then continue willy-nilly. Determine in advance when you will want to tack back. If you are close to the lay line, the tack back will be on the lee bow of weather-quarter boats. It should certainly be on the lee bow of the nearest boat. Always avoid the weather-quarter position on the major tack (particularly near the lay line) in oscillating winds. The worst possible disaster is to bear away to go astern of a crossing boat and to emerge with her lifted and you headed. Then you want to tack but you can't (because of her bad air). You want to be on her lee bow for the next shift, and the only place you can be is on her weather quarter.

Although unstable air flows do not oscillate at precise intervals, there is a rough periodicity, which varies with wind velocity. In light air oscillations may occur at intervals of from ten to twenty minutes; in heavy air, at two-to-three-minute intervals. The final shift of any leg is a persistent shift and must be managed accordingly. Thus, in light air, a shift occurring five minutes before the mark is reached should be considered to be progressive and persistent, and if a lift begins, an immediate tack out of it is indicated. (The same shift occurring early in the leg would, of course, be an oscillating shift; it would be welcomed, and a tack would not be made.)

In a 1975 Soling Winter Series race we started on port into clear and increasing (through light) air. As we approached the starboard lay line, in the lead with no more than five minutes to go to the mark, a backing shift developed, with no immediate drop in wind strength (Figure 52). We decided that this shift would persist and progress for the remainder of the leg and therefore tacked toward it. Several boats on our weather quarter had gained considerably in the back, but we crossed them all before we tacked back, inside and to weather of the entire fleet and within two hundred feet of the mark. Unfortunately, however, the wind was now dying rapidly, and when we came to a near halt fifty feet below the lay line, more than ten minutes had elapsed since our first tack. Besides running out of air, we had run out of time. What little wind remained oscillated to its earlier veered position, and three boats that we had thought to be completely controlled crossed us at the mark. The duration of an oscillation is as important as its direction.

In sum, then, early in the leg, follow the indications of the compass; late in the leg, watch the opposition. If late in the leg, both of you receive the same shift, tack in accordance with the compass—only modifying the timing of the tack to (1) stay close to an important opponent or (2) avoid tacking away in a minor shift. If you

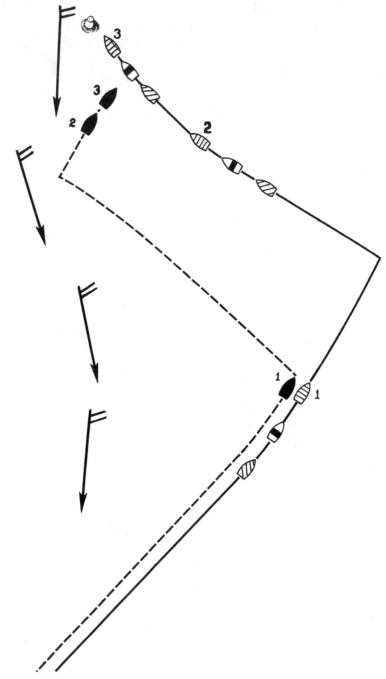

FIGURE 52

receive a shift different from your opponent's, the same principles apply except that you should tack at the beginning of a terminal lift if you are not laying the mark. If your opponent receives a shift and you do not, you should tack to cover him if (1) he is lifted on the same tack or (2) he is headed on the opposite tack. When small heading oscillations appear or when sailing a direction approximately halfway between the extremes, continue a tack toward the rhumb line and tack from a tack that takes the boat away from the the rhumb line. This will postpone arrival at the lay line, prolong the opportunity to gain from a subsequent shift, and decrease the likelihood that an opponent far to the opposite side of the course will make a dramatic gain in a final shift in his direction.

37. The One-Leg Beat

The one-leg beat, usually created by a big shift undetected or ignored by the race committee, adversely affects every boat in the fleet—except the one in the lead. Boats astern are deprived of the option to tack, are forced to make their gains on the same tack by passing either to windward or to leeward, are faced with the certainty of major loss if they are unable to escape the backwind and blanket zones of the boats ahead. (When this is the situation throughout the leg, the start often determines the outcome.) The problem must be dealt with in race after race, not just on one-leg beats, but whenever the option of tacking is lost—because of proximity to the layline, or because one side of the beat is heavily advantaged. Under these circumstances, the first concern must be to continue the tack in the appropriate direction. The second concern must be to gain on the boats advantageously positioned ahead and to leeward. The third concern must be to avoid the major loss which is likely to result from the disturbance of the air flow by boats ahead.

I often remember the start of a race in the 1959 CDA Regatta at Kingston when I was caught on the weather quarter of the most leeward boat in the fleet just after the start. I wanted the clear air that only the boat ahead possessed. I bore off sharply, planed across her stern and went through her wind shadow at about 45° to her course, emerging a boat length to leeward in clear air. Because *Salute* was such a great boat to windward, I was dead ahead within another minute and went on to win the race. Beating even a few Canadians usually isn't easy; beating fifty of them at once is an accomplishment worthy of remembrance. Unfortunately, the memory has served me ill on many subsequent occasions.

In a regatta at Essex, near the end of a long beat in light and highly variable air, St. John Martin broke into the lead and tacked a boat length ahead of me (Figure 53). We were nearly laying the mark in a lift, and a third boat, which I needed to cover, was astern on the same tack. To tack away from St. John made no sense under the circumstances. To attempt to break through to windward seemed equally foolish, since pinching is extremely inefficient in light air and St. John was obviously pointing higher than anyone else in the fleet. Some quirk of memory must have recalled that victory in Kingston, and I bore away to break through to leeward. I went but little faster as I bore off, and by the time I had broken through both backwind and blanket zones, I was four boat lengths to leeward. Needless to say, St. John rounded the weather mark far ahead. I obviously would have been wiser to stay where I was, dead astern. Although I undoubtedly would have dropped aft from this position, I wouldn't have lost four boat lengths.

The attack to leeward from astern is rarely successful. It should be attempted only in strong air when a significant increase in speed can be attained by displacing the sails from the centerline and bearing away to a close reach. Little increase in speed results from bearing away in light air, and little increase in speed results from bearing away in any air in most displacement boats. Unless the boat is moving at high speed, the blanket zone cannot be traversed except where it narrows far to leeward. In order to be moving at high speed you must initiate the maneuver free of backwind, i.e., to windward of dead astern. An abrupt bearing away at a marked angle to the course in a gust from close astern and to weather may result in a major increase in boat speed. But that speed must be carried through both backwind and blanket zones and out the far side. In light air or heavy boats, no such acceleration is obtainable.

The far better option (and in most conditions and most boats, the only one) is to break through to windward. You must acquire

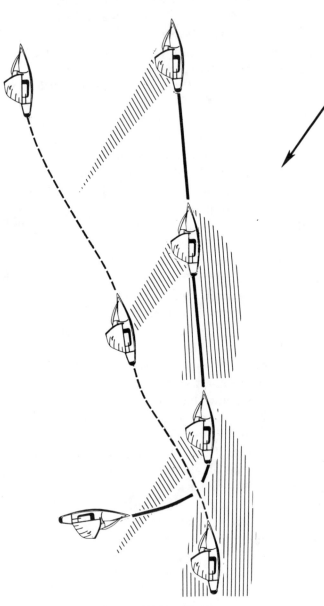

FIGURE 53

the capability of lifting out on a boat ahead or ahead and to leeward. This requires shifting to "pointing gear" (flattened sails and tightened leeches) when a boat ahead is blocking the preferred course. The first requirement is to lift out of her backwind. Once sufficiently far to windward, a shift back to "go gear" may permit passing. At the least, the maneuver permits continuing the preferred course and prevents the major loss that would result from continuing in backwind—and the greater loss that would result from an unsuccessful attempt to break through to leeward.

When on the preferred tack, you must be alert for a boat tacking into a damaging position on the lee bow. Other boats have an interest in preventing you from continuing unimpeded on the preferred tack, and in acquiring the position you have selected. As one of them tacks into a position ahead or ahead and to leeward, you must prepare to escape. When a boat initiates a tack that will be completed very close to leeward or dead ahead, a smooth luff, 10° or more above close-hauled, should be undertaken. If the tack will be completed farther to leeward (half a boat length or more), you should crack off a little in anticipation, from a position far enough away to avoid violating rule 34. By so doing, you will induce the tacking boat to tack farther to leeward and you will acquire a head of steam that will facilitate the subsequent luff. Such a response requires careful observation of boats approaching on the opposite tack and a talent for judging their intentions and their relative position.

Recently, we started from a line that permitted us to lay the weather mark. We couldn't resist the temptation to start near the weather end, which was farther upwind, but, of course, found half the fleet on our lee bow as the gun went. We had clear air, however, and with the boom displaced to the corner of the transom and the jib slightly eased, drove down across them until those close to leeward had been forced to tack away. The only remaining boat to leeward was several boat lengths farther down, so we decided to hold a fast, but more close-hauled course thereafter. As we approached the mark, we saw that we wouldn't be able to lay it in the weather-bow current. We trimmed in closely, and after a short tack rounded well in the lead. On the second round the wind had shifted another 10°, so we cracked off with the board well up and roared up the leg. Using a range on the distant shore, we realized that this sailing angle wouldn't quite lay the mark, so we hardened up for the last quarter mile. We had gained another hundred yards on our nearest competitor, who had worked his way to weather at the start of the leg.

Ahead and to leeward is the place to be on a one-leg beat; in a lift everyone lays the mark, and in a header, the leeward boat gains the most. Working to weather offers no advantage. At the initiation of a one-leg beat, go for speed, moving as rapidly as possible in the general direction of the mark. It will pay to bear away across the bows of any boats that are immediate threats, so as to be ahead and to leeward of them. Should it be ultimately evident that a higher course will be necessary to lay the mark, harden up for it. And it may never be necessary; if there is a lift (extending the one that produced the one-leg beat in the first place), or if there is a header, the race is won!

38. The Starboard-Tack Parade

Blind adherence to port rounding may be disappearing; we may soon be having an occasional fling at the tactical subtleties of rounding weather marks to starboard. Until that day comes, however, we are faced with the starboard-tack parade—boat after boat, bow to transom, on the starboard-tack lay line, approaching the weather mark which is shortly to be rounded to port. Two-thirds of the way up the weather leg, most helmsmen seem willing to settle for a seemingly safe berth in this starboard-tack parade. By so doing they relinquish all hopes of improving their position on that windward leg. Once they are on the lay line no shift, no alteration in current or wind velocity, can benefit them. They sail in the backwind and wake of all the boats ahead for a prolonged period. They have difficulty in judging the lay line from afar, and often find themselves overstanding. And if they have not in fact overstood, they may sink to leeward in the disturbed air and water, and unable to lay the mark, be forced to tack again—often under particularly difficult circumstances. It hardly seems reasonable for the majority of those in the fleet to handicap themselves in this manner—but they do.

For the more courageous, a far better route is available. Not the port-tack lay line, certainly. That has some of the disadvantages of the starboard-tack lay line, and in addition, the boat following that course is committed to approaching the starboard-tack parade, willy-nilly, at the mark—with few options remaining. The ideal approach to the mark is indeed on starboard tack, but from a few hundred feet to leeward of the lay line—far enough away from the parade to insure clear air. From this position a gain from either a heading or a lifting shift is possible. From this position the lay line can be determined when close aboard the mark. From this position the starboard-tack parade can be closely observed and the ideal moment to enter it can be selected as the situation develops. As each boat in the parade slows the boat astern (particularly in light air), the openings between boats widen, so the opportunities to enter the parade improve progressively. And the closer to the mark the parade is entered, the better the helmsmen of the entering boat is able to judge the lay line.

Approaching the weather mark to leeward of the starboard-tack lay line is justified because usually a boat can tack to leeward of the parade when close aboard the mark (Figure 54). If tacking to leeward is possible, significant gains are possible—as boats slowed in the parade are passed and an inside overlap on the nearest boat is acquired. The elements essential to tacking to leeward successfully in a large fleet are timing and speed. If the tack can be completed without the windward boat overriding, it will almost always be successful—even if it is completed, as may be necessary, a boat width below the lay line. With a smooth tack and clear air, even a course slightly below the lay line will in most boats permit a luff around the mark. Thus the port-tack approach should be timed, by bearing away if necessary, so that the tack is made ahead and to leeward of an approaching starboard tacker and as far as possible from other boats ahead and to windward. In many instances the starboard tackers have overstood, either from necessity (because they feared falling into the backwind of a boat ahead) or inadvertently (because they were unable to judge the lay line accurately from afar). If the water is smooth and the wind moderate to strong, a tack to leeward is more likely to be successful, because it will then cause little loss of speed. If the current is against the wind, the starboard tackers will be swept to weather, leaving even more room for a tack to leeward. And, of course, the closer to the mark the tack is made, the shorter will be the time during which the adverse effects of disturbed air will operate.

When the mark is near, the parade is widely spaced, the nearest approaching boat is overstanding, and the current is setting to windward, tacking to leeward should always be attempted. In smooth water and moderate to strong air, it should usually be attempted even if an ideal position on the lee bow of a starboard tacker is not obtainable. A high-performance boat that can be tacked smoothly into position facilitates the maneuver. When the traffic is dense, the safest place to tack is within a few boat lengths of the mark. The decisive question should be, Can speed be maintained to the mark? A lack of speed means an increase in leeway—and failure to lay the mark.

The rights of a boat tacking to leeward are limited only minimally. She is just required to complete her tack without interfering with boats to weather (rule 41). As soon as her tack is completed, she acquires the rights of a boat clear ahead or of a leeward boat, and weather boats must keep clear. While the port-tack boat is approaching the parade, and while she is tacking, the starboard-tack boat must not so alter course as to balk her; the starboard tacker may not bear down from her overstanding position even if she is about to round the mark (rule 34). The boat tacking to leeward acquires luffing rights if her tack is completed forward of the mast-abeam position (rule 38). She may luff (head to wind if she pleases), beginning as soon as she completes her tack, to prevent the boat to windward from overriding her. Within two boat lengths of the mark, she acquires an inside overlap as she tacks to leeward and therefore is entitled to room to round the mark—even if she cannot lay it (rule 42.2(b))! She may luff (head to wind if she pleases, even without luffing rights!) in order to round the mark, and the windward boat must give her room (rule 42.1). The latter may even be forced to tack to provide that room. If the windward boat does not tack and the leeward boat hits the mark, the windward boat may be disqualified. (Presumably, if a third boat is approaching close to windward, the intervening boat will be restricted to a luff head to wind; she cannot tack if by so doing she interferes with a boat on a tack.) Although some frightful donnybrooks may result, the leeward boat is justified in demanding room, and boats to windward must be alert to that possibility even when the leeward boat is not laying the mark.

In some circumstances a tack to leeward of the starboard-tack parade will obviously be doomed to failure and even a terminal luff to round the mark will be unsuccessful. Then a hole between the approaching starboard tackers must be sought and a tack to weather planned, even if it cannot be made until several boats have been allowed to pass ahead. This is, of course, the hazard that all the boats on the lay line have sought to avoid by their early entry into the parade. This route must be adopted in light air when a tack to leeward in disturbed air will result in an inability to clear the mark. It is the only route when the parade is encountered far from the mark; prolonged exposure to the backwind and wake of boats ahead would result in failure to lay. And it is the only route when the current is with the wind or when the seas are large and leeway is excessive. In these circumstances many places may be gained if boats ahead, unable to clear the mark, are forced to jibe away beneath it. And of course, when the approaching starboard-tack boat is herself under-standing, a position to weather must be accepted. The complications that may result from being pinned down to the port-tack lay line by a boat close to weather are too disastrous to be risked.

The distance from the mark at which the starboard-tack parade is entered determines what tactics are to be applied. Close to the mark, a tack to leeward will be successful in most conditions. Passing through the parade and tacking to weather will be required only in very light air, lumpy seas or adverse current. Far from the mark, a tack to leeward of the parade will rarely be successful, and it should be attempted only if no additional boats can be expected to cross and tack ahead, the wind is moderate to strong, the sea is

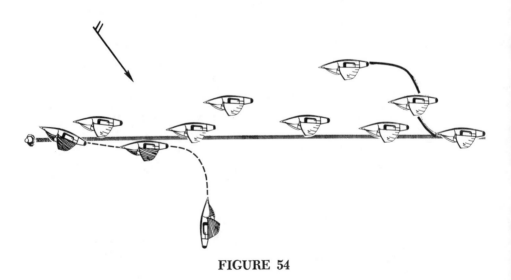

FIGURE 54

smooth, and the current is favorable. If forced to the lay line early (a circumstance to be avoided whenever possible), unless in the lead and in favorable current, one should usually tack to weather of neighboring boats. The slowing induced by the backwind, blanket, and wake of the boats which will eventually appear ahead will be more adverse than the extra distance sailed to weather. Being caught within the starboard-tack parade by a boat tacking on one's lee or weather bow will cause not only slowing but a marked increase in leeway. Near the mark, this may be accepted and compensated for by a forward movement of the draft and a freeing of the leeches of both main and jib. Far from the mark, it should be corrected as soon as it is detected by a tack to a position to windward of the backwind and wake of the nearest neighbor (Figure 54).

39. Approaching the Weather Mark

We avoided the crush at the port end of a typical CORK, 1973, starting line (heavily favored port end, short line, 60 boats, and almost no wind) and limped across well to leeward of about fifteen boats (half of which had started legally). Buddy Melges was about a hundred yards dead to weather, so we spent the long port tack testing our boat speed. He tacked away first, we followed, and near the weather mark, he looked as if he would barely cross us on port. Should we tack under him and enter the starboard-tack parade early, or should we pass astern, tack on his weather quarter, and enter close to the mark? In the light air, if we tacked to leeward, he would override us and then dictate all that followed. We went astern, tacked on his weather quarter, and looked for a hole. Another boat tacked on our lee bow. Buddy drove off behind three approaching starboard tackers, crossed the parade, and tacked well to windward of the lay line. Our new neighbor to leeward hailed us about, as the first of the three right-of-way boats demanded a response. We were forced to tack—below the lay line—and seconds later had to luff around the mark. As we barely cleared, the three starboard tackers luffed with us, slowed, but drove over and past. As they set their spinnakers just to weather of us, we lost what little air remained, and the boat which had hailed us about slipped past to weather. When we were finally able to obtain clear air and fill the spinnaker, we looked around for Buddy. He was in fifth place, about six boats and two hundred yards ahead. His approach to the mark had provided safety, speed, clear air, and departure in the optimum position.

Because free air and water on the reaches permits the leaders to separate from the followers by insurmountable margins, the most important mark is the weather mark, and the rounding of this mark should be planned as carefully as the start. Buddy demonstrated that, as at the start, the position in which the boat departs from the rounding is more important than the timing and position of her approach. In light air, it is necessary to sacrifice initial position to assure the retention of clear air and speed. In moderate to strong wind, because clear air and speed are readily recoverable, a more daring approach becomes feasible. In planning the rounding, the first consideration must be which side of the reach is advantaged. Unless this is the leeward side, it will be necessary to be the most windward of a group of rounding boats, or at least to have clear air and luffing rights to leeward. The retention of speed in the rounding requires the avoidance of the starboard-tack parade until near the mark, a smooth gradual tack into position, and proper sail trim without stalling as the boat is gradually borne away around the mark. The approach plan must ultimately be determined by safety—by what the rules allow. A careful consideration, in advance, of the circumstances in which approaching boats are likely to be met will permit a rounding that is safe *and* provides an opportunity to reach the advantageous side of the reach. The first weather mark is not the place for risk-taking—the possible losses are far too great.

There are four basic gambits which may be used in mark rounding when other boats are present and an open position in the lay-line parade has not been acquired. Which of the four is to be adopted is determined by the circumstances of the meeting with other boats: (1) meeting when each boat is on an opposite lay line, (2) meeting within the lay lines, (3) meeting between two port-tack boats within risk of collision of one or more starboard-tack boats (only distinctive when the rounding is to port), and (4) meeting when one boat is on the lay line and the other is not. The site of the meeting in relation to the two-boat-lengths circle is not significant; a tack must take place in each instance, and rule 42.2(*b*) specifically

exempts boats from the usual overlap restrictions when one of them
has completed a tack within two boat lengths of a mark.

Whether the rounding is to port or to starboard, meeting situation (1)—boats on opposite lay lines—is governed by the tacking
rule (rule 41) and if an inside position is acquired, by the mark-
rounding rule (rule 42). However, a tack may be completed to
leeward of the boat on the opposite lay line and a subsequent luff
used to round the mark. The limitation on this gambit is the need
for moderate to strong air and smooth water, not the rule. A variant
of situation (1) appears when the boat approaching on one lay line
crosses ahead and tacks to windward of the boat on the other lay
line. It is then possible, particularly in light air when a tack causes
significant slowing, for the boat on the rounding lay line to slip
into an inside overlap before the windward boat begins to round
(Figure 55). We encountered this situation in the final race of the
1973 Swiss Soling Championships series. At the last mark, which had
become a windward mark when the down-valley wind of the Alpine
lake supplanted the up-valley flow in late afternoon, our only significant rival crossed us on port within two boat lengths of the mark.
In the glassy calm he came to an almost complete stop as he tacked;
we slipped in to leeward and were bow to bow by the time he began
to round. Despite his vociferous protestations, only the tone of which

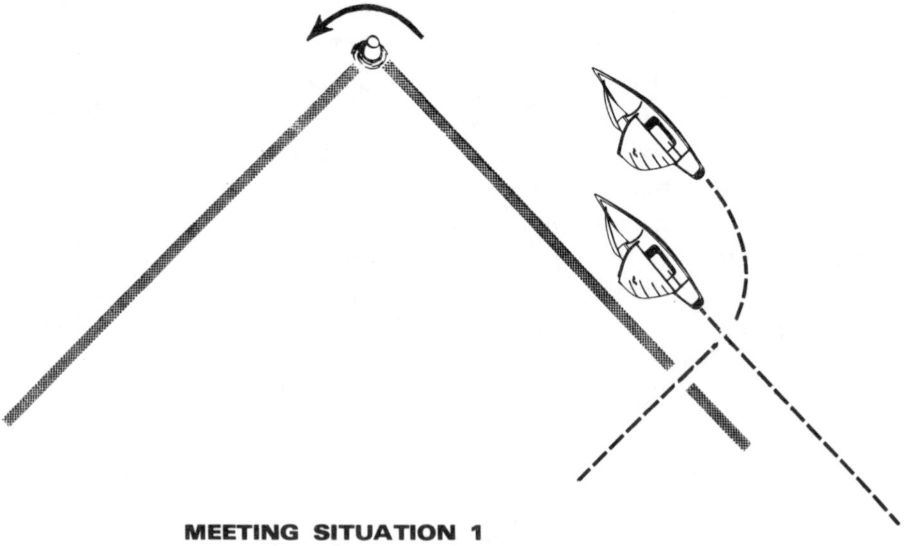

MEETING SITUATION 1

FIGURE 55

was decipherable to us, he had to give us the room, and the opportunity to win the series.

The resolution of meeting situation (2)—both boats within the lay lines—depends upon whether the rounding is to port or to starboard. *If the rounding is to starboard* and the mark is near, it will almost always pay to acquire the inside position, parallel and close to windward of the opposing boat (Figure 56). Even when she is a boat length or more ahead, she will be restricted from tacking by the limitations of the tacking rule (rule 41) and will be forced beyond the lay line by the windward boat. Successful resolution of the situation thus requires that the boat ahead always tack to cover to windward and that the boat astern, hoping the boat ahead will not

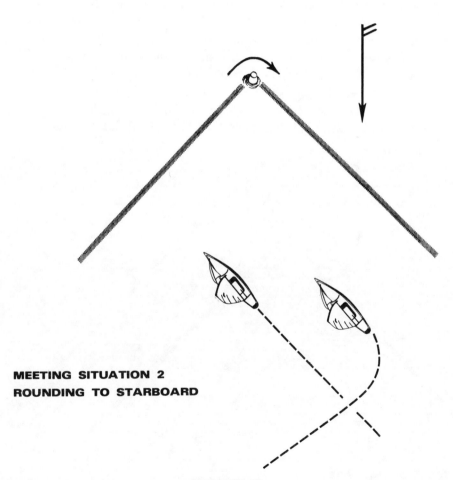

MEETING SITUATION 2
ROUNDING TO STARBOARD

FIGURE 56

follow this course, tack as soon as she reaches a position to windward. (To be sure, these techniques are appropriate only when the
boats are close.) *If the rounding is to port* and other boats are in the
vicinity, the disadvantages of being close to another boat approaching the lay line outweigh the advantages of the inside-to-windward
position. An outside, leeward, port-tack boat can call for room to
tack if she cannot clear an approaching starboard tacker. And an
outside, leeward, starboard-tack boat forced to the port-tack lay
line may impede the boat inside to windward when she attempts
to round in the teeth of the starboard-tack parade.

   Similarly, the problems inherent in meeting situation (3)—when
two port-tack boats approach one or more starboard tackers—result
in a need for caution. As two port-tack boats approach a right-of-
way boat (or boats), one or both may be required to take an evasive
action which will affect the other. In an Annapolis Winter Series
race, I crossed ahead and tacked inside, to weather, of a port-tack
boat that was a hundred yards from the starboard-tack lay line. As
we approached that lay line side by side, one slightly overstanding
starboard tacker could be seen to be in risk of collision with us
(Figure 57). I assumed that if the boat to leeward did not interfere,

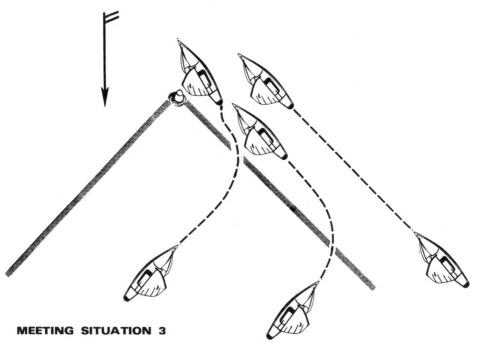

MEETING SITUATION 3

FIGURE 57

I could complete a tack to leeward of the starboard tacker and, in the smooth water, luff successfully around the mark. I watched the port-tack boat closely to see which of her three options she would select. It became evident that she was not going to bear away astern of the starboard boat and, immediately thereafter, that she was going to tack without a hail for room. I hailed to point out that I was not required to begin my tack until she completed hers. As I tacked, I saw that a collision would occur unless she luffed. I completed my tack, luffed up to shoot around the mark, and then bore away abruptly to clear my stern. The turn caused my stern to collide with the bow of the windward boat—whose tack had been so close that she was unable subsequently to keep clear. Alone, either of us could have tacked safely beneath the starboard tacker; together, we were at risk. The leeward port-tack boat had created the risk by tacking as she did and by failing to luff sufficiently far to weather as I tacked beneath her.

The leeward of two (or more) port-tack boats approaching the starboard-tack parade controls the destinies of her windward neighbors. Her first option—and, in light air (Figure 58), usually her best (see Chapter 38, "The Starboard-Tack Parade")—is to bear away to pass astern of a starboard tacker (Figure 58). However, she must then give room to her overlapped neighbors to pass astern of the right-of-way obstruction with her, if they so desire (rule 42). By so doing these neighbors can subsequently prevent her from tacking until they elect to tack. Frequently, however, the windward port-tack boats will elect to tack to leeward of the starboard tacker—a desirable result for the leeward boat.

Her second option is to hail the neighbor to windward for room to tack (rule 43). As soon as the windward boat is hailed, she must either tack or hail, "You tack" (if she feels she can cross ahead of the starboard tacker and not interfere with the tack of the leeward boat). In either case, the leeward boat is in control—she determines when the windward boat tacks, and need not tack herself until the windward boat has almost completed her tack. By properly timing her hail, she can force the windward boat to tack short of the lay line and then tack herself on the lay line (or just beneath it to permit a luff around the mark). In this manner the (originally) windward boat may be forced into a jibe and return as the leeward boat rounds inside the starboard tacker.

If the leeward boat chooses not to hail—her third option—she leaves herself vulnerable to one of two undesirable consequences:

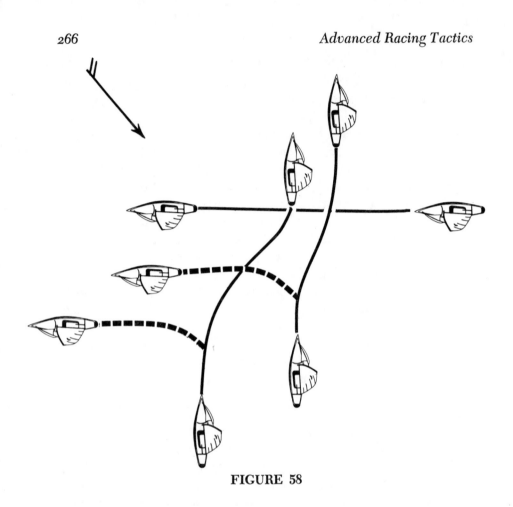

FIGURE 58

(1) The windward boat may hail for room to pass astern of the starboard tacker. Unless the leeward boat then immediately hails for room to tack (an overriding demand), she must give the room and accept the control. (2) If the windward boat elects to tack to leeward of the starboard tacker, she is not required to do so until the leeward boat completes her tack (if she tacks) (rule 41.2). Thus the advantage is transferred to the windward boat; she has the option of tacking last, presumably as close to the lay line as she desires (or at least considerably closer than she would have had to tack if she had been hailed). Each boat must, of course, complete her tack without interfering with the starboard tacker. But each, if forward of the mast-abeam position when she completes her tack, acquires luffing rights in relation to boats to windward (rule 38), and should exercise them, if necessary, as soon as she does complete her tack. (And

with or without luffing rights as an inside boat, each may luff to round the mark.)

The choice of a method for managing meeting situation (4)—when one boat is on the lay line and the other is not—depends, of course, upon whether the rounding is to port or starboard. With a port rounding, the situation is typical of any entry into the starboard-tack parade. The basic principle is to pass astern and tack to weather when (1) the air is light, (2) the sea is lumpy, (3) the current is with the wind or (4) the mark is distant. Only if the air is moderate to heavy, with the sea smooth and the current favorable, should a tack to leeward of an approaching starboard tacker be dared at a significant distance from the mark. And if a tack to leeward is attempted, it should be made close beneath the starboard tacker to guarantee subsequent control.

The meeting of a starboard-tack boat with a port-tack boat on the port-tack lay line, when the rounding is to starboard, is subject to entirely different rules and consequences. A boat approaching a

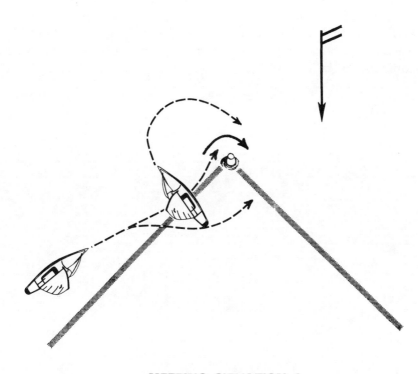

MEETING SITUATION 4

FIGURE 59

starboard rounding on starboard tack should make sure that she is the closest to the lay line of all starboard-tack boats (or that she is on the lay line). Boats to leeward will be prevented from tacking until after the inside windward boat has done so, and a boat dead astern on the lay line can be forced outside when the leader luffs at the mark. When only one boat is crossing on starboard, the port-tack boat has the advantage (Figure 59). The starboard-tack boat may not alter course or tack so as to obstruct the port-tack boat (rules 34 and 41), but must instead cross and tack to weather of the port-tack boat. If the port-tack boat is close, she may be able to break through to leeward as her opponent tacks beyond the lay line. The port-tack boat may reduce her speed or alter her course as required. By proper timing she may bear away below the starboard tacker and then luff up to clear the mark, ahead and to leeward. The starboard-tack boat may thwart this maneuver by altering her speed. If the port-tack boat slows with the intention of slipping astern, the starboard-tack boat may also slow (but not "alter course") enough to prevent the port-tack boat from clearing the mark.

An effective rounding to an advantageous position with speed and in clear air requires control over neighboring boats. The possible meeting situations which will determine how this control is to be acquired must be analyzed in advance.

40. The Second and Third Beats

Starting technique determines the outcome of the first beat. Success in the second and third beats depends upon more basic abilities. Away from the congestion of the start, boat-speed differences become apparent. Freed of the necessity of avoiding disturbed air, the helmsman can exercise his strategic competence and tactical skill. The essence of the first beat is defense—the avoidance of major mistakes; the essence of the second and third beats is offense—taking on the competition one on one. The fleet has opened up, the air is clear, and the visibility is good. It becomes possible to see the development of shifts and to deal with them appropriately. Alertness to the progress of the competition is essential as a guide to strategy, but conservatism is no longer appropriate. The closer the boat is to the finish line, the more the watchword becomes attack.

In a recent Fall Soling Bowl on the Chesapeake, we noted that on the left side of the first beat, near shore, the northerly air flow was backed considerably (Figure 60). As we started up the second beat we were fourth (having worked through the fleet after a late start due to a breakdown). We tacked in synchrony with the boats ahead in some early oscillations and seemed to be leaving the boats

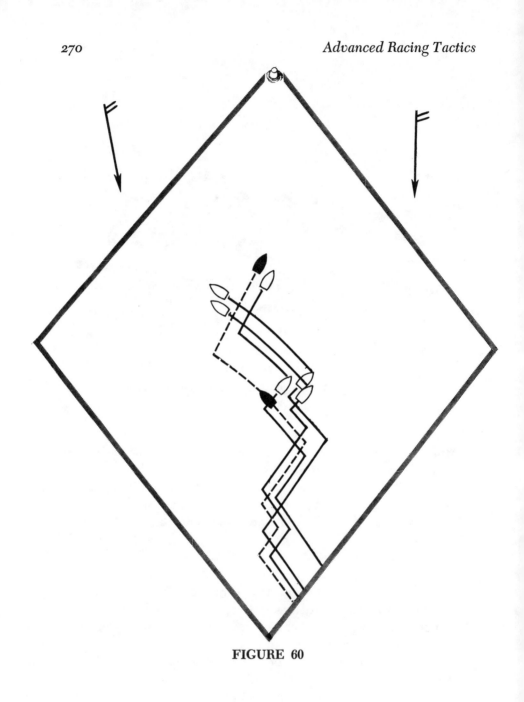

FIGURE 60

that were astern. We were looking for a chance to gain. The third of the three boats ahead tacked to port in a slight back, and the other two tacked to cover. Continuing on starboard would give us a chance to enter the more backed air ahead of the three boats ahead. Tacking with them could do no more than prevent a loss that might result from an oscillating veer. The odds strongly favored continuing on starboard *particularly when the boats ahead were on port.* We continued, and the wind backed progressively. Half a mile farther, we tacked to cross them all and went on to win with ease.

The second and third beats must be planned as meticulously as the first. When one side of the first beat is markedly advantaged, there is a tendency to assume that the same situation will exist on the subsequent beat. The strategic determinants of advantage are likely to change, however. Oscillations which may have made one side advantageous will probably not do so again. On the first beat a developing sea breeze may result in a veer, but on the second beat an oscillation back to the weather-system wind will be more likely than a further veer. The effects of factors that remain constant (current, shoreline) must be reconsidered in the light of data collected on the first round. A member of the crew should remind the helmsman of the state of the strategic determinants as the leeward mark is approached. Has a shift (or shifts) been noted on the preceding beat or on the reaches? Is the wind dying or increasing? What is the direction and strength of the current? Having been reminded, the helmsman can be relied upon to consider the ODSSSIC factors so as to identify the advantageous side of the beat ahead.

This identification permits the choice of the initial tack. And this choice must be made before the leeward mark has been reached, since it determines whether or not an inside overlap will be required. If a major difference in current exists—when one tack is into shore and the other is up the channel—the proper selection is obvious. In light air the selection is often equally obvious—the correct tack is the one toward the wind. If a squall appears on the horizon, the tack should be taken toward it. In an oscillating wind flow the lifted tack should be detectable at the end of the reach. Is the spinnaker pole being trimmed farther forward or farther aft as the mark is approached? The selection of the preferable tack is more difficult in the presence of a persistent shift. Have changes in the ODSSSIC factors appeared that indicate a persistent shift to come? Did a persistent shift appear during the first round? If so, has it been completed or is it still progressing? If it began early in the first

round and if the wind velocity has stabilized since, a completed persistent shift should be presumed. The favored tack is then away
from the completed shift, toward the expected oscillation to the
original direction. When there is doubt, the tack lifted to the wind
on the first beat should be selected. An oscillation is statistically more
likely than a progressive persistent shift.

The manner of approaching and leaving the leeward mark will
depend upon the plan. If the left side of the beat is preferred, the
approach must be designed to obtain the inside overlap. Being
trapped outside not only makes a tack in the desired direction impossible but permits the opponent to tack first and acquire a position ahead and to leeward on the preferred tack. If an inside overlap
has been acquired, the rounding must be made so that the boat
emerges high on the wind, above the course of any boat astern that
might prevent a tack. If an inside overlap cannot be obtained, it is
better to drop back and round dead astern rather than outside
(Figure 61). From this position a tack can be made without inter-

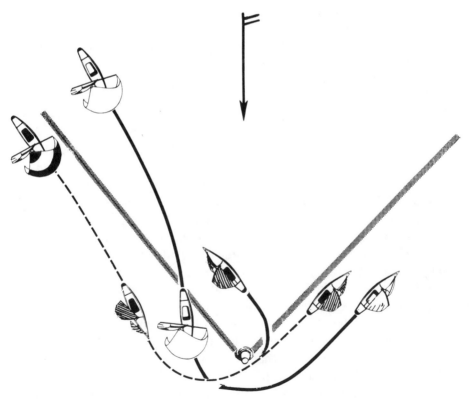

FIGURE 61

ference and the boat ahead can be prevented from tacking until released. If trapped outside, a luff after rounding may force the inside boat about and permit an early tack. Unless the advantage of a tack to port is absolute, it should be postponed until the congestion near the mark has been left astern. Boats coming down the second reach or approaching the leeward mark on port jibe at the end of the run are coming in along the starboard-tack course. An immediate tack will take the boat directly into their disturbed air and water.

If the right side of the beat is preferred, the approach to the leeward mark should facilitate continuing port tack. An inside overlap should be avoided unless it will assure emerging clear ahead. If an inside position has been adopted well in advance of rounding, an attempt should be made to force the outside boat wide, so that she can be overridden during the turn. A minimal overlap should be relinquished in preference to a wide, smooth rounding, which should be continued into clear air above the course of the boat ahead. If rounding outside, one should force the inside boat into a tight, slowing turn. Then, if clear air is not obtainable, one should crack off to leeward. If several boats are close ahead and the right side of the course is strongly advantaged, the sails should be trimmed to permit lifting out above the disturbed air. Failure to lift above boats close ahead will result in falling astern and to leeward, with the risk of being overridden by additional boats from astern. If the advantage of the right side is less obvious, a short tack to obtain clear air is justified, but it should be continued no more than a few boat lengths.

Success in all rounding maneuvers requires organization, freedom from preoccupation with the mechanics of boat handling. Each crew member must understand the priorities (jib trim comes first but must be synchronized with mainsail trim), and the helmsman must concentrate on steering. As the rounding is completed, trim must be for "starting gear": draft full and forward, leeches open and twisted, boom to leeward of center line.

Once the boat is on the preferred tack, subsequent strategic decisions will depend upon the behavior of competitors on the weather quarter. Careful observation will indicate whether they are receiving a different wind or a shift to their side of the course. If the presence of a varying current or of light air dictated the selection of the original tack, that tack should be continued unless a major shift to the opposite side of the course *and* a major increase in wind velocity develop. However, in moderate or heavy air, the appearance of a lifting shift requires a reevaluation of the plan. If the evidence suggests that the shift will progress, an immediate tack is in order.

On the second and third beats, the risks of gain and loss should be evaluated. Will fewer boats be lost if you continue the lifted tack and the shift turns out to be progressive and persistent, or if you tack and the shift is, after all, only an oscillation? Where are the major competitors? A tack away from the course clearly indicated as preferable by the plan should not be made until the expected gain has been achieved—or until there is clear evidence that the original decision was in error.

The second and third beats are opportunities for gain, and should be managed accordingly. When a gain has been acquired, a tack should be made to consolidate it. When boats on the weather quarter fall in astern, a tack should be made to cross them. But if the original tack was the preferred one, a tack back should be made before they reach a position ahead and to leeward—a position from which they could gain. As the lay line draws near, a tack should be made in plenty of time to establish a position ahead and to leeward on the approach tack. One should approach the lay line no closer than is necessary to assure against a major gain by a boat astern continuing toward it. If a boat on the weather quarter will be close when a crossing tack is attempted, such a tack should be made well before the lay line is reached. The opposing boat may then be forced to the wrong tack if you are on starboard, or may elect the wrong tack to cover if you are on port. It is surprising how often only a single covering tack is made by an opponent, with the result that when you tack back to the preferred tack, cover is relinquished and the opponent continues the disadvantageous tack. It is as if many sailors are embarrassed to cover closely or feel that being concerned to cover closely is an indication of weakness. Clearly, a tack should not be made to cover an opponent proceeding in the wrong direction; instead, you should pass astern, if necessary, and let her go. But once you have been forced to cover, keep up the cover; tack back and stay with the opponent.

On an Olympic course the termination of the second beat is a weather mark whose rounding initiates a run. The termination of the third beat is the finish. At the finish, position relative to neighboring boats is of course all-important; at the second weather mark, it is of little consequence. On the run, a position astern may result in blanketing the boat ahead and passing her; at the least it provides freedom to jibe away. What matters at the second weather mark is freedom to assume the preferred jibe. If a jibe will be necessary, rounding in an outside, overlapped position must be avoided. If the rounding tack is to be continued, rounding in an inside overlapped position is undesirable, but if it must be done, a course high on the wind for a brief period afterward will usually rectify matters. In light air, the worst possible rounding is the one that results after a tack beneath an approaching starboard tacker which requires a luff to round the mark. The approach to the second weather mark should be designed to maintain clear air and to acquire the maximum possible gain from late shifts (this means avoiding the starboard-tack parade), with little regard for the opposition. The boat should be fully prepared to assume the preferred jibe and should be sailed at high speed into the desired position.

v. *Reaching*

41. Leaving the Weather Mark

Sailboat racing at 6 knots hardly impresses the uninitiated as requiring split-second action and precision. But there are crucial moments in the race when the acquisition of speed or position, a frac-
tion of a second ahead of a competitor, can spell the difference between victory and defeat—and the commencement of the reach is
one of these moments. The speed of a boat reaching well, with her
hull and all her sails trimmed properly, may be double that of a boat
improperly trimmed, with her spinnaker half hoisted. Once the lead
has been attained, once the competitor has been passed and the fleet
settles down to the reaching parade, positions become fixed. Thereafter, usually the leaders increase their leads, and the tailenders, in
the wake and the backwind and blanket zones of the boats ahead,
increase their losses. Thus the rounding of the weather mark and
the acquisition of speed and position on the reach are critical, and
each boat must be prepared for them.

We race Solings on one or two weekends each month in the
winter. This is good racing—many short races in varied conditions,
with opportunities for both experts and neophytes to perfect their
racing skills. Good crew work is at a premium; on a short reach one

mistake in hoisting, jibing, or dropping the spinnaker may be disastrous. Minor variations in technique in leaving the weather mark are often decisive. As has been frequently noted, the great advantage of windward ability is that it results in a leading position on the first reach. And in modern boats, with their relatively high performance, proper exploitation of the reaching legs by the leading boat may produce a lead of hundreds of yards. The reverse side of this coin is, of course, the possibility of insurmountable loss by the following boats. But the same breakaway technique that provides a big gain to a leader may prevent a big loss when utilized by a follower. In a recent Winter Series regatta every race seemed to be won (or lost) at the start of the first reach. The winning boat arrived first at the weather mark in only three of the nine races but had the lead by the end of the reaching leg in every one of them.

The transition at every mark—the approach and the departure—must be thought out in advance. A plan for the reach formulated in strategic terms before the start must be translated into specific tactical details as the weather mark is approached. Will you want to go high or low initially? to hold up to get a better position to weather? to bear off to avoid the more adverse current to windward? Look around. How many boats will be rounding close ahead or close astern? How will you deal with the ones who will round with you? The optimal plan for the reach must be considered before arrival at the weather mark, but such consideration should not dictate the approach to the mark. You should be free to make any possible maneuver, and preferably the best possible maneuver, on the approach without regard to spinnaker preparations or other reaching requirements. The boat must be so organized that anything is possible, from any approach position. On a boat such as a Soling this means that it must be possible to hoist the spinnaker pole on either tack and to tack the boat with the spinnaker pole up. The spinnaker itself, fastened to sheets and halyard in advance, must be ready for hoisting immediately, without the delays attendant upon hooking up turtles, uncleating sheets, feeding out the spinnaker, and so on. If conditions warrant, the spinnaker should be going up as the mark is rounded.

A smooth, gradual turn is essential to the maintenance of speed. The centerboard (if present) should be raised approximately halfway, before or as the mark is rounded. The usual mistake is the failure to ease the main—by means of sheet or traveler or both—as the turn is made. The marked angulation of the rudder required to accomplish the turn in the presence of a stalled main nearly stops the boat. An excellent technique is to place a removable pin in the mainsheet that will stop the released line at an appropriate position. Then the mainsheet can be released as the mark is rounded and subsequently ignored until the boat is squared away, with the spinnaker drawing. The jib sheet can be released to a knot, since on most boats it never need be released farther. The easing of both sheets at the rounding is the minimum essential. Simultaneous easing of the main outhaul (to a knot or with a highfield lever) and the main Cunningham (to a knot) should be possible. A backstay (or the running backstays, if present), should be released as the spinnaker is hoisted. While the skipper (or middle man) is releasing main and jib, the spinnaker should be going up and the guy pulled around (to a mark on the line), and the sheet should be tended as soon as the tack reaches the pole. The most important element of this sequence is the steering; the skipper must be able to do his part in handling the sails without being distracted from his primary concern. The more gradually the boat is turned, the better its speed will be retained; and the more appropriately the sails are eased, the more readily increased speed will be acquired on the reach. Only if maximum speed is carried into the rounding will adjacent boats be dealt with successfully.

A rhumb-line course is appropriate only when the sailing angle is a beam reach or broader, the wind strength is moderate and steady, there are no other boats nearby, and there is no significant advantage to one side of the course. In all other circumstances, a decision must be made in advance on whether to deviate to windward or to leeward as the mark is rounded. If the wind or current velocity on one side of the course differs significantly from that on the other, deviation to the advantageous side will be required. The wind strength will determine the optimal sailing angle, and may require a deviation to windward or to leeward (particularly in very heavy or very light air). The helmsman should estimate the sailing angle in advance by considering both the wind strength and the effect of previously observed shifts. If the spinnaker cannot be carried at the sailing angle of the rhumb line, the reach should be sailed in two segments. The jib reach may be taken first, so that the spinnaker may be retained through the jibe, or—if spinnaker-handling techniques permit easy hoisting and lowering—an initial deviation to leeward may be utilized to escape neighboring boats. (See Chapter 43, "High or Low," and Chapter 44, "When Not to Set the Spinnaker.") The wind strength will determine the boat speed to be expected—which in turn may justify an early deviation to leeward to reserve the best speed for the end of the leg, or an early deviation to windward if the wind is light and variable or increasing. If planing is possible, the initial deviation must be to the direction that best facilitates planing. "It doesn't matter which way you're going if you're planing and the others aren't!" The boat can always be brought back up to the rhumb line later, when the wind strength changes—the course being up in the lulls, down in the gusts.

An awareness of boats rounding ahead and astern permits an early determination of the degree to which the boat should be borne away as the mark is rounded. If a boat has rounded close ahead, the best maneuver is to hold a course to windward of her. As she bears away to the straight-line course and/or sets her spinnaker, it may be possible to shoot across her stern and take her air (Figure 62). Hoisting the spinnaker is then delayed until the boat to leeward has

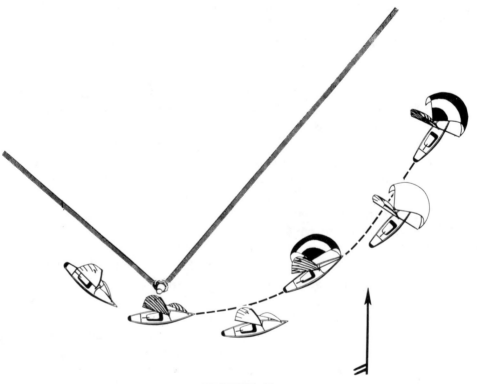

FIGURE 62

been blanketed. The boat close ahead usually has the advantage unless she luffs too sharply; then the boat astern should bear away, set her spinnaker, and with everything properly trimmed, attempt to ride through to leeward as the boat ahead sets her spinnaker. If a single boat is rounding close astern, it is equally essential to hold high, to convince the follower that she cannot override. Again, hoisting the spinnaker is delayed until the boat astern gives up and bears away to hoist hers. When a large number of boats are rounding ahead, it may be possible to catch the leeward ones as they are caught by their neighbors overriding them to weather. Once blanketed, a boat will be slowed for a protracted period; she may then be passed back by one windward boat after another. If many boats are rounding close astern, it may be assumed that each will luff the boat astern of her to windward of the course. To enter into this sequence of progressive deviations from the course is to give advantage to the boats to leeward. The better technique is to bear away to leeward initially (Figure 63), far enough to reduce the effects of blanketing, expecting to lose a boat or two but to get back all, and then some, later in the leg as the windward boats bear away to the jibe mark. Regardless of the reason (and there are many) for taking a route to leeward, if that course is desirable, it should be assumed immediately—but only by means of a controlled, gradual bearing away that preserves speed.

Think through the rounding in advance, be prepared for it, preserve speed by trimming sails properly, and then shoot through the competition to the strategically ideal reaching course.

Determinants of the Reaching Course

1. The presence of other boats

2. An advantage to one side of the course due to
   Wind-velocity variations
   Wind shifts (including the appearance of a new wind)
   Current variations

3. An adverse or deviating current which alters
   Course and heading angle
   Duration of exposure
   Apparent wind

4. Wind velocity and fluctuations in velocity

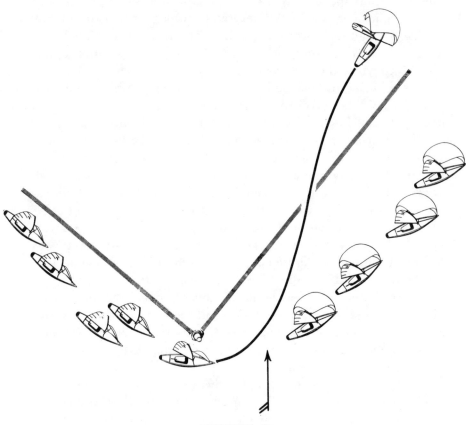

FIGURE 63

5. The range of sailing angles which permit spinnaker use, affected by
    Wind velocity
    Performance characteristics of boat and spinnaker

42. Up the Reach (Strategic Considerations)

The race plan, which provided for the use of a particular spinnaker at a particular sailing angle and in a particular wind strength on the first reach, must be reevaluated as the windward mark is approached. What are the strategic considerations? Has the wind changed in strength or direction since the plan was established? Will it change in strength or direction on the reach? Will it be stronger on one side of the reach than the other? Will a current be stronger on one side of the reach than the other? Will it be unfavorable? These are the significant strategic considerations that will determine the course to be undertaken as the mark is rounded. They must receive first priority; tactical considerations may necessitate an initially different course, but as soon as possible the course on the strategically advantageous side must be adapted.

A change in either wind strength or direction may so alter the sailing angle for the reach that the spinnaker cannot be carried, or a different spinnaker must be selected, or the leg must be sailed partially with and partially without the spinnaker. If the wind is dying, an initial deviation to leeward, with a light spinnaker and light sheets, may be required; whereas if the wind is increasing, an initial deviation to windward, followed by the set of a heavy reaching spinnaker late in the leg, may be required. If the wind has been oscillating, and a backing oscillation appears as the mark is rounded to port, there is no need to be panicked into a luffing match. The boat can be permitted to shoot off to leeward with the spinnaker up, since the following veer will bring her back to the rhumb line. If a persistent back is occurring, however, it may be wiser to forgo the spinnaker and maintain a position ahead and but slightly to leeward, with jib alone, until the progress of the shift has been resolved. If the wind continues to back, the advantages of being to leeward will be negated, since boats to windward then acquire an improving (or at least an unchanging) sailing angle as they bear away to the mark at the end of the leg. But if a persistent veer occurs, the sailing angle will progressively deteriorate as the reach progresses, and a position to leeward, which reserves the best sailing angle for last, will be extremely beneficial.

If the wind is significantly stronger on one side of the reach than the other (nearer a shoreline to windward, for instance), this advantage must be sought. If a new wind is expected during the course of the reach, will it merely change the reaching angle so as to modify the use of the spinnaker, or will a period or zone of calm interrupt the leg? If the latter is encountered, it may be wise to forgo the spinnaker, retaining the greater maneuverability (and often speed) provided by the jib, at least until the new wind arrives. Will the new wind change the reach into a beat or into a run? If the reach will become a beat (Figure 64), a position upwind in the new wind must be sought; therefore, a major deviation from the rhumb line toward the new wind is justified. If the reach will become a broad reach or a run, a position downwind in the new wind, *which will provide a better sailing angle,* must be sought (The latter prescription is consistent with the recommendation to deviate to leeward if the sailing angle will deteriorate as a reach progresses, and with the recommendation to jibe away from the shift if a persistent shift is expected on a run.)

Current is strategically significant anywhere on the course if it varies in strength or if it is unfavorable. The possibility that a shoal or dredged channel, or a variation in depth due to the proximity of a shoreline, will produce a major difference in current strength between the two sides of the reach must be considered in advance (and taken into account in the race plan prior to the start). If the difference is great, considerations of tactics, wind strength, and

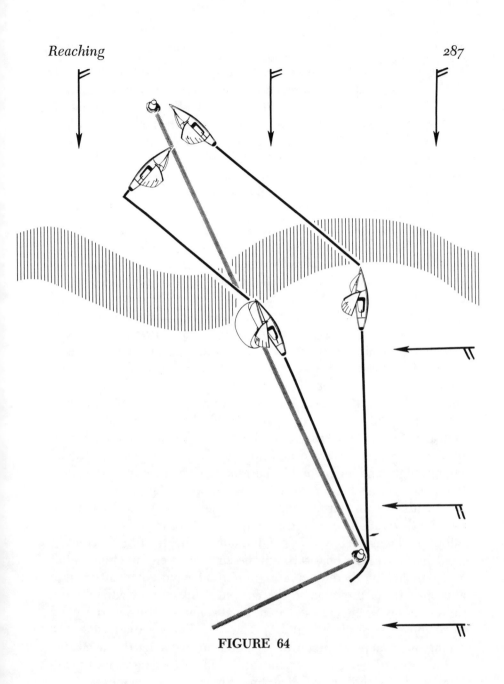

FIGURE 64

sailing angle must be ignored and the favorable side of the reach selected immediately. If the current is unfavorable, the duration of the leg will be extended and the effect of minor variations in boat speed due to disturbances in the air and changes in sailing angle will be magnified. Since a reduction in speed caused by disturbed wind will result in major losses during an extended leg, tactical considerations will initially be of overriding importance.

The next most significant effect of current is its tendency to deviate the boat to one side or the other of the rhumb line. If the shortest straight-line course is to be maintained, the plan for the leg must include an immediate deviation either to windward or to leeward, and a range must be obtained (usually with the mark ahead and a fixed object beyond) for verification that the straight line is being sailed. This deviation may require the use of a special spinnaker (or no spinnaker), which must be planned in advance. Since most helmsmen fail to recognize the current effect, the straight-line course usually has the additional advantage of providing clear air. When a boat is deviated unawares by the current, not only is the leg extended but the latter portion must be sailed up-current. While sailing such a prolonged up-current segment, a boat will be markedly slowed, compared with a boat on the rhumb line, and a major loss will result. In light air the speed of boats that initially deviate to leeward and approach the mark at an improved sailing angle and in favorable current is dramatically better than the speed of boats bearing away up-current on the approach.

An adverse current not only affects the course sailed by increasing any deviation from the direct up-current course but affects the sailing angles as well. As was pointed out in Chapter 16 ("Current"), a current moves the boat through the air in a given direction and at a given velocity, thereby creating a current wind equal in strength and opposite in direction to the current. This current wind, acting uniformly on all boats in the area, amalgamates with the true wind to produce the resultant wind in which the boats actually sail. The sailing angle depends upon the relationship between the wind due to the forward movement of the boat and this amalgamated resultant wind. As the vector diagram (Figure 65) indicates, the resultant wind varies chiefly with the boat's heading, and at all sailing angles is increased by the adverse current. This means that a course high on the wind after an initial leeward deviation is more advantaged, and a course low on the wind after an initial windward deviation is more disadvantaged. Although any deviation from the

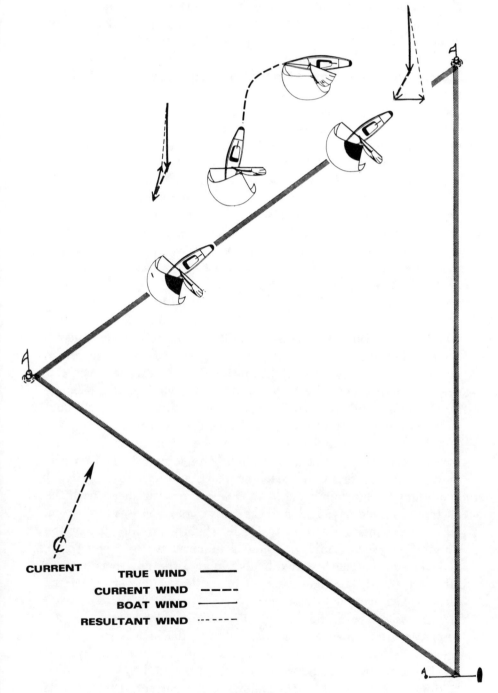

CURRENT

TRUE WIND ————
CURRENT WIND ————
BOAT WIND ————
RESULTANT WIND ————

FIGURE 65

rhumb line is undesirable, a deviation to windward which results in a subsequent deviation farther downwind is particularly to be avoided. The duration of the entire leg is increased by adverse current, but the segments sailed more slowly are especially prolonged. Major losses result from sailing at a disadvantageous angle for a period longer than one's competitors. This situation will occur, and the effect will be exaggerated by the adverse current, if the disadvantageous sailing angle is assumed in disturbed air or during a period when the wind strength has diminished. If deviation to acquire clear air on an up-current reach is necessary, it too should be to leeward (and as slight as possible), so that a markedly improved sailing angle will be available at the crucial termination of the leg, when the rest of the fleet will be broad reaching or running into the mark. A course high on the wind may then produce dramatic gains as the competition congeals into a mass of overlapping Dacron and nylon, unable to resist the adverse current.

In the Weymouth Town Trophy race, at Lowestoft, I rounded the weather mark with a good lead over eighty-four starters and bore off against the tide (Figure 65). Unable to see the mark, I sailed well to windward of the straight-line course until my followers rounded and bore away correctly on the direct course to the mark, which was almost straight up-tide. I bore away to cover, but discovered that now the "followers," down wind at a far better sailing angle, and up-current, were already ahead. Even without knowing the location of the mark, I should have realized that I had best be to leeward and up-tide. From that vantage point I could have covered the fleet at a faster sailing angle and worked out the most direct course to the reaching mark at my leisure. When I finally got to the rhumb line, two boats were well ahead with the clear air I should have had, and the mass of the fleet was just astern, taking my wind. I jibed away to the slightly up-tide side of the rhumb line, cleared my air, found a hundred feet of open space, and jibed back. The first two boats rounded the jibe mark a mere fifty feet ahead, but they were off in the favorable current of the second reach—never to be caught.

Some sacrifice of the straight-line course may have to be accepted to attain clear air and the boat speed which is so essential against the current. Look for an opening to leeward initially, and break free as quickly as possible. Get clear air, and then keep it while holding as straight a course (allowing for current deviation) as possible thereafter.

43. High or Low (Wind-Strength Considerations)

Success on the reach is largely determined by which side of the course is selected—the high or the low. When other boats are close, the decision must be reached prior to rounding the mark, so that deviation in the proper direction can be undertaken immediately. A deviation to leeward may not be made within three lengths of a boat overtaking to leeward (rule 39); therefore, it must be initiated before boats close astern round the mark. If a windward boat or boats will override as a deviation to leeward is undertaken, that deviation should be as expeditious as possible, to permit separation and reduce interference. A deviation to windward too should be made immediately; otherwise it will result in the boat's being overridden by a rival close astern, or it will initiate a prolonged luffing match. Once a deviant course has been entered upon, it must (almost always!) be continued ; to recross the rhumb line to the opposite side of the course and then deviate back again at the mark would significantly lengthen the course and eliminate all the advantages originally obtained. So the first decision must be the right one, reached after careful analysis of all the relevant factors.

Which course will permit arrival at the next mark in the shortest possible time? If a clear strategic advantage exists, it must be the overriding consideration. If there is no major strategic difference between the sides of the course, the choice will be determined by the presence of other boats and by variations in the wind flow.

We raced one April in the worst of sailing conditions. The water was still so cold that a conduction inversion persisted above its surface. The sea breeze that rocked the trees above was unable to reach into the sailing layer except in erratic patches that barely disturbed the glassy calm. After little but confusion on the windward leg, we encountered opportunities to gain or lose the entire fleet on the reaches. In the first race we rounded the jibe mark in the midst of the fleet and bore off on the broad reach in an attempt to escape to leeward (Figure 66). There was little wind anywhere, and what existed seemed to be dying. One boat went past to windward, and while we were caught in her blanket, several others slipped ahead. Eventually we got to leeward of the fleet, and with clear air (what little there was), were able to work farther and farther to leeward. While the others luffed each other increasingly to windward and disturbed what little wind remained, we pulled even. Halfway down the leg, we had regained our initial position. As the boats to windward bore away and slowed, we took the lead. At the leeward mark we were fifty yards ahead.

The same technique worked well, if less dramatically, in the following race; but the next morning, in even less wind, it was disastrous. We dropped from third to sixth on the same leg, with the wind from approximately the same direction. As we bore away, a sharp puff appeared and surged one boat past. We labored in her

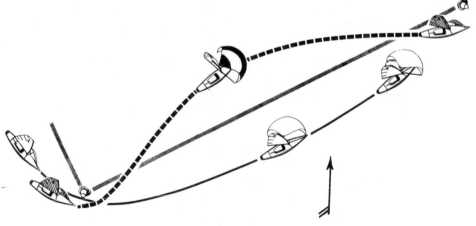

FIGURE 66

blanket as two others gained. New puffs materialized, which the windward boats caught but which never came down to us. From our leeward position we gained in the lulls, but not enough to compensate for the losses experienced in the puffs.

Because there is a justifiable tendency for each boat to move to weather of the rhumb line so as to protect her weather quarter, the entire fleet tends to sail the reach in a great circle. During the early portion of the leg, boats are deviating to weather of the rhumb line, and because of their better sailing angle, moving faster than those on the rhumb line. During the latter portion of the leg, boats are turning back to the rhumb line, and because of their poorer sailing angle, moving slower than those on the rhumb line. For boats adhering to this pattern, the crucial part of the leg, the approach to the jibe mark, is thus sailed at the least speed, affording a major opportunity for competitors to leeward to gain and establish an inside overlap at the turn. The traditional solution to this problem is to deviate to leeward initially, ignoring the apparent gains of boats to weather during the early part of the leg, so as to profit from the faster sailing angle at its termination. Deviation to leeward is by no means uniformly successful, however; if it were, everyone would be following that course. Early losses due to blanketing, and the continual receipt of disturbed air thereafter, may more than offset the advantages of the leeward course. It must be used selectively, not whenever the fleet is large and deviates to windward.

As my experience in the April races suggest, deviating to leeward of the fleet provides a faster course in light air if the wind is steady or dying, but deviating to windward provides a faster course if the wind is variable or increasing. In light air, major differences in speed may result from slight variations in the clearness of the air and in the sailing angle. In stronger air, when all boats sail at nearly the same speed, much less advantage is obtained from an improved sailing angle. Because the deviation of the leg is prolonged by light air, the effects of speed differences are magnified. Boats bearing away back to the rhumb line in dying air are extremely vulnerable; they may move at less than half the speed of boats in clear air at a higher sailing angle to leeward. However, where puffs and gusts intermittently reach the surface, boats to windward receive each gust first and are able to ride it to leeward until it dissipates. Boats to leeward receive the gust only after it has been disturbed by the boats to windward. As the wind increases, differences in speed due to variations in sailing angle diminish; deviation to leeward is less likely to be advantageous.

Rules for Reaching

(These are to be applied in the absence of a major strategic advantage on the opposite side of the course, and when the sailing angle and wind strength permit.)

1. When the wind is moderate and steady and no other boats are close, sail the rhumb line.

2. When the wind is markedly variable in velocity, sail up in the lulls, down in the gusts. Deviate to windward initially (Figurge 67).

3. When the wind is light and dying or persistently shifting aft, sail to leeward of the rhumb line, saving the advantageous segment for late in the leg, when the wind will be lighter or would otherwise provide a poorer sailing angle. Deviate to leeward initially.

4. When the wind is light and increasing or persistently shifting forward, sail to windward of the rhumb line, saving the disadvantageous segment for late in the leg, when the wind will be stronger or would otherwise provide a better sailing angle. Deviate to windward initially (Figure 67).

5. When the wind is strong, sail so as to facilitate planing or surfing. Deviate back to the rhumb line while planing and when the wind decreases.

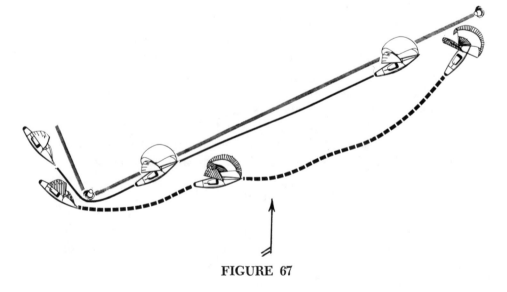

FIGURE 67

44. When Not to Set the Spinnaker
(Sailing-Angle Considerations)

I remember that soon after George O'Day published his pronouncement concerning spinnaker use—"When in doubt, don't!"—he capsized in a Princess Elizabeth series race (International 14's, Bermuda, 1958), just when he had set his spinnaker. (Experts—never
listen to them, and particularly never follow their example!) I am,
therefore, reluctant to discuss this matter in print, since in the near
future I will undoubtedly risk a spinnaker set at some inappropriate
time—and my pronouncement also may be remembered. O'Day's
error was, of course, not in setting but in capsizing; the episode may
serve as a reminder that the platform upon which the spinnaker is
set determines the range of its usefulness. At 25 knots on a close
reach, the risk of capsizing an International 14 may outweigh the
advantages of the spinnaker, while the risk of broaching a Soling
must be accepted to obtain those advantages. But the principles
apply to all. In decisions on whether to set the spinnaker, the heading angle of the boat is the prime consideration, and there is always
a limiting angle. Wind velocity—particularly as it influences the
heading angle—is the second consideration. The wind speed may be
either too great or too slight to justify its use. The wind produced by

the movement of the boat in a current, as well as variations induced by the boat's own speed, may prevent the efficient functioning of the spinnaker at heading angles that might otherwise seem appropriate.

Your own experience is the best indicator of the reaching angles in various wind strengths that permit you to set *your* spinnaker in *your* boat. Before the start, if possible, the heading angle for each reach should be checked and sailed (preferably with the spinnaker set) to determine whether a spinnaker should be set, and if so, which one. When a triangular course is sailed, however, the spinnaker gear should be set up for the first reach regardless of the expected heading angle. The wind direction (or its strength) may change, permitting the spinnaker to be set on the actual reach even though prior evaluation indicated otherwise. The delay resulting from rerigging the gear after rounding the weather mark will be disastrous when others are able to set immediately. If the reach is too tight, it may be possible to sail high at first and set the spinnaker later on the leg or at least before arrival at the jibe mark (so that the gear can be jibed at the mark).

Whether the spinnaker can be set on a close reach is determined by the relationship between the wind velocity and the heading angle. As wind velocity increases, boat speed rises less rapidly (until planing occurs); therefore, as the wind increases, the apparent wind moves aft for any given heading angle. The spinnaker may be used in moderate air at a heading angle 10°–20° higher than in very light air. In drifting conditions, it may be impossible to use the spinnaker on a reach that in moderate air would readily justify it. As the wind increases beyond the velocity at which the boat can be kept level with full hiking, heeling results in decreased efficiency. Thus the heading angle at which the spinnaker may be successfully used increases again at wind speeds above 10 or 12 knots (depending upon the boat). The spinnaker may be used on the closest possible reach in moderate air and only on progressively broader reaches in lighter or heavier air. In non-planing boats under spinnaker the highest possible angle, and the maximum possible reaching speed, are achieved when heeling, yawing, and leeway are just controllable by maximum hiking power (hiking pays). In planing boats, at slightly higher wind speeds, dramatic increases in speed shift the apparent wind forward and thus prevent spinnaker use at maximum reaching speeds.

At sailing angles that prevent spinnaker use or planing on the rhumb line, the reach is best sailed in two segments, one at a higher sailing angle than the other. The question then becomes, Which segment should be sailed first? The usual answer is to sail the slower segment first, with the greatest speed reserved for the termination of the reach. If raising and lowering the spinnaker is difficult, the best course may be to deviate to windward without the spinnaker at first and then, when the sailing angle is appropriate, to bear away and set it. The difficulty of lowering and resetting after the jibe is usually regarded as resulting in slowing in excess of the gains possible from an early set. In planing boats, however, the general view is that it is best to get planing first, which most often means bearing away below the rhumb line, and to worry about getting back to the course later. This technique usually works because (1) there is no spinnaker to lower and rehoist; (2) the wind fluctuates in planing conditions so one can come back up to the rhumb line in the light spots; and (3) it is possible to sail a higher course while planing than while initiating planing. This philosophy may well be applicable to boats that are unable to plane and to keelboats that set spinnakers on close reaches.

In large fleets, as we know, it is essential to take what you can get when you can get it. Hence, in some conditions, when the weather mark is rounded in close company, it may be better to break away at top speed immediately than to reserve the advantage for later. In moderate to heavy air, nearby boats may be nearly impossible to pass once they are properly trimmed. The wake of boats ahead traps the followers into a fixed relationship which no improvement in sailing angle, acquisition of clear air, or deviation to windward or leeward can overcome. An immediate spinnaker set while bearing away to leeward may provide the one chance to separate from the group (Figure 68). Although difficulty may be experienced in getting up to the mark later, boats that have been locked into the wake and the disturbed air of their neighbors will never catch up. The spinnaker should be capable of being lowered to windward, so that if it cannot be carried back to the rhumb line, it will be properly rigged for setting on the subsequent reach. Usually, however, the wind will let up sufficiently so that after an initial escape to leeward, segments of the course can be sailed high enough to permit a return. And (a fact that will never be recognized until the technique is tried) once the boat is up to speed with the crew in a full hike and the sails set for a balanced trim (with the main ragging, if necessary, through a released vang), she will sail far

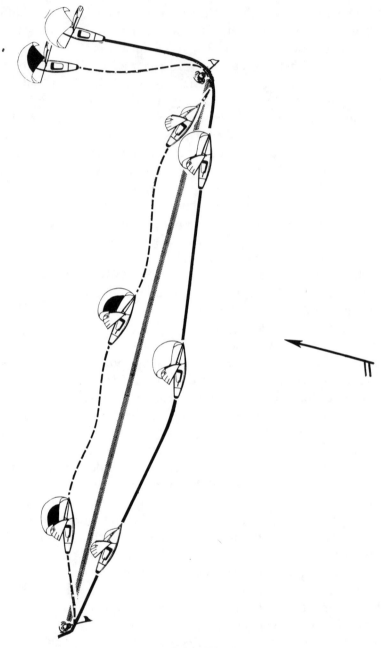

FIGURE 68

higher than was expected. Once stabilized, on her feet and going, she will make far less leeway than boats laying over along the rhumb line. I have been mistaken more often when I went high initially, intending a delayed set, only to end up watching boats streak through to leeward, than when I set the spinnaker, only to find that I could not get back up to the rhumb line.

Two-Segment Reaches

(These principles are to be followed when the sailing angle is so close that the possibility of setting the spinnaker, or of planing on the rhumb line, is doubtful.)

Go high initially without the spinnaker, set later,

1. When the wind is light but increasing.

2. When the wind is light to moderate, particularly if it is variable.

3. When the wind is expected to shift forward (persistently or after an oscillating veer).

Go low initially, setting the spinnaker immediately,

1. When the wind is light and dying.

2. When the wind is strong, and planing or surfing is possible.

3. When the wind is expected to shift aft (persistently or after an oscillating back).

The greatest difficulty in deciding whether the spinnaker should be set is experienced in very light air. On a run, sail shape is of minor importance; function is dependent chiefly on projected area consequent to drag. But on a reach, when lift is sought, an improperly set spinnaker is a detriment. The jib, which can be made to retain some shape by heeling and is stabilized by its stay, is far more efficient than a collapsed spinnaker. The boat cannot be positioned to give the spinnaker shape; attached flow on its leeward surface is required. The essence of successful use of the spinnaker in light air is keeping it full; collapse results not only in a period without beneficial effect but in the waste of additional power, to re-expand the sail. The spinnaker must be set with the sheet eased and the pole down and forward to keep the entire sail and its luff as full as possible. The boat should be headed off the wind sufficiently to prevent a risk of collapse. The jib should always be lowered in these circumstances, since disturbed flow in its lee, particularly if it is allowed to stall, will prevent the spinnaker from lifting.

Setting the spinnaker is particularly hazardous if the wind is not only light but subject to marked variations in direction. If the spinnaker collapses with each shift, precious time and energy are wasted before the sail can be refilled and thrust reacquired—and usually by the time the sail has been refilled, the wind shifts again, and the entire process must be repeated. The greatest light-air problem occurs when the shifts are oscillations of approximately 180°. These are to be found when (1) a favorable current approximately equals the wind velocity, (2) a sea breeze is developing under an offshore weather-system wind, or (3) a downslope (katabatic) wind is flowing beneath an upslope (anabatic) wind on a lake surrounded by large hills. In such circumstances the spinnaker may function beautifully in one wind and, of course, be not only useless but severely damaging when the wind reverses. Frequently, a zone of calm exists between the two winds that can be negotiated under spinnaker only with great difficulty.

At Essex, where the velocity of the current frequently exceeds the velocity of the wind, a downriver sail is often a series of alternating 2-knot runs, as the wind increases, and 2-knot beats, as the wind lets up. The spinnaker, which seems required when the breeze appears, is a real handicap when it dies, and particularly when its speed drops below that of the current. At Annapolis, where the southerly sea breeze often extends up to Severn, pushing a zone of calm beneath the overflowing weather-system northerly, a similar series of oscillations between the two winds produces 180° shifts. The spinnaker is again the wrong sail until the zone of calm has been passed and the wind astern is well established.

On the Vierwaldstättersee (where I won the Swiss Soling Championship in 1973), the midday upslope flow is characteristically pushed off the water's surface by the downslope flow at about 4:00 P.M. Between the two winds, a zone of calm develops. In the final race of the Swiss series, we sailed into this zone as we approached the leeward mark (Figure 69). We doused the spinnaker and rounded the mark to windward, abeam of our closest rival. He set his spinnaker on the final "windward" leg; we did not. We were able to utilize what little wind was available and worked our way back into the upslope wind well in the lead.

As George O'Day said, "When in doubt, don't!"

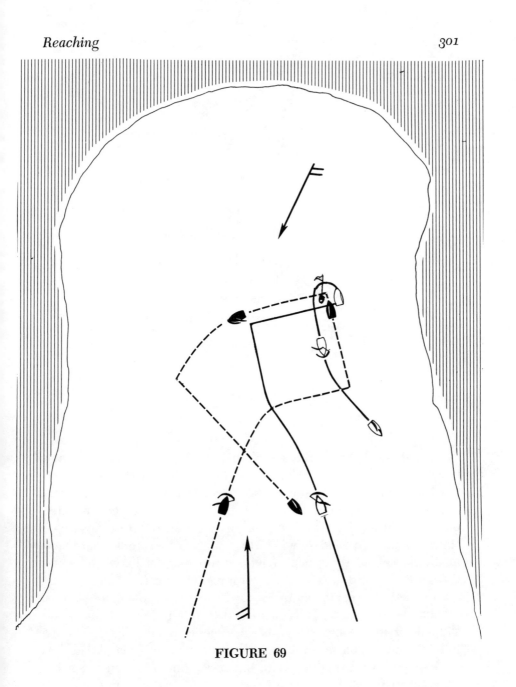

FIGURE 69

45. The Jibe Mark

In one of the light-air races at CORK, 1974, we labored through the flukes of the first beat to round the weather mark about twentieth (Figure 70). We broke off to leeward as the nearby boats luffed each other above the rhumb line. The mass of Dacron (ten boats within ten boat lengths) on our weather quarter was a constant threat. We held down farther and farther to leeward and finally had about three boat lengths of open water between us and the most leeward boats of the group. Periodically, boats of the group tried to break away to leeward and eased down closer to us. We barely, but successfully, managed to retain our clear air as we slipped off in the modest gusts and held a parallel course in the lulls. We were constantly tempted to come up to "consolidate," as we slipped ahead of the group, but each time the temptation became irresistible, the boats to windward closed up and changed our minds. When we were within about three hundred yards of the jibe mark, the wind dropped drastically, and boats both astern and to windward began to gain. We figured that if we didn't go up in the lull, we would be overriden by half the fleet. We went up a few boat lengths, broke ahead of the threatening boats to weather,

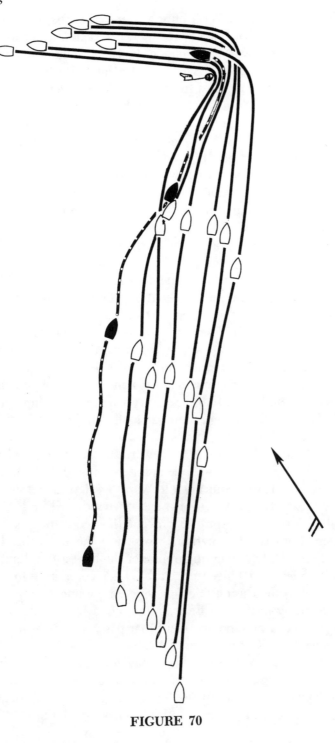

FIGURE 70

and bore away again. With only a hundred yards to go, one boat, formerly dead astern but now to leeward, acquired an inside overlap, and another was threatening. In the last hundred feet these two came up bow to bow with us, at a far better sailing angle. As we rounded, we were third from the mark, completely blanketed by the boats inside. We came to a near halt at the completion of our jibe, and boat after boat slipped inside and drove over us as we wallowed in successive blanket zones. Even boats that had been forced to round outside of us were able to slide to leeward and escape. The inside boat was two hundred yards ahead by the time we were up to speed, and we had lost over a dozen boats. We had violated the cardinal rule of the jibe mark: *Sacrifice anything to get or keep the inside overlap.*

All the advantages achieved early in the leg may be lost if an inside overlap is not acquired. As the weather mark is rounded, an immediate move must be made to the advantageous side of the leg. Regardless of the initial deviation, the boat must be worked to leeward, at least in the latter part of the leg, so as to obtain the inside overlap. The boat may be worked to leeward by two techniques. The first is to go up in the lulls, down in the gusts—and always down a little sooner and a little longer than neighboring boats. The second is to remain always on the lee bow of neighboring boats, going no higher than necessary when a boat threatens to pass to windward and holding as low as possible to block a boat threatening to pass to leeward.

If the initial deviation is to leeward, the acquisition of an inside overlap depends merely upon keeping far enough to leeward to prevent any boat from acquiring a leeward overlap. If the initial deviation is to windward, however, boats to windward and to leeward, ahead and astern, conspire to prevent the acquisition of a leeward position. Both the temptation to override the boat ahead and the seeming necessity of working up under the boat astern limit the urge to work to leeward. Once the boat has been committed to a course to windward to the rhumb line, allowing an opponent to pass to windward is rarely justifiable. Early in the leg, a luff should be vigorous enough to convince the opponent that passage to windward will not be allowed. This may prevent further threats. Late in the leg, a slight luff to make the opponent pay for her gain, followed by a bearing away to assure the retention of an inside overlap, may be more appropriate. Late in the leg, in large fleets with boats threatening from both to windward and to leeward, the best compromise is to give up those to windward so as to break any overlaps to lee-ward. In light air, this move should be made relatively early; in moderate to heavy air, or with few competitors about, it can be made late. Once the boat has been committed to a leeward course, the deviation should be carried to a position out of the direct wake of boats ahead and three or more boat lengths to leeward of any boat that is in a position to blanket. Be alert to gusts and to big waves; ride them down to leeward as far as possible before coming back up to the direct course. If there is a boat farther to leeward, gusts and waves must be used to ride down across her bow. Call out "Mast abeam" when appropriate, and then continue to press down to the degree the leeward boat permits. Once she has been overridden she will stop and fade astern, leaving the way to the in-side overlap wide open.

Boats above the rhumb line in the last few hundred yards must bear away to a progressively slower sailing angle. This slowing is exaggerated in light air or adverse current, when the reach is broad, and particularly when a large number of boats are approach-ing together. Boats approaching from below the lay line may be 40° higher on the wind than those above the lay line, and therefore even in traffic, will have a far faster approach. A boat bearing away gives up an overlap early (a line perpendicular to her transom extends far up the course). Thus slowed down and outside, the windward boats need not be feared. The modest losses incurred in bearing away to the leeward position are fully compensated for by the gains achieved from that position on the mark approach. The increased speed available to the leeward boat may enable her to win overlaps on boats that were far ahead in the middle of the leg. The acquisition of additional overlaps is not the purpose of the leeward position, however; the goal is the inside position on the turn. The danger for the leeward boat is another boat to leeward. *Once in a leeward position, it is essential not to come up too early.* Coming up early may result in being blanketed by the boats to windward, and the consequent slowing may permit a boat astern or to leeward to acquire an overlap not otherwise attainable. To be sandwiched be-tween boats inside and out, forced into a tight turn, and completely blanketed while doing so is disastrous. It is far better to settle for a position astern, so as to round inside.

Another potential disaster results from holding starboard jibe far down a very broad first reach. We followed Buddy Melges from about a hundred feet astern along such a course in a race at CORK,

1974 (Figure 71). Buddy jibed across the boats to leeward on which we had both made big gains. He was able to slip through all the starboard tackers and jibe back inside and to leeward of them. We continued on starboard just a few yards farther and then jibed. Unfortunately, we found a solid wall of boats on starboard as we headed back, and were forced to jibe again. We finally rounded outside of about four boats, having lost six or seven that had been well astern. By rounding wide and holding low after the rounding, we were able to reacquire clear air sooner than the boats that had fought their way to windward in the crowd. We recovered three of those we had lost, but Melges was now two hundred yards ahead, with ten boats between us.

Once the boat is within the two-boat-lengths circle, with the inside overlap established, the outside boats must be manipulated as effectively as possible. Rule 42 gives the advantage to the boat that has established an overlap in advance. If your overlap was acquired at the last moment, you are better advised to forgo the advantage than to force it. The outside boat will emerge ahead anyway, so a foul should not be risked. When there is doubt as to which boat has right-of-way, a collision must be avoided. It is always better to go into a protest meeting knowing that you cannot lose. If your inside overlap is well established, you should hail the boat outside to notify her that you will take all the room you need to round in "safety." The boat should be swung as widely as possible before the turn. This permits a smooth, gradual turn that preserves speed, facilitates the handling of the spinnaker, and forces outside boats to a longer, less controlled course which diminishes their chance of retaining clear air ahead and to leeward. It allows boats ahead to move out of the way, a result particularly desirable in heavy air. (Boats that mismanage the jibe and stall out dead ahead are major hazards.)

There is less concern at the jibe mark than at any other mark for the management of the leg to come. Being inside is far more important than moving immediately to the proper side of the second reach. The result is, if all goes well, emergence to windward of nearby boats after every jibe. Since this position usually permits overriding and blanketing boats that are overlapped, a move to leeward, if desired, is easily accomplished. When no other boat is close, the rounding should be made gradually, while the crew concentrates on keeping the spinnaker full. When one or more boats are rounding outside, the turn, though still kept as widely as possible,

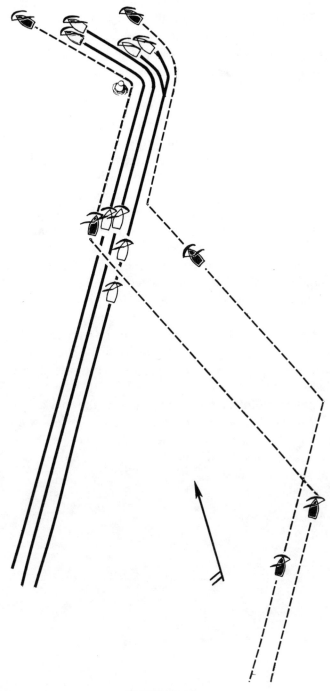

FIGURE 71

is necessarily more abrupt. The essential is to get the spinnaker around, full or collapsed, so that it will not be aback when swinging up on the wind. The same priority applies to rounding when a boat or boats are close astern. It is important to go as high as possible immediately. A collapsed spinnaker will not interfere with this maneuver, but one that is aback will. If an inside overlap has not been acquired, the turn should be smooth and wide while the crew concentrates on keeping the spinnaker full. If a boat rounds inside (unless she mishandles the rounding), the initial move should be to leeward of the rhumb line, for the reacquisition of clear air.

After rounding, a rapid breakaway with appropriate sail trim is the only concern. Next, the boat ahead must be considered. If a course to leeward of the rhumb line is preferable, a feint up that induces the opponent to luff should be followed by a bearing away with the first gust or advantageous wave. If a course to windward is preferable, the time to override the boat ahead is immediately after rounding, before she is organized. It may be impossible later; the remainder of the second reach often becomes a parade, with few changes in position. If the fleet is congested at the jibe mark, the wind will be markedly disturbed in its vicinity. What matters most after the rounding is separation from the disturbed air around the mark; a move to the preferable side of the second reach may be made later.

The crucial point of the reaches is the jibe mark. If the leaders are to be prevented from getting away and the followers are to be left astern—the desired outcome of the two reaches—an inside overlap must be obtained and a breakaway onto the second reach accomplished in clear air.

46. The Second Reach

On the reach the leaders, in clear air and water, are bound to gain, and will permanently leave behind any boat that makes a mistake. The first reach is the critical leg, and the jibe mark the critical turn. Here the essence is offense, and gains must be made relative to neighbors if the boat is to keep pace with the leaders. Once around the jibe mark, positions tend to become fixed. Boats have usually arrived among the company they deserve, and passing becomes extremely difficult. The essence of the second reach is therefore defense, the avoidance of mistakes. The major risk is excessive deviation from the rhumb line, due either to being forced to leeward while rounding the jibe mark or to being forced to windward by a luffing match. Both dangers must be guarded against. The watchword is holding, retaining both position and distance—the avoidance of loss with respect to the fleet through excessive involvement with neighboring boats. Let the competition be taken out by luffing matches. If the boat ahead is determined not to be passed, let her go. It is far better for both boats to keep pace with the leaders than for both to lose while one makes a gain relative only to the other.

The recommendations for the second reach made in Chapter 17

("Big Fleets") are, "Go high immediately. . . . Allow no boats to pass to windward. . . . Work to leeward in the gusts, but keep your wind clear." After rounding the jibe mark with an inside overlap to "go high" may be the only possible course. It is, in any event, the absolutely necessary course in traffic; any other will result in at least the loss of the boat immediately astern. All boats outside the innermost are dead to leeward and completely blanketed as they round. The immediate need is for clear air and the establishment of a position that will prevent loss for the remainder of the leg. Boats to leeward will be attempting to establish a safe leeward position, boats astern to override to windward. The only safe route is above the rhumb line, high enough to over ride boats to leeward and to intimidate those astern. On the second reach, the windward position is regularly justifiable, since it provides early advantage without sacrificing the inside position at the subsequent mark.

The choice of tactics while reaching depends upon variations in speed due to changes in wind strength and in sailing angle. Effective utilization of these variations requires recognition of the sailing angle that provides the greatest speed at the wind velocity available. In moderate air, peak speed in most high-performance boats is attained with the apparent wind just forward of abeam and the spinnaker pole a foot or two off the jibstay. If the wind decreases, the same speed can be attained only by sailing higher; if the wind increases, the same speed can be attained while sailing lower. Hence the standard recommendation to go up in the lulls, down in the gusts. The boat that is best able to utilize the gusts to get to leeward will usually be the most successful. She will maintain a near peak speed by coming up in the lulls without lengthening her course or being forced to approach the terminal mark at a broad angle. If the leg provides a very tight reach, a course on or above the rhumb line is required to prevent being overriden, but a faster course is available farther to leeward. When free of boats threatening from astern, the boat should be borne away to the rhumb line. In heavy air, peak speed is achieved with the apparent wind aft of abeam. In such conditions, a position to windward of the rhumb line permits riding off in the gusts and results in a far higher average speed. If the reach is broad, most boats will deviate to windward of the rhumb line and will therefore approach the leeward mark at less than optimal speed. In such conditions, after clear air has been established at the jibe mark, the boat must be worked to leeward, so that she will approach the leeward mark along the rhumb line or below it.

Luffing

Passing another boat to windward is accomplished by one of two techniques. The first, simplest, and most frequently utilized is the application of greater speed. If this advantage is available, the procedure is to lift higher in a gust, ride up to a position abeam to windward, and in subsequent variations—lulls or gusts—gradually work forward to a blanketing position. Once blanketed, the boat to leeward will fall rapidly astern. If a slower boat recognizes the greater speed of an opponent astern, she is well advised to grant her free passage. An initial luff to force the attacker to windward and so require that she pass at least a boat length to weather should be followed by concentration on the careful utilization of gusts to get down to leeward. To contend the passage of a superior boat is to delay the progress of both and to permit the remainder of the fleet to escape permanently. I have never seen a slower boat profit from a luffing match, but I have seen many, as a consequence of such involvement, lose what had been a position of contention.

Against a boat of equal ability, another technique must be used. Its success depends upon either mismanagement or surrender by the helmsman of the boat to leeward. (A properly managed boat of equal speed will never be passed to windward—and if the boat ahead is of superior speed, her helmsman need not even look astern.) As the boat proceeds down the reach, her course and sail trim should be continually modified to maintain maximum speed despite variations in wind strength and direction. Ordinarily this means that as the wind increases and the apparent wind moves aft (because there is less gain in boat speed than in wind speed), the boat should be borne away and the sails eased and that as the wind decreases and the apparent wind moves forward, the boat should be headed up and the sails trimmed in. If planing is initiated or terminated, the apparent wind will shift in the opposite direction and the sails should be trimmed in the opposite manner. If each boat makes these adjustments appropriately (and each experiences the same wind) passing of one by the other will be unlikely. The better utilization of wind variations by the attacking boat may permit her to acquire a position to windward which blankets the boat ahead.

The boat astern may accomplish this by attacking in a gust. In light to moderate air her apparent wind will shift aft, so she may increase her speed by sailing higher. If the boat ahead ignores the gust or bears away, the attacking boat may be able to ride up into a blanketing position. The defense for this attack is to come up only if the windward boat is threatening to blanket. Bearing away in the gust, which permits coming back up in the subsequent lull, usually provides a net advantage. The attacking boat, coming up in the gust, usually loses in the subsequent lull more than she has gained. In heavy air, increased speed is acquired by bearing away and initiating planing or surfing; this speed can subsequently be maintained on the rhumb-line course. The attacking boat must, therefore, bear away to gain speed before coming up to pass to windward (Figure 72). If the boat ahead is very close, the attacker may be unable to bear away sufficiently to initiate planing. Therefore she does better to start the attack from a boat length or more astern, where there is room to initiate planing and freedom from the wake of the boat ahead. The usual mistake of the boat ahead is to come up *before she is planing* to luff an attacker that is already planing. This effort is doomed to failure; the boat ahead must bear away in the gust, initiate planing or surfing, and then come up to fend off the attacker. Ideally, the boat ahead should luff before the gust to place herself close to leeward of the attacker, bear away as the gust hits, and then come back up when planing. The attacker should essentially do the same thing. Her hope of success is in initiating planing sooner and maintaining it longer than the boat to leeward. Her justification for attempting the attack is that the apparent wind of the non-planing boat to leeward shifts aft as the gust hits (while her own apparent wind, if she is planing or surfing, shifts forward) and that she may reach a position directly to windward of the leeward boat before she is abeam.

If the reach is beam or broad and one other boat is nearby after the jibe mark has been rounded, an immediate luff to a close reach is appropriate. This should be continued no higher and no longer than is necessary to override or discourage the opponent. As soon as this situation has been resolved, the boat should be taken down to the rhumb line or to leeward of it, (particularly if the wind is light). If the reach is tight, the close reach above the rhumb line should be maintained to prevent being overriden and to allow for riding the gusts down to the rhumb line. If many other boats are nearby, break away from the jibe mark to windward of the rhumb line and establish the best possible position relative to nearby boats. As soon as the maximum gain has been obtained, begin to work to leeward. If a boat ahead indicates her willingness to luff in response to your threat from astern, let her go. (I remember Kirk Cooper, of

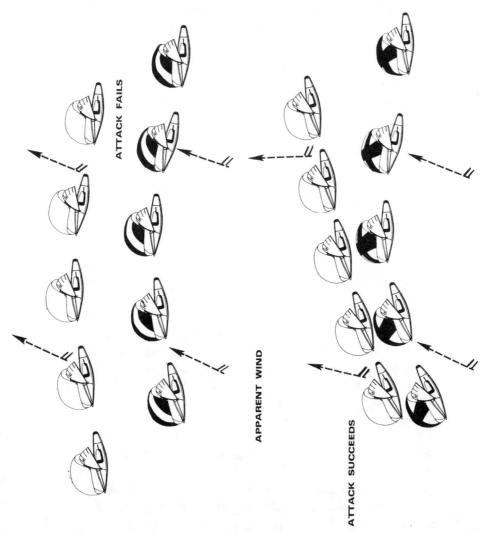

FIGURE 72

Bermuda, telling me at CORK that he would take me all the way to St. George's if I attempted to pass him to windward. I let him go—and caught him on the subsequent leg.) If you are in the early part of the leg and the reach is broad, attempt instead to break through to leeward. Feint up in a lull to force the boat ahead up, and then bear away in a gust. Try to slip down two or three boat lengths to leeward while riding her stern wave. Breaking through will be impossible unless you are three or more boat lengths to leeward, out of the significant blanket zone. Late in the leg, or when the reach is tight or the air heavy, settle for a position astern. *Attempt to drive over to windward only if you are confident of your superiority either in boat speed or in reaching skill.*

The Leeward Mark

The recommendations for the rounding of the leeward mark, at the end of the reach, are as follows:

> Determine in advance the advantageous side of the subsequent beat.

> Do not be concerned to obtain an inside overlap unless the left side of the beat is clearly preferable. However, do not allow an opponent to obtain an inside overlap if you are approaching the mark on or above the rhumb line.

> Prepare for a good, smooth rounding and for the proper sail trim to initiate the beat.

The advantageous side of the beat is ascertained by a consideration of the ODSSSIC factors—which should be reexamined as the leeward mark is approached. If the left side of the beat is heavily favored, an inside position should be obtained. The leeward mark is distinguished from the jibe mark, however, by the much slighter significance of the inside position. An outside and astern position is undesirable at any rounding, but at the leeward mark an outside and ahead position can be parlayed into an advantage, by luffing, if a tack to the left side of the beat will be required. Hence, the approach should not be compromised by the effort to obtain an inside position unless an immediate tack is essential.

In some circumstances, the leeward mark must be approached from wide to leeward; if the wind is light, the reach broad, or the current adverse, boats approaching on the rhumb line or above it are progressively slowed because they blanket each other. A boat coming in from a position well to leeward of the rhumb line and the blanket zones of the boats to windward may move at twice their speed. If the reach is so broad that the mark cannot be laid without bearing off below an optimal downwind course, a jibe, preferably to starboard, should be planned well in advance of the approach. This will permit approaching the mark high on the wind. The gains resulting even from an approach on port after jibing far outweigh the modest advantage obtained by seeking an inside overlap.

Although obtaining an inside overlap is usually not necessary, preventing the acquisition of one is sometimes essential. In light air, particularly, the late acquisition of an overlap by a competitor who is close aboard may be extremely detrimental. Speed is markedly reduced if the mark is approached from a position on or above the rhumb line which necessitates a 90° (or greater) turn. A boat acquiring an inside overlap in this position can easily override the outside boat and leave her wallowing astern (to be overridden by additional competitors in many instances). To prevent the acquisition of an overlap, a boat approaching the leeward mark from on or above the rhumb line should luff as high as is necessary. Or if she recognizes that the overlap cannot be prevented or broken she should swing wide, so as to preserve her speed and to allow the inside boat to move completely ahead. Either of these maneuvers is usually safe, since a luff cannot result in the loss of the inside position and a wide swing inside the two-boat-lengths circle cannot relinquish an additional overlap. When approaching on or above the rhumb line, the possibility of gaining or permitting an overlap must be recognized well in advance. Failure to gain one results in little loss, but permitting one may result in disaster.

The leeward mark is a major site for the use of "slow up and win" tactics. In favorable current, a swing wide to drop astern of inside boats may permit an approach across their sterns inside and up-current. If the inside position is desirable, the boat that has already obtained it may be wise to drop the spinnaker early or let the pole go forward on the approach (Figure 73). The outside boat too may try a "slow up and win" tactic; it is sensible for her to swing out or collapse her spinnaker early as a preliminary to an attempt to cross astern and acquire the inside overlap. For the inside boat the best defense, which can sensibly be utilized even if the outside boat is not actively threatening, is to slow to the extent necessary to keep the outside boat well overlapped. The best rounding of the leeward

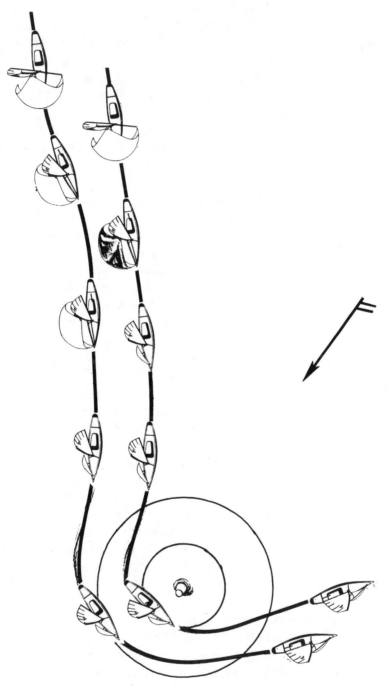

FIGURE 73

mark is one made inside and ahead of the nearest competitor; this provides freedom to choose between continuing and tacking, and prevents the opponent from enjoying that freedom except after significant loss.

VI. *Running*

47. Starting the Run

The run, like the beat, permits boats to separate widely from each other, to sail courses of greatly varied length, and to experience conditions that differ markedly in their effects upon boat speed. In most conditions, most boats sail a run faster at some angle to the dead-downwind course. Deviations up to 20° produce marked increases in boat speed with but minimal increases in distance sailed. Therefore, unless the dead-downwind course is at a marked angle to the rhumb line (in which case all boats will assume the same jibe), a choice among jibes exists. The jibe selected must provide a course not only faster than the dead-downwind course but faster or shorter than the course on the other jibe. Variations in course length, although of minor importance in relation to the rhumb line, become of major significance in the relationship between boats approaching from opposite sides of the rhumb line at 40° to each other. Usually of yet greater significance is the difference in speed between boats sailing in different wind strengths or currents on opposite sides of the run. And most significant of all is the effect of wind shifts which require one boat to adopt a longer course than her opponent's to obtain the same sailing angle, or to sail the same length course at a poorer

angle than her opponent on the opposite side of the run. As important as the selection of the first tack on the windward leg is the selection of the first jibe on the run. (See "Rules for Downwind Strategy," pp. 85–88.)

Determinants of the Initial Jibe

1. *The median wind direction*—which if at an angle to the rhumb
   line causes one jibe at an optimal sailing angle to be closer to
   the rhumb line than the other

2. *Variations in wind velocity, waves, and/or current*—which
   cause one side of the run to be advantaged compared with the
   other

3. *An expected subsequent wind shift*—which if one of a series of
   oscillations merely requires that the jibe best aligned with the
   rhumb line be assumed, but which if persistent requires that
   the initial jibe be away from the anticipated direction of the
   shift

4. *The apparent wind velocity*—which if reduced by light air or
   favorable current will require that clear air be obtained at a
   large angle to the dead-downwind course regardless of which
   jibe is preferred

5. *The presence of other boats*—which may require that a temporarily less favorable jibe or sailing angle be assumed to avoid
   loss or permit gain

As the weather mark is approached, pertinent data must be collected and reviewed. The direction of the wind that will be present
at the time of rounding must be determined, and if oscillating shifts
have been detected on the beat, the median wind must be ascertained. The dead-downwind course in the wind expected at the
time of rounding, or the dead-downwind course in the median wind,
can then be calculated. These headings, and headings 10°, 15°, or
20° to either side, appropriate to expected sailing angles, should be
recorded in a suitable location. If a persistent shift has occurred,
the dead-downwind heading recorded before the start should be
changed. If the shift was greater than 20°, the run will consist of
but one jibe—at an optimal sailing angle, on the rhumb line. Even
a shift of less than 20° will cause one jibe to be better aligned with
the rhumb line than the other. The better-aligned jibe will provide

not only a shorter course to the leeward mark but also the advantageous position from which to receive any subsequent shift. If the original shift progresses, the mark will be laid at an even better sailing angle. If a shift in the opposite direction appears, the jibe required will carry the boat back toward the rhumb line, rather than away from it.

The course should be surveyed before the weather mark is reached. Is the wind evenly distributed? Are there flat spots off to one side? Are the waves (which will provide opportunities for surfing) larger on one side of the course? Will there be variations in the current across the course? If a previous shift or a poorly designed course has caused one jibe to be far better aligned with the rhumb line than the other, that jibe should be assumed initially. If it is not obvious that one jibe is aligned better with the rhumb line than the other, the jibe toward the advantageous side of the course should be assumed initially. Insurmountable gains and losses develop rapidly when one boat is sailing toward an advantage and the other is sailing 40° or more away from it—particularly if the latter is also sailing away from the rhumb line.

The third consideration before the mark is rounded is the possibility of a shift or shifts appearing during the run. If the wind has been oscillating on the beat, it will be oscillating on the run. The recording of the median downwind heading (and of headings on each side) permits an immediate determination of which jibe will carry the boat most directly to leeward. Although this is usually the jibe best aligned with the rhumb line, and is detectable by direct observation of the oscillating shift present as the mark is rounded, compass confirmation is invaluable (particuarly as the leg progresses). The compass heading should be checked as soon as the boat is on course. If the heading is at an angle to the rhumb line greater than expected—greater than that of the opposite jibe—the boat should be jibed immediately. If a persistent shift is *expected*, an entirely opposite solution is required (Figure 74). Regardless of which jibe is better aligned with the rhumb line, the jibe away from the expected direction of the shift must be assumed initially. This places the boat in the optimal position to benefit from the shift by providing a higher, faster sailing angle on the jibe back to the rhumb line.

The true-wind velocity and the strength and direction of the current wind determine the apparent-wind velocity, and the apparent-wind velocity determines the sailing angle required to achieve the

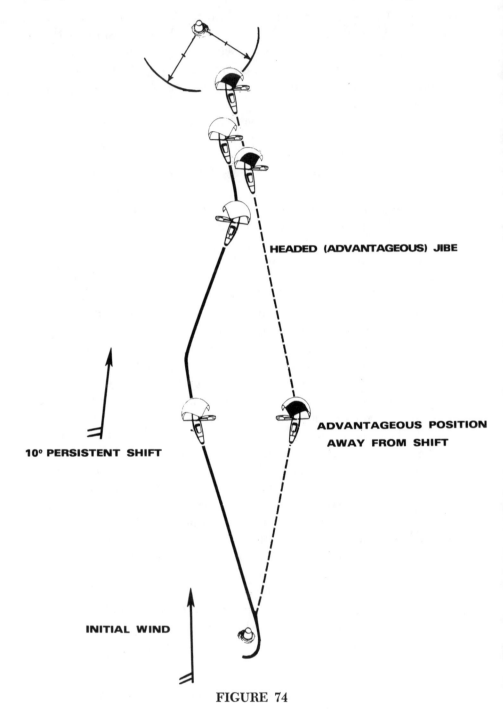

HEADED (ADVANTAGEOUS) JIBE

ADVANTAGEOUS POSITION
AWAY FROM SHIFT

10° PERSISTENT SHIFT

INITIAL WIND

FIGURE 74

optimum "speed made good" (Vmg) to leeward. In general (but to a degree varying with the innate capabilities of the boat), the lower the apparent-wind velocity the greater the deviation from the dead-downwind course required, and vice versa. Opportunities to surf or plane will require a greater deviation at high wind speeds than would otherwise be appropriate. In very light air or very heavy air the necessity of maintaining optimal speed often overrides the need to assume the advantageous jibe.

If the presence of other boats prevents acquisition of the optimal sailing angle on the preferred jibe, it may be wise to forgo the jibe advantage to attain freedom of maneuver on the opposite jibe. Breaking away from the congestion at the mark (which requires maximum speed) must be the first consideration when substantial speed variations are possible. The preferred jibe can be assumed a little later, after the boats ahead have been overridden or planed through. The plan to assume the preferred jibe must not so dominate the rounding procedure that boats astern are lost, or boats ahead which could be caught are allowed to escape.

The weather mark should be rounded in a manner that facilitates acquisition of the selected jibe. If a jibe to port is contemplated, the rounding should be inside—or wide and astern—of another boat rounding simultaneously. Observation of the side on which boats have hoisted their spinnaker poles or placed their turtles will indicate the probable distribution of neighbors after rounding and may suggest the means of reaching a desired position in relation to them. One's own gear and spinnaker-hoisting techniques should accommodate a set on either jibe. If the pole and lines have been set up on the wrong side, the minimum necessity is an ability to jibe while hoisting.

The mark should be rounded gradually, and the main and jib eased synchronously to preserve speed. The turn away from the wind produces an apparent wind from to leeward proportional to the speed of the turn. This not only slows the boat but seriously hampers the initial filling of the spinnaker. The rounding in light air and/or favorable current should be made very gradually and to a course higher on the wind than will ultimately be utilized (Figure 75). This means rounding so as to pass other boats to windward if they are close ahead, or so as to preserve clear air at a higher sailing angle ahead of them if they are close astern—regardless of which jibe is thereby assumed. The boat which turns fully to a dead-downwind course as she rounds is at the mercy of all her nearby

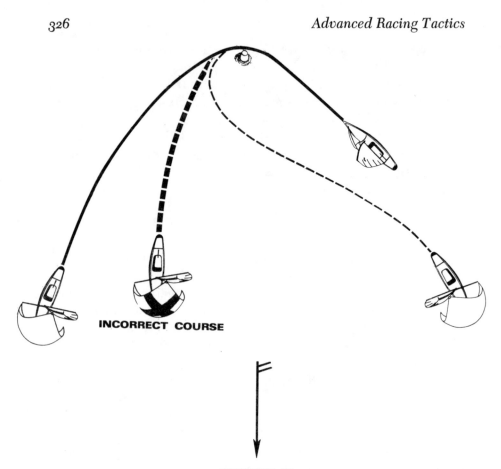

INCORRECT COURSE

FIGURE 75

competitors. As she sets and her spinnaker fails to fill, she will stop and be passed—and left.

While his boat rounds the weather mark, the helmsman should be as free as possible from involvement in boat handling, so that he can continually watch the competition. If he becomes preoccupied with sail trim, he may inadvertently allow himself to be trapped in the blanket of a boat astern or even sail the wrong jibe for several minutes. Having made his first decision, determining the jibe upon which to initiate the run, he must look about to insure that his decision was correct. He must also be on the alert for boats with right-of-way, both those ahead and to leeward on the run and those still approaching the weather mark. The boat in the lead may have been able to ignore the risks of meeting her competitors for an extended period prior to the initiation of the run. But at this point (and at the initiation of the subsequent beat) the paths of the boat ahead and those astern cross. Some race committees use an offset mark to guide those initiating the run away from the direct path of those coming up the beat. The boat leaving the weather mark on starboard jibe is at risk of disqualification from boats beating on starboard tack; the boat leaving on port is at risk of disqualification from every boat on the windward leg.

48. Tacking Downwind

On the run, the purpose of sailing a course not on the rhumb line is to increase speed; the technique utilizes the increased speed provided by sailing higher on the wind to compensate for the increased distance sailed. At some ideal angle to the apparent wind, the greatest speed in relation to the distance to be sailed will be achieved. This optimal angle will depend not only on inherent characteristics of the boat (which must be learned through experience) but upon wind velocity and current. In general, the more responsive the boat, the less the advantage of deviation from the dead-downwind course; a light boat with a very large sail area, such as the International 14, needs to deviate only in very light air and in marginal planing conditions. Less responsive boats, such as the Soling, need to deviate from the dead-downwind course in almost all conditions (though Bruce Goldsmith seems to sail dead to leeward, heeled to weather, in moderate air with as much success as his deviating rivals). Each helmsman must learn how much deviation his boat requires in each wind strength and must recognize the need to deviate farther when the wind drops and to deviate less when it blows harder. Since few runs are set exactly downwind, responsive boats can usually be sailed the entire leg at a reasonable sailing angle on one jibe. The art of tacking downwind is therefore only perfected in classes which must deviate 15° or 20° to achieve optimal speed.

The ideal deviation from the dead-downwind course decreases from a large angle (60° for some boats) in very light air to almost nothing in moderate winds (for most boats). Then, for planing boats, it abruptly increases in marginal planing conditions to a large angle (as large as is necessary to permit planing), and thereafter gradually diminishes once again to almost nothing, in winds so strong that planing is possible dead before the wind. In general, the greater the increase in speed possible, the greater will be the deviation required for maximal progress to leeward. In very light air and in marginal planing conditions the disparity between boat speed dead downwind and on a broad reach is great, and therefore the optimal deviation is large. In moderate air when boats are achieving "maximal displacement hull speed" on all downwind courses, and in strong winds when boats are planing at almost equal speeds on all downwind courses, the disparity between boat speeds at various deviations from dead downwind is minimal and the optimal deviation is small. Few boats sail well dead downwind in any condition, however, and since deviations up to 5° from dead downwind increase the distance sailed only infinitesimally, sailing slightly above dead downwind, even in moderate and heavy air, is almost always desirable.

The optimal deviation also varies with the current, since the current alters the strength of the apparent wind and therefore the disparity between boat speed dead downwind and broad reaching for a given true-wind velocity. In an adverse current the apparent wind of boats sailing to leeward is increased, and therefore the disparity in boat speed between boats sailing dead downwind and those broad reaching is reduced. Tacking downwind is conducted at small angles of deviation in an adverse current, with the deviation inversely proportional to the velocity of the current. In a favorable current the apparent wind of boats sailing to leeward is decreased, and therefore the disparity in boat speed between boats sailing dead downwind and those broad reaching is increased. Tacking downwind is conducted at large angles of deviation in favorable current, with the deviation directly proportional to the velocity of the current (Figure 76).

In the presence of a current, the wind in which a boat sails is a combination of the true wind, the wind due to the forward move-

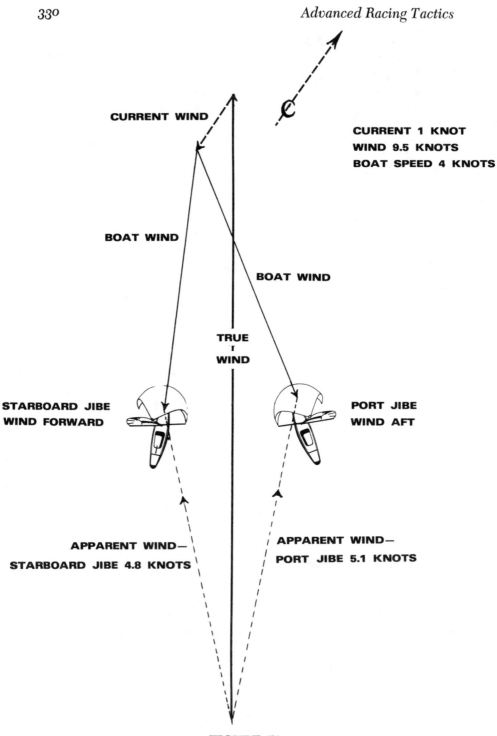

CURRENT WIND

C

CURRENT 1 KNOT
WIND 9.5 KNOTS
BOAT SPEED 4 KNOTS

BOAT WIND

BOAT WIND

TRUE
WIND

STARBOARD JIBE
WIND FORWARD

PORT JIBE
WIND AFT

APPARENT WIND—
STARBOARD JIBE 4.8 KNOTS

APPARENT WIND—
PORT JIBE 5.1 KNOTS

FIGURE 76

ment of the boat, and the wind due to the movement of the boat through the air caused by the current. For a boat sailing downwind in a 2-knot current acting in the same direction as a 2-knot wind, the net wind available is zero. If the wind drops, the current wind exceeds the true wind and the course becomes a beat to "windward." If the wind increases, the true wind exceeds the current wind and the course becomes a run—in extremely light air. It is thus not surprising that on the run, as the wind varies and is obstructed by interfering boats, there are occasional flat spots, and sometimes the wind comes from dead ahead even when the remainder of the fleet still has it aft. All boats must tack downwind when running with a strong current; in a wind flow but slightly greater than the current flow, the sails will not even fill on a dead-downwind course. For the boat to attain a speed greater than that of the current, she must be turned higher on the wind until the sails fill effectively (and until she is at least as high as the competition). Marked lateral deviation is required to obtain adequate boat speed, but because the duration of the run is reduced in favorable current, the actual distance deviated is minimized and clear air is readily acquired. The danger in tacking downwind with the current is in failing to jibe back to the rhumb line in time. This may result in sailing a longer course or, at the worst, in being swept past the mark.

The boat speed achieved is determined by the angle of the boat's course to the dead-downwind course, not by the deviation from the rhumb line. The course optimally deviated from the dead-downwind course will usually be better aligned with the rhumb line on one jibe than on the other. As in sailing to windward, it is better to take the jibe which is directed more toward the mark (closer to the rhumb line) initially. The time of the jibe and the angle of return to the mark can be more accurately judged from close aboard toward the end of the leg, and any wind shift is likely to provide an improved course, shorter and/or higher on the wind, for either ultimate jibe. The angle of the course to the rhumb line will be different on each jibe (if the true wind is not aligned with the rhumb line), and the shorter jibe back may be at a fairly marked angle to the rhumb line. Knowledge of the compass heading for the dead-downwind course insures that each jibe will be conducted at the same angle to the true wind. A course for the opposite jibe can be estimated in advance, and the jibe can be made when, at the appropriate bearing, a clear course back to the rhumb line is available.

It must be remembered that there is no fixed optimal angle of

deviation. As the wind velocity (which determines the angle) varies, so must the angle be varied. The angle which provides optimal
speed in the gust cannot be appropriate to the lull. If the wind decreases and the same sailing angle is continued, the boat will be
sailing at less than optimal speed. As we know, when the wind increases, the apparent wind initially shifts aft, and when the wind
decreases, the apparent wind initially shifts forward. This means
that speed will not change immediately and that the sailing angle
need not be changed significantly in response to a transient variation in wind velocity. However, once boat speed has increased or
decreased in response to an alteration in wind velocity, a change in
direction is required. Although a jibe is initially selected at a particular angle to the downwind course, its conduct is subject to continuous variation—up in the lulls, down in the gusts (Figure 77).

As the boat is sailed along on what appears to be the preferred
course, the compass should be frequently checked to insure that the
jibe continues to be the one best aligned with the median dead-
downwind course. Each time the wind changes in velocity or direction, a change in heading to maintain optimal speed will be possible
or required. If it becomes feasible to keep the boat sailing at an
optimal speed on a course below the original, the jibe (and the
lower course) should be continued. If in order to keep the boat sailing at optimal speed a course above the original is required, the possibility of a jibe must be considered. The lifted course may be at
such an angle to the median downwind course that the opposite jibe
becomes the preferred one. If the changes in wind direction are due
to oscillating shifts, the boat should be jibed on lifts and continued
on course in headers; that is, the response should be opposite to
those desirable when she is tacked to windward in similar conditions (Figure 77). In general, and in the absence of a persistent shift,
this technique keeps the boat on the major jibe (the course best
aligned with the rhumb line) and on the shortest course to the mark
while sailing at the optimal speed (the course best aligned with
the median downwind course). As in sailing to windward, the maintenance of optimal speed requires continual minor variations in
heading—up in the lifts, down in the headers; a jibe should be undertaken only when the lift is sufficiently great for the opposite jibe
to become preferable. Also, as in sailing to windward, variations in
wind velocity must not be confused with variations in wind direction. The risk is that a lull (requiring a more lifted course) will be
confused with a lifting shift and seem to necessitate a jibe. Just as

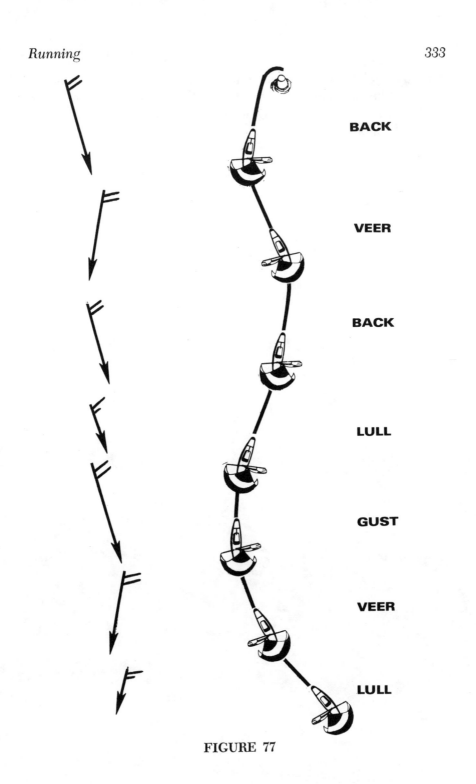

FIGURE 77

a tack should never be undertaken, in sailing to windward, when an apparent header is accompanied by a lull, so a jibe should never be undertaken, in sailing downwind, when an apparent lift is accompanied by a lull.

49. Downwind Strategy

Tacking downwind is a more complicated procedure than tacking to windward. Tacking to windward is precisely limited by the windward ability of the boat; the course can be improved only if the wind shifts. Tacking to leeward has no such limitation, since the boat can be sailed over the full range of possible courses. The course selected will vary not only with the boat's ability, the wind strength, and the current, but also with the occurrence of wind shifts. However, few sailors analyze their course to leeward in the manner that they analyze their course to windward. They tend to shrug off the large gains and losses commonly experienced when tacking downwind as the consequences of unpredictable variations in wind strength and direction. In fact, the results of tacking downwind are chiefly dependent upon wind shifts, and these effects are determined, just as they are to windward, by whether the shifts are persistent or oscillating. The tendency of some sailors to handle all shifts alike when sailing to windward, courting disaster by treating a persistent shift as an oscillating one, has its exact counterpart in their behavior when tacking downwind, with equally disastrous results.

A late-afternoon veer in the sea breeze caught us napping in the fourth race of the New England Soling Regatta. We had finally overtaken Ken Baxter and were leading him and the fleet by about four boat lengths halfway down the final run (Figure 78). All of our dangerous competitors (we thought) were on port jibe with us and they were deviating farther to the south of the rhumb line than we. Our spinnaker was optimally filled and we were sailing at an angle to the rhumb line as low as that of our competitors. All seemed well. Three-quarters of a mile from the finish we noticed that we were being headed slightly, that the wind was veering, and that we could sail even closer to the rhumb line at the same sailing angle. A glance astern revealed that the two boats which had rounded the last mark seventh and eighth, about a quarter mile astern, were the only boats on the opposite jibe, and they scarcely looked threatening. I should have known better. That little port-jibe header was the beginning of a 30° persistent veer, the late-afternoon sea-breeze veer—and we were sailing toward it.

Dave Curtis, 150 yards astern, jibed to starboard a few minutes after the veer commenced—and we should have gone with him. The nearby boats were still on port, however, so we waited until he had crossed our stern, and then followed suit. Both of us sailed across the paths of the majority of the fleet at a progressively poorer angle to the rhumb line as we watched Jim Gardner and Bill Pattison (the two who had taken starboard jibe initially) roaring up toward us on port jibe from a position far to the north of the rhumb line. As we approached the finish line they both crossed us, high on the wind, poles against their forestays, moving at seemingly twice our speed to finish first and second. We jibed back to port just ahead of Dave Curtis and salvaged third by less than a boat length. Ken Baxter, who had held port tack toward the veer long after we had jibed to starboard, had dropped from second to ninth, and Peter Warren, who had gone wind (velocity) hunting to the south, but jibed back sooner than Ken, barely beat him in for eighth.

We were team racing in 14's off Annapolis recently in a fitful easterly which threatened to be replaced by a southeasterly sea breeze (Figure 79). Bob Reeves had led the opposing team in the preceding races, so we elected to control him at the start of this one. We successfully forced him down the line, tacked back to an excellent weather-end start ourselves, picked him up again as he came out of the pack, held him back up the weather leg, and rounded the weather mark just ahead of him, in sixth place. The next leg was a

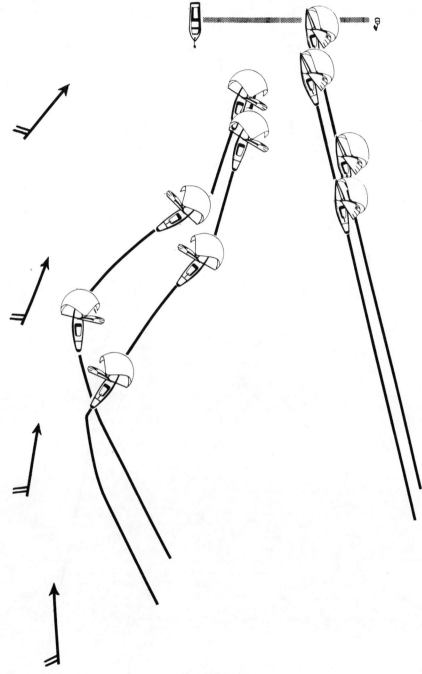

FIGURE 78

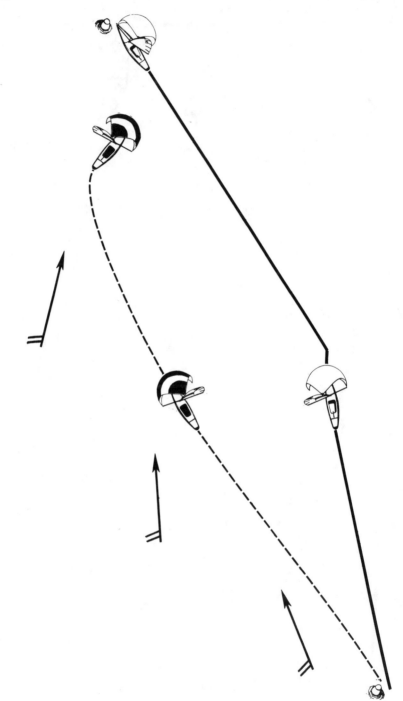

FIGURE 79

very broad reach on starboard tack. In expectation of the southeasterly sea breeze we decided to turn Bob over to a teammate ahead
and to jibe off to the southeast. The sea breeze filled in as expected,
but it was as strong down to leeward where Bob was as it was far to
windward where we were. And halfway down the leg, as we headed
back to the mark from to port of the rhumb line, we were dead before the wind, while Bob, who had initially held above the rhumb
line to starboard, was high on the wind on port jibe. We moved up
to a poor fourth, ahead of some boats which had imitated our move
toward the sea breeze, but Bob had sailed through to leeward of
almost the entire fleet and was a close second at the mark. We had
jibed toward the new wind, had sailed the early part of the leg in a
breeze that was progressively farther ahead, and had lost. Bob had
held a jibe away from the new wind, had sailed initially in a breeze
that was progressively farther astern, and had left us far behind.

Success or failure on the run is usually determined by the manner of dealing with wind shifts. The handling of oscillating shifts is
essentially analogous to their management in sailing to windward.
Regardless of the direct rhumb-line course, when oscillating shifts
are occurring, the jibe which takes the boat more directly downwind (in relation to the *median* wind direction) is selected. A header
is desired because in it the boat can be sailed more directly downwind at an appropriate angle to the apparent wind. The boat is jibed
on lifts rather than tacked on headers, and is continued on the
headed jibe until another lift appears. It is essential to jibe whenever the boat has to be headed significantly higher (i.e., lifted) to
maintain a given boat speed. When a significant course deviation is
possible or required to keep the spinnaker properly filled, a wind
shift may be presumed. If it is a header, the boat is borne away to a
more desirable, more directly downwind course; if it is a lift of such
magnitude that the opposite jibe becomes more directly downwind,
the boat is jibed.

This technique, appropriate to most wind flows, in which at least
small oscillations are to be expected, is entirely inappropriate to the
management of a persistent shift. In an oscillating wind flow, the
course sailed downwind can be significantly shortened by a switch
in jibes with each major shift. The wind velocity may require a sailing angle of 10°–20° to the dead-downwind course, but the rhumb-
line course can be approximated on alternate jibes. The optimal sailing angle at the best running speed can be obtained on starboard
jibe in a back, on port jibe in a veer. This technique is consistent

with the basic principle of initiating the run on the jibe that permits approximating the rhumb line at the best sailing angle. With two good reasons for sailing the headed jibe, most sailors do so continuously—and few are prepared for a persistent shift.

When sailing to windward in a progressive persistent shift, early advantage must be sacrificed to gain optimal position for the return tack to the mark after the shift has occurred. The correct method is to sail toward the direction of the expected shift, continuing on into the header as the shift appears until the lay line for the opposite tack is approached. The final tack to the mark is then made in the desirable lift. The persistent shift downwind must be managed similarly. If such a shift is expected, the inclination to jibe on a lift (as in oscillating winds) must be resisted. The technique must be to *sail away from the direction of the expected shift as it appears or progresses until the lay line is reached*—until the mark can be laid on the opposite jibe at the optimal angle to the apparent wind. The final jibe to the mark is then made in a desirable header.

In contrast to the multiple jibes required in the management of oscillating shifts, a single jibe away from the shift and a single jibe back to the mark are appropriate to the management of a persistent shift. The timing of the jibe back depends upon whether the shift is a single more or less instantaneous event or, as is more common, a progressive change in one direction. If the shift takes place abruptly, as it may with a frontal passage, the jibe back to the mark should be made as soon as the shift occurs, or if it is small and a good sailing angle cannot be obtained immediately, as soon as the lay line that provides the optimal sailing angle is reached. If the shift is progressive, the jibe back will be progressively headed, providing a course higher and higher on the wind, faster and faster. In this situation, the jibe back should be made short of the apparent lay line, with the expectation that the progressive header will let the boat down to the mark at the same optimal sailing angle—and that distance will be saved. It obviously does not pay to continue the lifted jibe at a marked angle to the rhumb line any farther than necessary.

If wind shifts are to be properly managed, the boat must be sailed in a manner that permits their detection. The compass heading of the dead-downwind course must be noted in advance, so that the proper jibe can be assumed initially. Thereafter, the boat should be sailed at the optimal angle to the wind, with the spinnaker pole fixed. The helmsman must learn to adjust his course to keep the spinnaker properly oriented to the wind (with rapid, minor variations in wind strength and direction dealt with by modifications of sheet trim only). The boat must be steered up in the lulls, down in the gusts, and these variations in wind velocity recognized for what they are. When the boat has to be headed up to accommodate a change in wind direction, the compass heading must be checked. If the new heading is beyond the recorded optimal angle to the median downwind direction, the boat should be jibed—unless a persistent shift is expected. This possibility should be reviewed before the first jibe. If a persistent shift is expected, the first jibe must be taken away from the expected shift and must be continued until the mark can be laid at the optimal sailing angle on the opposite jibe. Compass headings are as important downwind as they are upwind. If a progressive trend in one direction beyond the expected range is detected at any time during the leg, a progressive persistent shift must be suspected. Then the lifted jibe must be continued until the nature of the shift has been clarified.

50. Tactics on the Run

The helmsman must have a continued awareness of the relationship of the competing boats to a sighting from his boat perpendicular
to the median downwind line. Boats behind such a sighting are
astern, boats ahead, are ahead. Boats that were previously astern but
are now abeam on this perpendicular sighting have gained and
must be presumed to have been sailing a better course. Relative
position must be continually evaluated as an indication of the appropriateness of the jibe. If boats on the opposite jibe are gaining
in relation to the perpendicular to the downwind line, a jibe may
be in order. Just as a tack is either right or wrong in sailing to windward, so a jibe is either right or wrong in sailing to leeward.

On the run, gains and losses between boats (which may be
scattered widely across the course) depend upon five factors:

1. Wind interference, chiefly due to blanketing, by adjacent boats

2. The angle to the apparent wind at which the boat is sailed

3. Differences in wind velocity and/or current across the course

4. Oscillating shifts

5. A persistent shift

Since differences in boat speed are slight in most running situations, performance differences can usually be assumed to be due to tactical or strategic factors.

The initial move while rounding the weather mark must be designed for obtaining clean air, especially when many boats are rounding close together. A smooth rounding into clear air may provide an essential breakaway, but a move toward the preferred side of the course must be undertaken immediately thereafter. Subsequently, while the appropriate jibe is maintained, boats astern and to windward must be watched, so that their blanket zones can be avoided. It may be necessary to sail lower or higher than is optimal in order to escape being blanketed. Unless there is no clear advantage to continuing the same jibe, a jibe should not be utilized to avoid blanketing. Deliberate attempts at blanketing a boat ahead should be made only when defeating that boat would mean a significant scoring difference in the series. Usually attempts at blanketing result in slowing, failure to comply with strategic considerations, and net losses in relation to other boats. On the approach to the leeward mark, however, blanketing can be an extremely effective weapon. In planning the approach the goals must be first, to avoid being blanketed (at least until the two-boat-lengths circle is reached), and second, to blanket boats just ahead when that maneuver is integral to the preferred rounding procedure.

If boats sailing at a higher angle are gaining, a greater angle to the downwind course may be preferable. If boats sailing at a lower angle are gaining, a smaller angle may be appropriate. Each boat has an optimal sailing angle for running in each of the many possible wind conditions. Although an approximation of this optimal angle, usually between 10° and 20° to the dead-downwind course, should be assumed initially, only constant checks of gains and losses with respect to neighboring boats determine whether it is indeed being maintained.

Continuous observation of other boats must also be utilized as a method of detecting advantages of place or wind direction. A jibe opposite to that of the majority of nearby competitors, required initially to obtain clear air, should not be continued without a clear indication of its advantage. A gain by competitors on the opposite side of the course may be evidence of an advantage due to stronger wind or less current. If the gain is not associated with a change in wind direction, the opposite side of the course must be presumed to be advantaged and a jibe in that direction is indicated. If there are oscillating shifts, gains by competitors may be presumed to be due to such shifts (which may or may not be uniform across the course). As in sailing to windward is oscillating winds, changes in course should be made in accordance with the indications of the compass, not with reference to the competition. The possibility of a persistent shift must be constantly considered and the compass constantly observed to detect its appearance. If the compass indicates a heading outside the range of expected oscillations, a persistent shift should be suspected. If competitors are gaining because of a persistent shift that is expected to progress, a jibe toward the advantageous side of the course should be undertaken immediately.

If a persistent shift occurs, the resultant gain or loss will be determined by (1) whether the shift is completed more or less instantaneously or is progressive, (2) how far the boat has progressed from the rhumb line when the shift occurs, and (3) whether the boat is jibed immediately or is continued on the same jibe. If the shift is completed instantaneously, no action can be taken that will alter its effect. The farther the boat has sailed from the rhumb line, the more beneficial (or damaging) will be its effect. If a shift is marked in degree, the jibe toward it may be more appropriate than the jibe away. The initial loss due to sailing away from the shift at a wide angle to the rhumb line will not be offset by the better sailing angle on the jibe back.

Any shift that appears when the boat is well to the side of the course toward it will be disadvantageous. Continuation of the headed jibe at the optimal sailing angle will take the boat parallel to the rhumb line (or away from it) on a significantly lengthened course. Sailing directly to the mark nearly dead downwind will result in an even greater loss because of reduced speed. If the shift can be expected to progress, the only solution is to jibe away from it as soon as it is recognized (Figure 80). The longer the jibe toward the shift is continued, the longer will be the resultant course, if the shift progresses farther. The jibe toward the rhumb line should be discontinued short of the lay line, since farther progression of the shift will permit the boat to be gradually headed down to the mark at the optimal sailing angle.

For example, two boats initially on opposite jibes are returning toward the mark and the rhumb line, each at 20° to the dead-downwind course. If a 20° shift occurs, one boat will be sailing dead downwind, on a very slow course, and the other will be sailing at 40° to the dead-downwind course, at an excellent sailing angle. For

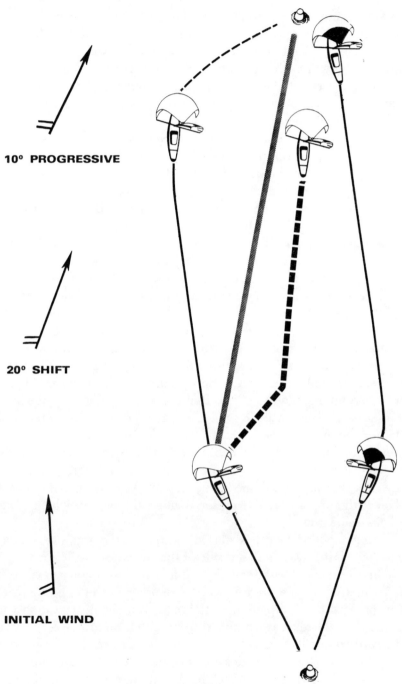

10° PROGRESSIVE

20° SHIFT

INITIAL WIND

FIGURE 80

the disadvantaged boat to maintain her speed she must head up an additional 20°, to approach her opponent at a 60° angle. She must give up either speed or distance. If the shift is expected to be progressive, she will do better to give up the distance and get across to the favored side of the course immediately; otherwise, boat after boat may be lost as she creeps up to the mark with the wind dead aft—or sails a longer and longer course.

As the leeward mark is approached, the timing of the final jibe to lay the mark at the optimal angle must be decided. If the boat is being sailed at 20° to the dead-downwind course (this being the optimal sailing angle), the optimal angle on the opposite jibe is 40° to the course, and the boat should be jibed before the mark bears at that angle. The optimal sailing angle must be continued right to the mark, since peak speed is essential when other boats may be interfering with clear air. If the final jibe was made too soon or a shift occurs, it is tempting to bear away below that optimal angle to lay the mark. But it is far better to jibe again, twice if necessary, to maintain peak speed. (Jibing should be so well executed that no loss results even when it is done repeatedly.) If oscillating shifts are occurring, you need only make sure that you remain continuously on the headed jibe until the leeward mark is approached. Then it is necessary to look ahead to decide which jibe will be preferable just prior to rounding, and to sail a lifted jibe a little longer, or jibe away from a headed jibe a little sooner, in order to be on the preferable jibe for the crucial final minutes. If you find yourself on the wrong side of the mark in the final shift, and there is inadequate time for the arrival of a saving return oscillation, you had best jibe toward any close competition immediately. In this way you may be able to blanket the opposition and preserve an inside overlap which would otherwise be lost.

If a competing boat has started the run on the opposite jibe and the wind shifts away from her side of the course, she will jibe toward you at an excellent sailing angle. If the shift can be presumed to be an oscillating one (to be followed by another in the opposite direction prior to the completion of the leg), you should continue your jibe. But if the shift is presumed to be a persistent one, or the last of a series of oscillations, you should jibe back toward the opponent's trajectory and then jibe back on that trajectory to cover her. This response will require approaching her at a marked angle to the rhumb line, with a loss of distance down course. But it (1) prevents further loss if the shift progresses in the same direction and (2) permits you to stay to windward of her, to blanket her if she passes you. If this situation develops near the mark and she is laying the mark at a good sailing angle, the covering jibe should be made to retain the inside position at the mark. If she is astern, jibe inside of her trajectory and be alert to her probable immediate attempt to cross your stern. If she is ahead but laying the mark at a good angle, jibe so as to blanket her; and if jibing to starboard, attempt to break the overlap later. If she is sailing above the mark, jibe so as to retain an inside position and to lay the mark at the optimal angle.

51. Approaching the Leeward Mark

On a run at CORK., 1974, we had gained considerably in the moderate but shifty air by continuing starboard jibe well to the right of the rhumb line (Figure 81). We jibed back to approach the leeward mark at a good sailing angle and looked about. Fabio Albarelli was approaching on a collision course; Syd Dakin, also on starboard jibe, was a more distant threat; and beyond Syd were two other boats which, though farther back, could be dangerous. We bore away a bit as Albarelli closed with us, and he jibed onto our weather quarter. We stayed low to retain our relatively clear air and slowly worked ahead. Now Syd Dakin appeared, charging toward us high on the wind. We couldn't come up to cross his stern without falling into Albarelli's wind shadow, so we bore away and prepared to make an emergency jibe if necessary. Dakin brought his bow almost up to ours and jibed on top of us, assuring himself an inside position at the mark, now only a few hundred feet away, and control over us and Albarelli. He evidently failed to consider the two boats on the starboard-jibe lay line, however. As Dakin jibed, a line perpendicular to his transom swung 40° to fall far astern of these boats (which had seemed safely astern). He had to give both of them room at the

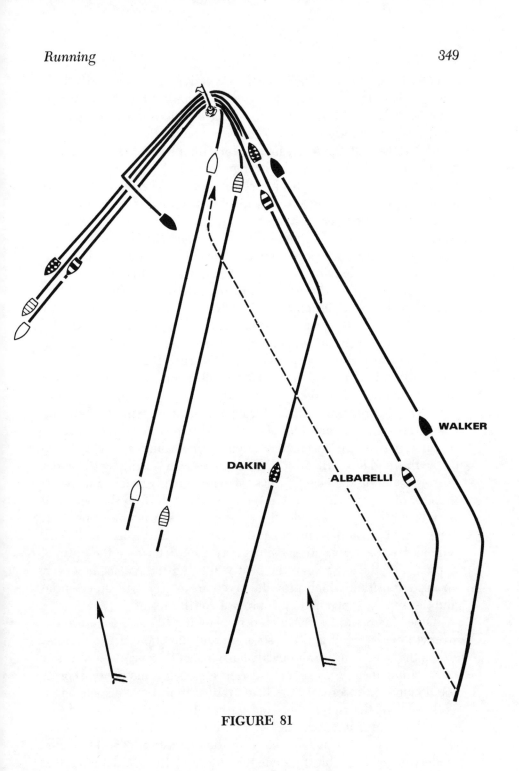

FIGURE 81

mark, and as we rounded fourth, slowed and outside, Albarelli swung up inside of us and drove over. We had lost four boats in two minutes and were starting the final beat unable to tack, in bad air.

It is obvious that looking ahead should be continuous and should be undertaken, at the least, long before the jibe to port on the approach to the leeward mark. Recognition of the presence of four boats to be met en route back to the mark would have dictated an early port jibe, crossing just ahead of Albarelli and just astern of Dakin, and a jibe back to starboard directly ahead of the two inside boats on the lay line. We would then have had the latter controlled astern, and with an inside overlap on Dakin, acquired as he jibed, would have rounded first, in clear air, with freedom to tack.

At some point on the run, well in advance of its completion, two matters must be determined—the advantageous side of the next beat, and the best means of approaching the leeward mark. The latter will be primarily dependent on the former, which must be established in terms of experience on the run. Has the wind been oscillating, and if so, which oscillation will be present as the leeward mark is rounded? Has there been evidence of a persistent shift, and if so, will it progress farther during the beat or will the beat be characterized by a persistent shift toward the earlier direction? For instance, has a veer been associated with an increase in velocity on the run, and if so, will an additional increase in velocity with farther veering occur on the beat? Or has the wind already reached its maximum probable velocity, so that the only likely shift on the beat will be a back? If the right side of the beat will be advantageous or at least not disadvantageous, an inside position at the leeward mark will not be necessary; other factors may then determine the optimal approach. If the left side of the beat will be advantageous, however, an inside position which provides freedom to tack will be essential and the approach planned must provide for this result.

Other factors to be considered in planning the approach are the strength of the wind and the strength and direction of the current. When the wind is light, and particularly when the current is adverse, the maintenance of clear air to the last possible moment becomes the dominant concern. As the boats return from their dispersion on both sides of the rhumb line and gather in line or at least side by side, the wind is markedly deviated and disturbed in the vicinity of the mark. Each boat is blanketed by the one astern. The blanketed leaders may be unable to stem the tide and thus find themselves halted a few yards from the mark as the fleet piles up astern. In these circumstances, the zone of disturbed air must be avoided until the last possible moment and then must be traversed at high speed as far to leeward as possible (Figure 82). This means that if the rounding is to port the approach must be on port jibe at a very high sailing angle, with the boat coming in from far to the right of the rhumb line in order to pass well to leeward of the mark and of the fleet jammed up close to it. An attempt to come in on starboard jibe at a similar sailing angle would require entry into the worst of the disturbed air, might mean colliding with boats unable to give the required room, and might result in subsequent entrapment. In adverse current, the spinnaker should be retained until after the mark has been rounded and the beat has actually commenced. In light air without an adverse current, it may be better to come in on a jib reach, dispensing with the spinnaker in order to obtain an even higher sailing angle.

A wide rounding is also necessary in favorable current, to avoid being swept past the mark as the turn is made. If one or more boats have an inside overlap, a turn out must be made close to (or at) the two-boat-lengths circle, so that the actual rounding can be made across their sterns and close to the mark. In heavy air the same principles apply, since boats rounding sharply close to the mark will make marked leeway as they turn onto the beat with little hydrodynamic side force and initially inadequate sail trim. Again a wide rounding is necessary and a position astern of inside boats is better than an inside overlap.

When several boats approach a leeward mark (to be rounded to port) on port jibe in line astern, each may select a preferred rounding to facilitate tacking or continuing the rounding tack. The acquisition of an inside overlap may provide little advantage except that it permits an early tack. However, when several boats approach on starboard jibe or dead downwind, an inside overlap may provide a tremendous advantage to the boat astern and be disastrous to the boat ahead. A 180° turn dead to leeward of an inside boat results in a major loss for the outside boat—and leaves her barely moving because of the sharp turn, blanketed, and unable to tack away to escape. When approaching the leeward mark on starboard jibe or dead downwind, one must be alert to the advantage to be gained by acquiring an overlap and even more alert to the danger of allowing a boat astern to acquire such an overlap. The risk is particularly great when a number of boats are approaching together and there is a chance of being blanketed by one and overlapped by another. For

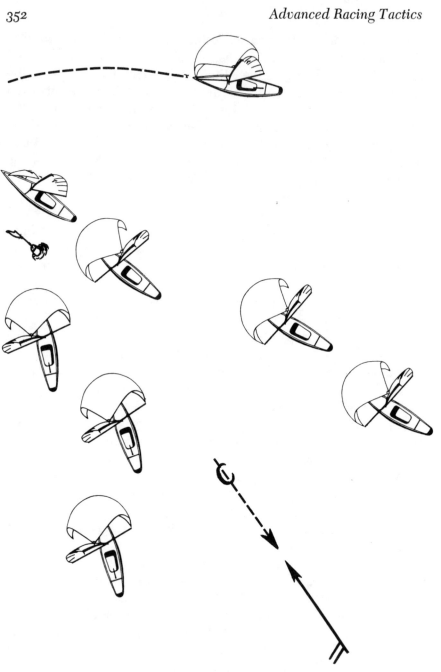

FIGURE 82

these reasons, in the company of many boats, it is always better to approach from a wide angle. The higher the approach angle, the less opportunity any boat astern has to obtain a blanketing position.

I recently led an entire race only to approach the leeward mark in dying air and with the nearest three boats close aboard. All four of us were on starboard jibe above the lay line. The two nearest were on my weather quarter threatening to blanket, but outside, while the third was dead astern. I allowed the two outside boats to blanket me so as to pin them outside, and then jibed. But the boat astern jibed simultaneously, picked up the blanket relinquished by the others, and surged between my stern and the mark. If no other boats had been nearby, I could have hailed (before we reached the two-boat-lengths circle) that I was taking her the wrong side of the mark (a gambit rarely useful except in team racing) and continued with her past the mark (rule 42.1(a)(iv)). This would have meant an additional jibe, a close-hauled course back to the mark, mass confusion in the spinnaker handling, and the loss of two boats. A luff outside the two-boat-lengths circle that will permit breaking the overlap after a jibe away is usually justified, but not one close to the two-boat-lengths circle that requires continuance beyond the mark. I settled for the sandwiched position, dropped from first to third immediately, lost a hundred feet to the boat that had rounded inside, and barely scraped back into second on the short beat to the finish.

The boat that is ahead on starboard jibe or dead downwind (or that intends to approach the mark on starboard jibe) must be aware of the dangers and avoid an approach that will permit the boat astern to blanket her. If the boat astern on the approach jibe is assuming a weather-quarter position, the boat ahead must hold high enough to prevent the acquisition of an overlap. This may require a longer course and an additional final jibe at the two-boat-lengths circle. The best gambit for the boat astern is to maintain a position close astern or to leeward and astern on a penultimate starboard jibe. If the boat ahead jibes beyond the ideal lay line, the boat astern can easily jibe into an inside blanketing position on the approach jibe. If the boat ahead jibes short of the ideal lay line, the boat astern blankets her readily on the nearly dead-downwind course. The boat ahead should do her best to lure her opponent into a position overlapped to windward on the penultimate jibe; she can then jibe into a position inside and to windward of the boat astern. The boat ahead must jibe first (since her opponent will be happy to

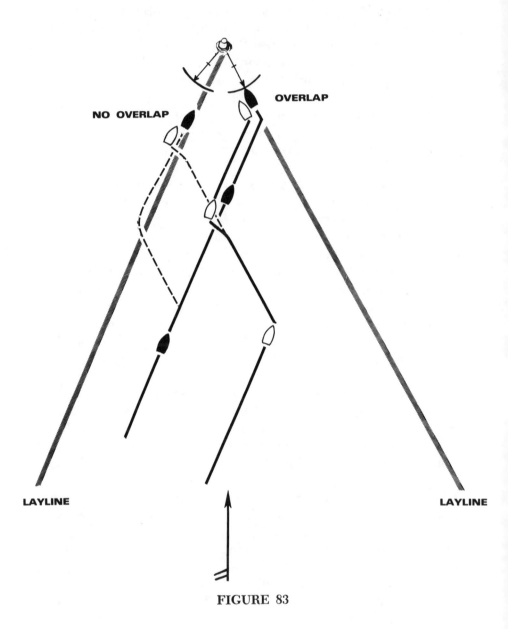

NO OVERLAP

OVERLAP

LAYLINE

LAYLINE

FIGURE 83

force her farther and farther beyond the ideal lay line), and she must do this on the ideal lay line, in order to retain maximum speed on the approach. She must utilize her spinnaker to the last possible moment and retain clear air until the two-boat-lengths circle is reached. As at the jibe mark, almost any sacrifice, any handicap, is acceptable for the sake of preventing an opponent on starboard jibe or dead downwind from acquiring an inside overlap.

If the right side of the run has been favored and the boat has been sailed to the right of the rhumb line, a time to return must be chosen. The return should not be so early that strategic advantage is sacrificed, but should not be so late that tactical advantage on the approach is relinquished. Preferably, the port jibe back should be undertaken when a hole appears that will permit crossing without deviation to go astern of starboard tackers. The ideal time is when a significant gain has been made that can be consolidated by the jibe back. If the mark is getting close, however, it is better to deviate to cross astern of nearby starboard tackers and of boats that were previously astern than to allow oneself to be blocked outside at the mark. The return port jibe should be carried beyond the trajectory of the most distant starboard tacker so as to assure being either dead ahead or inside at the mark (Figure 83). This maneuver is particularly effective in light air and whenever boats on starboard are more than two boat lengths above the lay line. The boat crossing close astern may acquire an overlap as she jibes and *will certainly acquire one as the boat ahead jibes!* The defense for the starboard tacker is to jibe ahead of the approaching opponent and then to jibe back slightly beyond the lay line. A boat crossing astern will be unlikely to gain an overlap if the boat ahead sails into the two-boat-lengths circle at a high sailing angle. A jibe outside the two-boat-lengths circle grants an inside overlap to a boat far astern on starboard; a jibe inside the circle grants nothing. If only one boat is in close contention, it may be wise to catch her as she crosses astern on port jibe rather than to jibe ahead of her. (She might subsequently jibe to a blanketing position and then break the overlap.) Since she will be high on the wind, you should be able to bear away just before she arrives, jibe at the instant her bow crosses your course, and complete the jibe before she can jibe. She will subsequently be trapped, unable to jibe because of your proximity, and forced to continue on port until you jibe back, with her clear astern.

VII. *Finishing*

52. Tactical Control

There are a number of circumstances in which it is possible to control a competitor. Such control is complete if the competitor is forced either to slow or to perform a course-lengthening maneuver. Partial control is less dramatic: the competitor is made to adopt a less advantageous course. To cover merely entails maintaining a position which will assure that any advantage accruing to the covered boat will also accrue to the covering boat. Partial-control techniques are frequently used when a single competitor threatens. Complete-control techniques cannot be maintained for long periods and therefore should be applied only at critical times, such as before reaching a lay line, before rounding a mark, or when approaching the finish line.

The only place where tactical control is regularly justified is near the finish line. There is never any justification for allowing a following competitor to pass nor for not attempting to control a competitor close ahead near the finish. A point lost can never be regained. The last leg must be managed initially for strategic advantage, but upon return from the chosen side of the course, a major concern must be to recognize the boats which will be in contention. Is there one close ahead that can be caught? Are there others close astern that could move ahead? If no boat is close ahead, the decision is simple: a controlling position with respect to the boat next astern must be acquired, to assure that she is beaten. If several boats are close astern and one or more are close ahead, it is better to concentrate on doing the strategically correct thing than to acquire a controlling position relative to one of the threatening boats. This is where recognition of the downwind end of the line (if finishing to windward) is so important. The first consideration must always be to sail the shortest course to the finish, with or without tactical control. If one boat is close ahead and another close astern, a chance to catch the one should not be taken at the risk of losing the other. The strategically correct position must be obtained first—the advantageous side of the shift on the course, the lay line to the downwind end—and control over the boat ahead attempted from that position.

Tactical control must be restrained. Preoccupation with neighboring boats is usually associated with a neglect of strategic considerations—considerations of far greater significance. The helmsman who, in second place, preoccupies himself with beating Boat Three may end up being passed by Boats Four and Five. Early in a series, except at the finish, specific competitors are best ignored. When an opportunity to consolidate appears, it should be taken. A chance to tack across the fleet, obtain a lee-bow position on the lay line, acquire an inside overlap at the jibe mark, is a chance to achieve a permanent gain in placement, and must be utilized. But such a move is made with a purpose—to provide subsequent advantage, such as clear air, a favorable course, an opportunity to separate from the fleet. It is not, and should not be, directed at beating a specific boat until late in a series, when scoring relationships begin to matter.

An equally important reason for restraining attempts at tactical control is philosophical. Most competitors assume that the early part of each race should be an opportunity to demonstrate skill in starting technique, strategic evaluation, and the attainment of boat speed —to sort out the competent from the less competent. Only late in the race, when boats are essentially paired and grouped on the basis of these skills, should one-on-one tactics be applied. This attitude is commendable, since in its absence skilled competitors could be deliberately obstructed by less skilled opponents early in the race and the series outcome would depend less upon individual ability and more upon the happenstance of which boats met on the course. The attitude also results in a desirable "live and let live" effect: "If I don't tack on your lee bow as we struggle up this first weather leg, you will be less likely to tack on mine the next time we meet." There is nothing in the rule book that requires such behavior, but sailboat racing would seriously deteriorate in its absence.

On the other hand, if tactical or strategic advantage requires a certain action, it should not be deferred because of the proximity of an innocent bystander. It makes no sense for one boat to diminish her own advantage in order to avoid injury to another (and the by-stander expects no such sacrifice). On the weather leg if a sudden header demands a tack, it should be made—regardless of the boat to leeward that is now tacking and will end up dead astern. To sail away from the next shift for several boat lengths in order to provide clear air for a competitor is not "sporting"; it is foolish (and perhaps condescending). Each competitor should expect only that his rivals behave in their own best interests and not single him out for injury for some extraneous reason. The saying "Nice guys finish last" is not appropriate to sailboat racing, but "Show me a good loser and I'll show you a loser" is.

If control is sought on the windward leg, a tack will be required. Care must be taken to accomplish this tack in such a manner that control is indeed achieved; a mismanaged tack can easily transfer control to the opponent. If control is not sought, the possibility that the opposing boat will seek it must be considered, and when she does, her tack must be parried appropriately. If the helmsman is unable to see the approaching boat, the crew must alert him to her presence and to her expected position at the moment of meeting. If she is on starboard, an avoiding maneuver may be required. If she is on port, she may tack to a lee-bow position even though this may be inconsistent with her own best interests. The likelihood of such a move will depend upon the disposition of her helmsman and the de-sirability of changing tacks. It is useful, therefore, for the crew to indicate which boat is approaching and to remind the helmsman of the probable advantages that tacking would give the opponent. If there is a strong reason for a boat to be on a particular tack, an op-ponent is likely to join her. Each meeting situation requires an appraisal of the reasons for continuing or not continuing the present tack—for the boat and for her opponent. As each opponent ap-proaches, compass calls must come through loud and clear and the strategy of the leg must be quickly reviewed.

Early in the race and early in each windward leg (but not just after the start), each boat is presumably on the tack that her helmsman considers preferable. If you have a good reason (and you should) for being on a particular tack, you should attempt to continue it and to avoid being forced by the opponent to tack. If you are on starboard and will cross ahead, do so. If you are on starboard and will cross astern, wave the opposing boat across. Slow up if necessary; do not give her any reason for tacking on your lee bow. If you are on starboard and will meet the opponent, be prepared for her to tack to your lee bow. If you are slightly ahead, you should plan to drive over her with slightly cracked sheets and eased sheet leads. If she is slightly ahead, you may wish to luff as she tacks, to obtain a position to windward of her backwind. If, as must be expected occasionally, she tacks to a controlling position, you must decide whether the advantages of continuing justify the loss that will result from being controlled. If they do not, a tack should be made immediately, before you are slowed. Such a tack should be continued no farther than necessary to obtain clear air.

If you are on port when you meet an opponent early in the leg, you must decide whether to risk crossing ahead or to bear away gradually with proper sail trim. An abrupt bearing away will result in a major loss in speed. When in doubt, bear away—properly. The crew member responsible for detecting starboard tackers should also be responsible for determining whether crossing can be safely accomplished. He is better able to make this determination than the helmsman, and if required to do so regularly, will soon become competent. It is *never* sensible to cross when in doubt. If caught in a close crossing, bear away abruptly, when your keel or centerboard has crossed the course of the opponent, so as to swing your stern out of her way. Never tack after your bow has crossed that course line. I have been amazed on a number of occasions by the effectiveness of bearing away. In a Soling race on Long Island Sound, Don Cohan crossed me so closely that I expected to hit him amidships. As he swung his stern away, my bow seemed to remain a constant six inches from his topsides until we were sailing parallel courses in opposite directions. I never altered my course and am pleased that he, and others, respect my helmsmanship sufficiently to dare such a maneuver. Unfortunately, not all sailors can be trusted to hold their courses precisely in this situation, and you may be disqualified as readily by an opponent who thought he had to bear away as by one who was forced to do so.

Later in the race, particularly when approaching the lay line or the finish line, control becomes important. When two boats meet, each regards the other as the one that must be defeated. On the first beat, resolution of the meeting determines position on the reach; on the last beat, it determines the score. Control at the end of the second beat is less significant, since usually a jibe can be used to obtain clear air at the start of a run.

After crossing well ahead, open cover may be utilized. When approaching the lay line, a tack is made abeam to weather (Figure 84), to enable the boat to stay between the opponent and the mark and to reduce the risk of overstanding. The leading boat then need not tack until her opponent is seen do so or until, close to the mark, she is certainly able to lay it. Covering from abeam to weather is also useful if a persistent shift to the opposite side of the course is possible (but unlikely). Tacking ahead and to windward should be done only near the finish or when dealing with a major contender late in a series. Since this maneuver will usually cause the opponent to tack, it should be used only for this purpose. Continued control will require a tacking duel. Also, a dead-to-windward position will result in a loss with any shift. Cover from ahead and to leeward should be used when a heading shift is expected (as it always is in oscillating winds). When on or paralleling the lay line, and whenever complete control is desired, the boat should make the covering tack dead ahead. A tack in this position has an almost maximally detrimental effect but is less likely to cause the opponent to tack. The tack should actually be made slightly to windward of dead ahead to allow for leeway at the completion of the tack and for the opponent's luff. Failure to take this precaution almost cost me a race in Bermuda when I tacked dead ahead beneath the starboard-tack lay line and allowed my opponent to luff into clear air to windward. I was almost prevented from tacking (to port) for the line.

If control is desired but tacking dead ahead is impossible, a lee-bow position must be sought. To be effective, the lee-bow position must be as close as possible to the course of the other boat. Since the tack should be made gradually to preserve speed, it should be initiated when the bow is a few feet to leeward of the course line of the opponent. (The exact distance desirable will depend upon the length and turning characteristics of the boat.) If the opponent luffs, as she should in smooth water, or attempts to drive over close aboard, the leeward boat should luff as soon as she completes her tack. If control is what matters, it should be obtained even if both boats luff to a halt. Unless success in acquiring the lee-bow position

WEATHER QUARTER

CLOSE ABEAM TO WINDWARD

LEEBOW

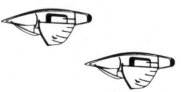

DEAD TO WINDWARD

FIGURE 84

can be expected, it should not be sought. Being driven over may cause the loss of more than one boat. Of course, if the opponent is on the lay line to the finish, the risk is justified.

The only opportunity for control remaining to the boat too far behind to acquire a lee-bow position is to cross astern and tack to a controlling position on the opponent's weather quarter. If acquired close aboard, this position may prevent the opponent from tacking, and if acquired short of the lay line, it may prevent the opponent from tacking until the weather boat tacks into the lead. A starboard-tack boat cannot bear away to cross astern (since this would constitute a balk—(rule 34) and is therefore unable readily to acquire a weather-quarter position. To be sure, she may pass astern without altering course, or may slow so as to do so. A port-tack boat is, of course, unrestricted; she may bear away from any position to pass astern. And as she bears away to pass astern, the crossing boat must hold her course. (The only alternative for the crossing boat is to tack to a lee-bow position before the opponent bears away, if they are within risk of collision.) When, near the finish, a starboard-tack boat that is not laying the line crosses a port-tack boat, she must presume that the port-tack boat will tack on her weather quarter (Figure 85). If the port-tack boat tacks immediately after she passes astern of the

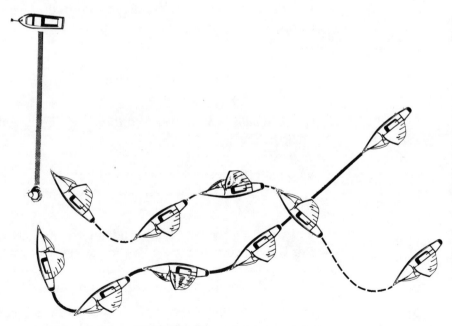

FIGURE 85

starboard tacker, she should be able to prevent the latter from tacking for at least a short period of time—and possibly until she has been forced beyond the lay line. If the starboard-tack boat tacks as the port-tack boat passes under her stern (and she cannot tack earlier), she will have to complete her tack before the port-tack boat initiates her tack. Of two boats tacking simultaneously, the one on the other's port side must keep clear (rule 41.4). Thus, the initially port-tack boat controls the situation from the time the starboard-tack boat elects to cross until, after both tack, the leeward of the two escapes ahead and tacks for the line. The starboard-tack boat is at significant risk of disqualification if she attempts to tack as the port-tack boat goes under her stern.

Be alert to situations involving meetings with other boats, and be prepared to respond in a way enabling you to continue your present tack or to take over control if you wish—instead of being *under* control.

I. CONTROL WHILE BEATING

A. *Complete Control:* The competitor is slowed or is forced to perform a course-lengthening maneuver. Utilized when approaching the lay line.

1. *Weather-Quarter or Close-Astern Position* (when the competitor is ahead)
ESCAPE:
a) Luff sharply
b) Bear away and tack to starboard
c) Jibe away

2. *Close Abeam-to-Windward Position* (when the competitor is behind)
ESCAPE:
a) Pinch to a lee-bow position and luff
b) Drop back and tack astern
c) Jibe away

B. *Partial Control:* By means of wind interference, the competitor is induced to assume a less advantageous course or is covered so as to prevent her subsequent acquisition of an advantageous course; the competitor is behind.

1. *Lee-Bow Position:* Forces the competitor to assume a disadvantageous tack or to slow. Utilized on the lay line or

early on a long tack. Provides partial control to the boat behind for a short period.

ESCAPE:

a) Tack away

b) Fall astern to a controlling "weather-quarter position"

2. *Dead-to-Windward Position:* Forces the competitor to assume a disadvantageous tack or to fall astern.

ESCAPE:

a) Tack away

b) Bear away

C. *Cover*

1. *Distant Abeam-to-Windward Position:* Covers the bulk of the fleet en masse without interference (which might induce tacking and fleet splitting).

ESCAPE: Optional

2. *Distant Ahead or Ahead-to-Leeward Position:* Covers the bulk of the fleet en masse without interference. Utilized to reach an area of strategic advantage first. Also utilized to enter oscillating shifts to maximum advantage.

ESCAPE: Optional

DANGER: Complete control by a boat moving up to "weather-quarter position"

II. CONTROL NEAR THE WEATHER MARK

1. *Weather-Quarter Position:* Forces the competitor beyond the lay line. Acquired by tacking inside.

2. *Close Abeam-to-Windward Position:* Forces the competitor beyond the lay line. Acquired by tacking inside.

3. *Lee-Bow Position on the Lay Line:* Holds competitors astern. Acquired by tacking beneath a crossing competitor. Provides an inside overlap while rounding.

4. *Starboard Tack:* Controls a port-tack competitor when rounding to port. Advantage limited when rounding to starboard by the loss of right-of-way while tacking. Always preferable when three or more boats meet.

5. *Tacking on the Competitor's Starboard Hand when Boats are Tacking Simultaneously:* Blocks the competitor's attempt to assume "close abeam-to-windward position."

III. CONTROL AT CROSSING

1. *Starboard Tack*, options:
   a) Cross ahead, tack to "Close abeam-to-windward position"
   b) Tack to "lee-bow position"
   c) Slow up to force the competitor to tack
   d) Cross astern, tack to "weather-quarter position"

2. *Port Tack*, options:
   a) Cross ahead, tack to "close abeam-to-windward position"
   b) Tack to "lee-bow position"
   c) Cross astern, tack to "weather-quarter position"

3. *Third Boat Present*, options:
   a) Induce the competitor to tack into the interference zone of the third boat or to permit escape by tacking from partial cover to avoid such interference
   b) Hail for room to tack to "weather-quarter position" to clear a third boat with right-of-way
   c) Demand room to pass astern of a third boat with right-of-way to acquire "close abeam-to-windward position"

53. The Finish Point

As a race-committee chairman, I am often closely exposed to the finishing practices of my competitors, and I am surprised at how few seem to attempt to finish at the nearest point on the finish line. In one race, after I had established the finish line and my crash boat had departed for other chores, the committee boat's anchor dragged. For the windward finish the committee-boat end of the line was clearly favored, but less than a third of the fleet finished at that end.

A windward finish line is like a starting line; regardless of the effort made by the committee, one end is almost always farther upwind than the other. And just as one point on the starting line, the end farther upwind, provides the shortest course to the windward mark, so one point on the finish line, the end farther downwind, provides the shortest course to the finish. At the start, many boats contend closely for the one best point; at the finish, usually only a few boats are in immediate contention—and apparently fewer still have helmsmen who recognize the advantage of seeking that downwind point.

In a windward finish, it is essential to decide as soon as possible which is the downwind end and to tack for that end. If the finish line is established before the start of the race, the downwind end can be detected in advance. However, if the wind shifts subsequently, the preferred end may change. When other competent sailors are finishing ahead (in other classes?), the preferred end becomes apparent early on the final leg. When the leg is a one-leg beat, the downwind end is obvious. Usually, however, the committee attempts to set a windward finish line across the wind, and it is then difficult to ascertain the downwind end until close aboard. It must always be assumed that the line is not squarely across the wind and that one end or the other is downwind. The general rule is that the tack most nearly perpendicular to the line (the tack that takes the boat to the line most directly) will take the boat to the downwind end of the line. The downwind end is the end which is to leeward on that tack. A boat approaching on the most perpendicular tack and overstanding the end of the line is overstanding the most downwind point on the line and has sailed a longer course than necessary.

When, as is usual, the downwind end of a windward finish line cannot be ascertained in advance, the boat should be tacked when the first lay line to an end mark is reached (Figure 86). To cross the lay line to either end may result in overstanding. But during an approach to one end on its lay line, the downwind end can be determined from reasonably close aboard *without overstanding.* The determination must be made when, on the lay line to one end of the line, the boat approaches the lay line to the other. If at that moment the other end looks closer, more downwind (that is, if the other tack appears more perpendicular to the finish line), the boat should be tacked. If the end being approached looks closer, more downwind, the tack should be continued. To continue beyond the lay line to the downwind end is to overstand and to give away valuable distance to a more observant (or luckier!) competitor. Ideally, the finish-line approach should be to the lay line to the starboard end on port tack. If the port end is subsequently recognized to be the downwind end, the tack toward it will be starboard, providing safe passage in the congestion. The final tack should be timed to hit the end of the line "on the nose": boats tacking on the lee bow will be unable to lay the mark; boats passing astern and tacking will be behind and overstanding.

The reason for this concern about identifying the downwind end is, of course, that unless care is taken, a boat or boats close ahead or astern may be granted an advantage and be lost when they could

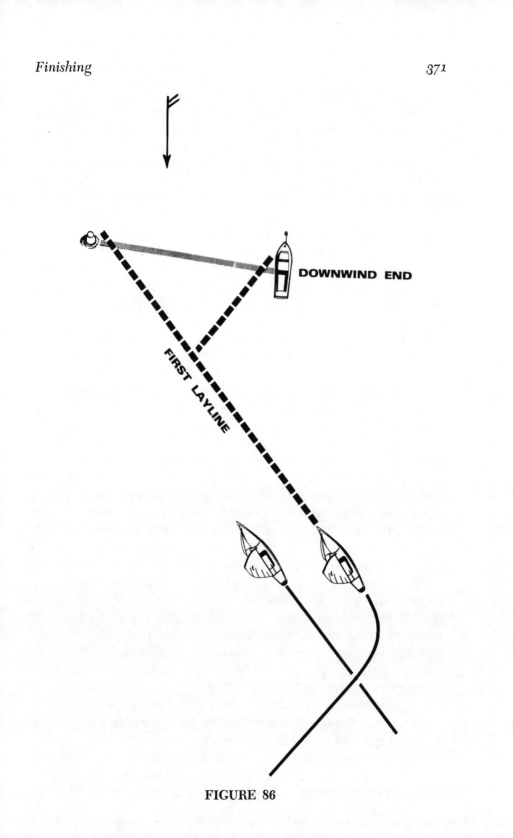

FIGURE 86

have been beaten. The skipper of a boat ahead will be able to determine the downwind end sooner than his competitor and unless he is inexperienced will take the appropriate tack to the finish. However, he may overstand the most downwind end before recognizing it and/or may be forced to continue the wrong tack. In this instance the downwind end may be selected by determining which tack is most likely to result in success in overtaking a boat ahead. If it is obvious that continuing astern, to windward or to leeward, will mean finishing astern, the other tack should be tried as soon as its lay line is reached. If many boats are close, however, the relationship to a particular boat must be ignored and instead every effort must be exercised to determine the downwind end. One or more of the nearby boats may fail to recognize it or may overstand it. If you are on the lay line to one end (as you should be) and all other nearby boats are on the same tack above the lay line, the tack should be continued unless the opposite end is clearly downwind. If the end being approached is, in fact, the downwind end, a major gain on the other boats, which are overstanding, will result. If it is not the downwind end, tacking and passing astern to reach the other end is not likely to be fruitful. The competition, closer to the line, can more readily recognize the downwind end and as readily tack to cover.

Inasmuch as the ideal approach to the finish line is on the lay line to one end, a close opponent should be blocked from acquiring this position. This means that control must be maintained from to windward. When crossing ahead near the finish but below the lay line, a control tack should be made dead to windward. When crossing close astern, a control tack should be made on the opponent's weather quarter. The lee-bow position must be avoided until on the layline—and even then this position will be hazardous if subsequently the other lay line is recognized to be the favored one. If trapped in a lee-bow position, the only resort is a luff, made strongly and sharply enough to force the opponent about (rule 38). The only control that matters is the control that prevents the opponent from tacking to the downwind end of the line.

No advantage over another boat is sufficient to warrant its continuance once the downwind end can be laid. I have frequently seen a boat, approaching the finish line on starboard, sail past the lay line to the downwind end in an attempt to catch her competitor port-starboard (Figure 87). If the starboard tacker crosses, the port tacker will bear off astern of her, and will certainly not be forced to

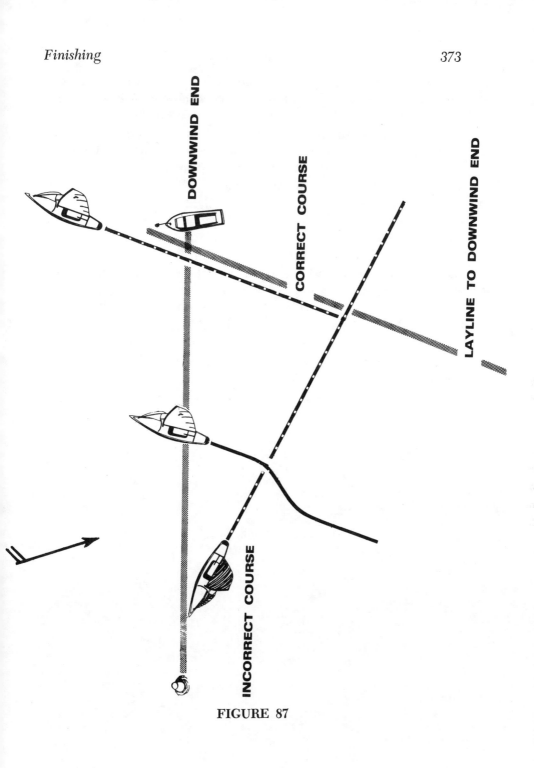

DOWNWIND END

CORRECT COURSE

LAYLINE TO DOWNWIND END

INCORRECT COURSE

FIGURE 87

tack. If the starboard tacker tacks on the lee bow of the port tacker, she may still reach the line first—but how much sooner she would have done so if she had tacked when she crossed the lay line! The ideal approach to the finish is on the port-tack lay line to the starboard end of the line not only because a tack, if required, will be to starboard but because port tack will provide no temptation to do anything except seek the downwind end!

Many series are won (or lost) by slight margins at the finish line. A point lost can never be regained. A member of the crew must be assigned the specific responsibility of determining the downwind end of the finish line. If possible, the initial approach should be on (or below) the lay line to the apparently downwind end. Repeated practice in the observation of boats finishing ahead, of flags, of waves, and of the lay of the committee boat will give the observer skill in determining the downwind end before the lay line to the opposite end is reached. That moment is decisive; either the boat must be tacked to one end, or the tack must be continued to the other.

Yacht Racing Rules
of the
International Yacht Racing Union,
1973–1976
Definitions

When a term defined is used in its defined sense it is printed in **bold** *type.*
All definitions and italicized notes rank as rules.

Racing—A yacht is **racing** from her preparatory signal until she has either **finished** and cleared the finishing line and finishing **marks** or retired, or until the race has been **cancelled, postponed** or **abandoned,** except that in match or team races, the sailing instructions may prescribe that a yacht is **racing** from any specified time before the preparatory signal.

Starting—A yacht **starts** when, after fulfilling her penalty obligations, if any, under rule 51.1(*c*), Sailing the Course, and after her starting signal, any part of her hull, crew or equipment first crosses the starting line in the direction of the course to the first **mark.**

Finishing—A yacht **finishes** when any part of her hull, or of her crew or equipment in normal position, crosses the finishing line from the direction of the course from the last **mark,** after fulfilling her penalty obligations, if any, under rule 52.2, Touching a Mark.

Luffing—Altering course towards the wind until head to wind.

Tacking—A yacht is **tacking** from the moment she is beyond head to wind until she has **borne away,** if beating to windward, to a **close-hauled** course; if not beating to windward, to the course on which her mainsail has filled.

Bearing Away—Altering course away from the wind until a yacht begins to **jibe.**

Jibing—A yacht begins to **jibe** at the moment when, with the wind aft, the foot of her mainsail crosses her centre line and completes the **jibe** when the mainsail has filled on the other **tack.**

On a Tack—A yacht is **on a tack** except when she is **tacking** or **jibing.** A yacht is on the **tack** (**starboard** or **port**) corresponding to her **windward** side.

Close-hauled—A yacht is **close-hauled** when sailing by the wind as close as she can lie with advantage in working to windward.

Clear Astern and **Clear Ahead; Overlap**—A yacht is **clear astern** of another when her hull and equipment in normal position are abaft an imaginary line projected abeam from the aftermost point of the other's hull and equipment in normal position. The other yacht is **clear ahead.** The yachts **overlap** if neither is **clear astern;** or if, although one is **clear astern, clear ahead** and **overlap** apply to yachts on opposite **tacks** only when they are subject to rule 42, Rounding or Passing Marks and Obstructions.

Leeward and **Windward**—The **leeward** side of a yacht is that on which she is, or, if **luffing** head to wind, was, carrying her mainsail. The opposite side is the **windward** side.

When neither of two yachts on the same **tack** is **clear astern,** the one on the **leeward** side of the other is the **leeward yacht.** The other is the **windward yacht.**

Proper course—A **proper course** is any course which a yacht might sail after the starting signal, in the absence of the other yacht or yachts affected, to **finish** as quickly as possible. The course sailed before **luffing** or **bearing away** is presumably, but not necessarily, that yacht's **proper course.** There is no **proper course** before the starting signal.

Mark—A **mark** is any object specified in the sailing instructions which a yacht must round or pass on a required side.

Every ordinary part of a **mark** ranks as part of it, including a flag, flagpole, boom or hoisted boat, but excluding ground tackle and any object either accidentally or temporarily attached to the **mark.**

Obstruction—An **obstruction** is any object, including craft under way, large enough to require a yacht, if not less than one overall length away from it, to make a substantial alteration of course to pass on one side or the other, or any object which can be passed on one side only, including a buoy when the yacht in question cannot safely pass between it and the shoal or object which it marks.

Cancellation—A **cancelled** race is one which the race committee decides will not be sailed thereafter.

Postponement—A **postponed** race is one which is not started at its scheduled time and which can be sailed at any time the race committee may decide.

Abandonment—An **abandoned** race is one which the race committee declares void at any time after the starting signal, and which can be resailed at its discretion.

Yacht Racing Rules
of the
International Yacht Racing Union,
1973–1976
Part IV

SAILING RULES WHEN YACHTS MEET

Helmsman's Rights and Obligations Concerning Right of Way

The rules of Part IV apply only between yachts which either are intending to race or are racing in the same or different races, and, except when rule 3.2(b)(ii) applies, replace the International Regulations for Preventing Collisions at Sea or Government Right-of-Way Rules applicable to the area concerned, from the time a yacht intending to race begins to sail about in the vicinity of the starting line until she has either finished or retired and has left the vicinity of the course.

SECTION A—RULES WHICH ALWAYS APPLY

31—Disqualification

1. A yacht may be disqualified or otherwise penalized for infringing a rule of Part IV only when the infringement occurs while she is **racing**, whether or not a collision results.

2. A yacht may be disqualified before or after she is **racing** for seriously hindering a yacht which is **racing**, or for infringing the sailing instructions.

32—Avoiding Collisions

A right-of-way yacht which fails to make a reasonable attempt to avoid a collision resulting in serious damage may be disqualified as well as the other yacht.

33—Retiring from Race

A yacht which realizes she has infringed a racing rule or a sailing instruction is under an obligation to retire promptly; but, when she persists in **racing**, other yachts shall continue to accord her such rights as she may have under the rules of Part IV.

34—Right-of-Way Yacht Altering Course

When one yacht is required to keep clear of another, the right-of-way yacht shall not so alter course as to prevent the other yacht from keeping clear; so as to increase any alteration of course required of the other yacht in order to keep clear; or so as to obstruct her while she is keeping clear, except:

(*a*) to the extent permitted by rule 38.1, Right-of-Way Yacht Luffing after Starting, and

(*b*) when assuming a **proper course** to **start,** unless subject to the second part of rule 44.1(*b*), Yachts Returning to Start.

35—Hailing

1.   Except when **luffing** under rule 38.1, Luffing after Starting, a right-of-way yacht which does not hail before or when making an alteration of course which may not be foreseen by the other yacht may be disqualified as well as the yacht required to keep clear when a collision resulting in serious damage occurs.

2.   A yacht which hails when claiming the establishment or termination of an **overlap** or insufficiency of room at a **mark** or **obstruction** thereby helps to support her claim for the purposes of rule 42, Rounding or Passing Marks and Obstructions.

SECTION B—OPPOSITE TACK RULE

36—Fundamental Rule

A **port-tack** yacht shall keep clear of a **starboard-tack** yacht.

SECTION C—SAME TACK RULES

37—Fundamental Rules

1.   A **windward yacht** shall keep clear of a **leeward yacht.**

2.   A yacht **clear astern** shall keep clear of a yacht **clear ahead.**

3.   A yacht which establishes an **overlap** to **leeward** from **clear astern** shall allow the **windward yacht** ample room and opportunity to keep clear, and during the existence of that **overlap** the **leeward yacht** shall not sail above her **proper course.**

38—Right-of-Way Yacht Luffing after Starting

1.   **Luffing Rights and Limitations.** After she has **started** and cleared the starting line, a yacht **clear ahead** or a **leeward yacht** may **luff** as she pleases, except that:—

A **leeward yacht** shall not sail above her **proper course** while an **over-lap** exists if, at any time during its existence, the helmsman of the **windward yacht** (when sighting abeam from his normal **station** and sailing no higher than the **leeward yacht**) has been abreast or forward of the mainmast of the **leeward yacht.**

2.   **Overlap Limitations.** For the purpose of this rule: An **overlap** does not exist unless the yachts are clearly within two overall lengths of the

longer yacht; and an **overlap** which exists between two yachts when the leading yacht **starts,** or when one or both of them completes a **tack** or **jibe,** shall be regarded as a new **overlap** beginning at that time.

3. **Hailing to Stop or Prevent a Luff.** When there is doubt, the **leeward yacht** may assume that she has the right to **luff** unless the helmsman of the **windward yacht** has hailed "Mast Abeam", or words to that effect. The **leeward yacht** shall be governed by such hail, and, if she deems it improper, her only remedy is to protest.

4. **Curtailing a Luff.** The **windward yacht** shall not cause a **luff** to be curtailed because of her proximity to the **leeward yacht** unless an **obstruction,** a third yacht or other object restricts her ability to respond.

5. **Luffing Two or More Yachts.** A yacht shall not **luff** unless she has the right to **luff** all yachts which would be affected by her **luff,** in which case they shall all respond even if an intervening yacht or yachts would not otherwise have the right to **luff.**

39—Sailing Below a Proper Course

A yacht which is on a free leg of the course shall not sail below her **proper course** when she is clearly within three of her overall lengths of either a **leeward yacht** or a yacht **clear astern** which is steering a course to pass to leeward.

40—Right-of-Way Yacht Luffing before Starting

Before a yacht has **started** and cleared the starting line, any **luff** on her part which causes another yacht to have to alter course to avoid a collision shall be carried out slowly and in such a way so as to give the **windward yacht** room and opportunity to keep clear, but the **leeward yacht** shall not so **luff** above a **close-hauled** course, unless the helmsman of the **windward yacht** (sighting abeam from his normal station) is abaft the mainmast of the **leeward yacht**. Rules 38.3, Hailing to Stop or Prevent a Luff; 38.4, Curtailing a Luff; and 38.5, Luffing Two or more Yachts, also apply.

SECTION D—CHANGING TACK RULES

41—Tacking or Jibing

1. A yacht which is either **tacking** or **jibing** shall keep clear of a yacht **on a tack.**

2. A yacht shall neither **tack** nor **jibe** into a position which will give her right of way unless she does so far enough from a yacht **on a tack** to enable this yacht to keep clear without having to begin to alter her course until after the tack or **jibe** has been completed.

3. A yacht which **tacks** or **jibes** has the onus of satisfying the Race Committee that she completed her **tack** or **jibe** in accordance with rule 41.2.

4. When two yachts are both **tacking** or both **jibing** at the same time, the one on the other's **port** side shall keep clear.

SECTION E—RULES OF EXCEPTION AND SPECIAL APPLICATION

When a rule of this section applies, to the extent to which it explicitly provides rights and obligations, it over-rides any conflicting rule of Part IV which precedes it except the rules of Section A—Rules Which Always Apply.

42—Rounding or Passing Marks and Obstructions

1. **Fundamental Rules Regarding Room.** When yachts either on the same **tack** or, after **starting** and clearing the starting line, on opposite **tacks,** are about to round or pass a **mark** on the same required side, with the exception of a starting **mark** surrounded by navigable water, or an **obstruction** on the same side:—

(*a*) When **Overlapped:**

(i) An outside yacht shall give each yacht **overlapping** her on the inside, room to round or pass the **mark** or **obstruction,** except as provided in rules 42.1(*a*)(iii), and (iv) and 42.3. Room includes room for an **overlapping** yacht to **tack** or **jibe** when either is an integral part of the rounding or passing maneuver.

(ii) When an inside yacht of two or more **overlapped** yachts either on opposite **tacks,** or on the same **tack** without **luffing** rights, will have to **jibe** in order most directly to assume a **proper course** to the next **mark,** she shall **jibe** at the first reasonable opportunity.

(iii) When two yachts on opposite **tacks** are on a **beat** or when one of them will have to **tack** either to round the **mark** or to avoid the **obstruction,** as between each other rule 42.1(*a*)(i), shall not apply and they are subject to rules 36, Opposite Tack Fundamental Rule, and 41, Tacking or Jibing.

(iv) An outside **leeward yacht** with luffing rights may take an inside yacht to windward of a **mark** provided that she hails to that effect and begins to **luff** before she is within two of her overall lengths of the **mark** and provided that she also passes to windward of it.

(*b*) When **Clear Astern** and **Clear Ahead:**

(i) A yacht **clear astern** shall keep clear in anticipation of and during the rounding or passing manoeuvre when the yacht **clear ahead** remains on the same **tack** or **jibes.**

(ii) A yacht **clear ahead** which **tacks** to round a **mark** is subject to rule 41, Tacking or Jibing, but a yacht **clear astern** shall not **luff** above **close-hauled** so as to prevent the yacht **clear ahead** from **tacking.**

2. **Restrictions on Establishing and Maintaining an Overlap**

(*a*) A yacht **clear astern** shall not establish an inside **overlap** and be

entitled to room under rule 42.1(*a*)(i) when the yacht **clear ahead:—**
(i) is within two of her overall lengths of the **mark** or **obstruction.**
except as provided in rules 42.2(*b*) and 42.2(*c*), or (ii) is unable
to give the required room.
(*b*) The two-lengths determinative above shall not apply to yachts, of
which one has completed a **tack** within two overall lengths of a
mark or an **obstruction.**
(*c*) A yacht **clear astern** may establish an **overlap** between the yacht
clear ahead and a continuing **obstruction** such as a shoal or the
shore, only when there is room for her to do so in safety.
(*d*)(i) A yacht **clear ahead** shall be under no obligation to give room
to a yacht **clear astern** before an **overlap** is established.
(ii) A yacht which claims an inside **overlap** has the onus of satisfying the Race Committee that the **overlap** was established in proper
time.
(*e*)(i) When an outside yacht is **overlapped** at the time she comes
within two or her overall lengths of a **mark**, or an **obstruction,** she
shall continue to be bound by rule 42.1(*a*)(i) to give room as required even though the **overlap** may thereafter be broken.
(ii) An outside yacht which claims to have broken an **overlap** has
the onus of satisfying the Race Committee that she became **clear
ahead** when she was more than two of her overall lengths from the
mark or an **obstruction.**
3. **At a Starting Mark Surrounded by Navigable Water**
When approaching the starting line to **start,** a **leeward yacht** shall be
under no obligation to give any **windward yacht** room to pass to leeward
of a starting **mark** surrounded by navigable water; but, after the starting
signal, a **leeward yacht** shall not deprive a **windward yacht** of room at
such a **mark** by sailing either above the course to the first **mark** or above
close-hauled.

43—Close-Hauled, Hailing for Room to Tack at Obstructions
1. **Hailing.** When two **close-hauled** yachts are on the same **tack** and
safe pilotage requires the yacht **clear ahead** or the **leeward yacht** to
make a substantial alteration of course to clear an **obstruction,** and if she
intends to **tack,** but cannot **tack** without colliding with the other yacht,
she shall hail the other yacht for room to **tack** and clear the other yacht,
but she shall not hail and **tack** simultaneously.
2. **Responding.** The hailed yacht at the earliest possible moment after
the hail shall either:—
(*a*) **tack,** in which case, the hailing yacht shall begin to **tack** either:—
(i) before the hailed yacht has completed her **tack,**
(ii) if she cannot then **tack** without colliding with the hailed yacht,
immediately she is able to **tack** and clear her, or
(*b*) reply "You **tack,**" or words to that effect, if in her opinion she can

keep clear without **tacking** or after postponing her **tack.** In this case:—
(i) the hailing yacht shall immediately **tack** and
(ii) the hailed yacht shall keep clear.
(iii) The onus shall lie on the hailed yacht which replied "You **tack**" to satisfy the Race Committee that she kept clear.
3. **Limitation on Right to Room when the Obstruction is a Mark.**
   (*a*) When the hailed yacht can fetch an **obstruction** which is also a **mark,** the hailing yacht shall not be entitled to room to **tack** and clear the other yacht and the hailed yacht shall immediately so inform the hailing yacht.
   (*b*) If, thereafter, the hailing yacht again hails for room to **tack** and clear the other yacht she shall, after receiving it, retire immediately.
   (*c*) If, after having refused to respond to a **hail** under rule 43.3(*a*), the hailed yacht fails to fetch, she shall retire immediately.

44—Yachts Returning to Start

1.(*a*) A premature starter when returning to **start,** or a yacht working into position from the course side of the starting line or its extensions, when the starting signal is made, shall keep clear of all yachts which are **starting,** or have **started,** correctly, until she is wholly on the pre-start side of the starting line or its extensions.
   (*b*) Thereafter, she shall be accorded the rights under the rules of Part IV of a yacht which is **starting** correctly; but if she thereby acquires right of way over another yacht which is **starting** correctly, she shall allow that yacht ample room and opportunity to keep clear.
2. A premature starter while continuing to sail the course and until it is obvious that she is returning to **start,** shall be accorded the rights under the rules of Part IV of a yacht which has **started.**

45—Yachts Re-rounding after Touching a Mark

1. A yacht which has touched a **mark** and is about to exonerate herself in accordance with rule 52.2, Touching a Mark, shall keep clear of all other yachts which are about to round or pass it or have rounded or passed it correctly, until she has rounded it completely and has cleared it and is on a **proper course** to the next **mark.**
2. A yacht which has touched a **mark,** while continuing to sail the course and until it is obvious that she is returning to round it completely in accordance with rule 52.2, Touching a Mark, shall be accorded rights under the rules of Part IV.

SECTION F—WHEN NOT UNDER WAY

46—Anchored, Aground or Capsized

1. A yacht under way shall keep clear of another yacht **racing** which is anchored, aground or capsized. Of two anchored yachts the one which anchored later shall keep clear, except that a yacht which is dragging shall keep clear of one which is not.

2. A yacht anchored or aground shall indicate the fact to any yacht which may be in danger of fouling her. Unless the size of the yachts or the weather conditions make some other signal necessary a hail is sufficient indication.

3. A yacht shall not be penalized for fouling a yacht in distress which she is attempting to assist or a yacht which goes aground or capsizes immediately ahead of her.

(Numbers 47 and 48 are spare numbers.)

Glossary

Abeam—At approximately right angles to the fore-and-aft line of a boat.

Abeam-to-Windward Position—The position of a boat parallel to, and to windward of, another boat when a line joining them amid ships would be at approximately right angles to the center lines of both boats.

Advantageous Current—Current flowing in the direction being sailed.

Advantageous Side—That side of the rhumb line which provides a faster course to the mark.

Advantageous Tack (or Jibe)—That tack (or jibe) which provides a shorter or faster course to the mark.

Adverse Current—Current flowing in the direction opposite to that being sailed.

Aerodynamic Force—The total force produced by the sails through deviation of the air flow.

Aggressiveness—Personality trait of a skipper who is bold and enterprising and enjoys the demonstration of his superiority.

Ahead-to-Leeward Position—The position of a boat parallel to, to leeward of, and ahead of another boat.

Angle of Incidence—The angle of a horizontal chord of a sail to the air flow (or of an underwater fin to the water flow).

Anticyclone—See *High (1)*.

Apparent Wind—The wind that impinges upon the sails, a combination of the true wind, the current wind, and the boat wind.

Approach Tack—The tack that is headed toward and will terminate at the starting line, the mark, the lay line, or the like.

Attached Flow—That portion of the air flow which bends to follow the contour of the leeward surface of a sail.

Back—A counterclockwise shift in wind direction.

Backwind—The turbulent air flow in the wake of the sails.

Balance—A stable state, resulting from the production of aerodynamic and hydrodynamic forces of equal strength and opposite alignment, which permits a boat to sail a straight course at the optimal rudder angle.

Barging—Approaching the starting line, in order to start, from a position to windward of the lay line to the end of the line.

Base Leg—The course taken by a boat prior to, and in preparation for, the assumption of the approach to the starting line.

Bear Away, to—To turn a boat away from the wind.

Beat—The course to the windward mark at a close-hauled sailing angle.

Beneath—To leeward of.

Blanket—The reduction and disturbance in the air flow to leeward of the sails.

Boat Speed—The ability of a boat to sail rapidly.

Boat Wind—The wind created by the forward movement of a boat.

Breakthrough, inversion—The dissipation of an inversion due to heating from below associated with a change in the velocity and direction of the surface wind.

Broach—An abrupt yaw associated with marked heeling consequent to a sudden disequilibrium between aerodynamic and hydrodynamic forces.

Clear Air—Air flow undisturbed by the presence of other boats.

Close-hauled Course—Course sailed by a boat attempting to make maximum progress to windward.

Completed Persistent Shift—Persistent shift that has ceased to progress prior to the commencement of a leg.

Confidence—Personality trait of a skipper who feels assured of winning.

Contender—A boat whose position or score gives her a reasonable chance of winning.

Cover, to—To maintain a position of advantage with respect to a competitor.

Cross-Current Tack—The tack more perpendicular to the current.

Current Stick—A stick weighted at one end so that it floats vertically, used to determine the direction and strength of flow.

Current Wind—The wind created by the current-induced movement of the boat.

Cyclone—See *Low* (*1*).

Data Collection—The acquisition prior to a race of pertinent information (wind direction, current strength, and the like).

Dead Ahead—The position of a boat directly ahead of another and on the same course.

Dead Downwind—directly to leeward.

Dead to Windward—Directly to windward.

Depression—See *Low* (*1*).

Determination—State of mind of a skipper who is resolute in his intention to win.

Dirty, or Disturbed, Air—The deviated, eddying air flow astern and to leeward of a competitor.

Disadvantageous Tack (or Jibe)—That tack (or jibe) which provides a longer or slower course to the mark.

Diurnal Variation—The variations in surface air flow resulting from the daily changes in surface temperature.

Down—See *Low* (*2*).

Down-current—In the direction toward which the current is flowing.

Downwind—To leeward; in the direction toward which the wind is flowing; opposite to the wind direction.

Downwind End—The end of the starting or finish line farther to leeward.

Draft—The depth (degree of concavity) of a horizontal cross section of a sail.

Drive—Personality trait of a skipper who persists vigorously and relentlessly in his efforts to win.

Favored End—The upwind end of the starting line.

Fluke—An unpredictable change in wind direction.

Flyer—Course opposite to that taken by the vast majority of the fleet.

Foot to—To sail rapidly by bearing away slightly below the close-hauled course.

Foredeck Man—The member of the crew responsible for jib and spinnaker trim.

Freedom to Tack—The ability of a boat to tack without interfering with a competitor.

Gust—A sudden, brief increase in wind velocity, usually the consequence of a downdraft from the upper air flow.

Headed Jibe—The jibe that is affected by a header, which may permit a boat to assume a direction more in line with the median wind while keeping the same sailing angle.

Headed Tack—The tack that is affected by a header, which forces a boat to point away from the median wind.

Header, or Heading Shift—A shift in wind direction toward the direction in which a boat is heading.

Heavy Air—An air flow with a velocity exceeding 20 knots.

High—(1) A weather system characterized by the presence of a dome of dense air flowing outward, clockwise, from its center; also "anticyclone."

(2) To windward or farther to windward; also "up."

High-Goal Setting—Personality trait of a skipper who intends to win major regattas.

Hole—A brief, localized reduction in wind velocity.

Hydrodynamic Force—The force, produced by the movement through the water of a hull and its fins, which opposes the aerodynamic force.

Inside—Between a competitor and the mark or the rhumb line.

Instability—A condition in which warm air beneath cold results in mixing, turbulence, and oscillating shifts.

Instructions—The rules, created by the race committee, which regulate the racing.

Interference—The consequence of the intervention of a competitor between a boat and the wind.

Inversion—A layering of warm air over cold air that separates one zone of air flow (or calm) above from another below.

Jibe Mark—The mark that terminates the first reach and requires a jibe to round.

Lay, to—To assume a course that permits passing the mark on the proper side.

Lay Line—The course that permits a close-hauled boat or a boat at an optimal sailing angle on the run to just clear the mark in the existing wind. The "new lay line" is the lay line after a wind shift.

Lee-Bow Effect—(1) The adverse effect of the backwind of a leeward boat upon the performance of a windward boat; a boat in the lee-bow position creates such an effect.

(2) The supposedly beneficial effect of current flowing from ahead and to leeward.

Leeward—On the side away from the wind.

Leeward End—See *Port End*.

Leeward Mark—The mark that terminates the second reach and/or the run and that initiates the second or third beat.

Leeway—The drift (or angle of drift) of a boat to leeward as it proceeds forward.

Lift, or Lifting shift—A shift in wind direction away from the direction in which a boat is heading.

Lifted Jibe—The jibe that is affected by a lift, which requires a boat, in order to retain the same sailing angle, to deviate away from the median downwind course.

Lifted Tack—The tack that is affected by a lift, which permits a boat to point closer to the median wind.

Light Air—An air flow with a velocity of less than 5 knots.

Low—(1) A weather system characterized by the presence of a low-density mass of air flowing inward, counterclockwise, toward its center; also "cyclone," "depression."

(2) To leeward or farther to leeward; also "down."

Lower Air Flow—The air flow at the surface; if from the same generating source, backed and slowed compared with the air flow above it.

Luff, to—To deviate toward the wind.

Luffing—(1) Altering course toward the wind.

(2) The technique by which a leeward boat forces a windward boat to windward.

Lull—A brief reduction in wind velocity, usually present at the base of an updraft.

Match-Race Tactics—Tactics designed to beat one boat without regard to the others.

Median Wind—The wind that flows at the median direction, midway between the extremes in the range of its oscillating shifts.

Mental Toughness—Personality trait of a skipper who is resistant to adversity and criticism.

Middle—A position near the rhumb line.

Middle Man—The member of a three-man crew responsible for navigation and support functions.

Moderate Air—An air flow with a velocity between 5 and 20 knots.

New Wind—A wind from a new source that appears during or following the presence of another wind.

Odsssic—An acronym (standing for *Oscillating, Dying, Sea breeze, Squall, Shoreline, Inversion, Current*), used as a reminder of the significant strategic factors.

One-Leg Beat—A windward leg the major portion of which is sailed on one tack.

On Port (or Starboard)—Sailing on the tack specified.

Optimal Sailing Angle (Running)—The sailing angle that permits the greatest progress downwind.

Oscillation, or Oscillating Shift—A wind shift that will be followed by a shift back to the original direction prior to the completion of the leg.

Outside—Beyond a competitor that is nearer the mark or the rhumb line.

Override, to—To pass rapidly to windward of another boat.

Overstanding—Adoption of an approach tack (or jibe) that clears the mark by a greater distance than necessary, consequent to sailing beyond the lay line.

Passive Sailing—The temporary acceptance of a position astern of another boat, designed to retain proximity while awaiting an opportunity to move ahead.

Persistent Shift—A shift in wind direction that is not followed by a return to the original direction prior to the completion of he leg.

Pinching—Heading closer to the wind despite an absolute loss in speed made good to windward.

Planing—The movement of a boat that has sufficient buoyant lift to rise upon her own bow wave and reduce her wave-making resistance.

Pointing—(1) Heading a boat at a specific angle to the apparent wind.
(2) Heading a close-hauled boat close to the apparent wind.

Port End—The end of the starting line that is to port (and to leeward of a starboard-tack boat) as the line is crossed; also "leeward end."

Port Tacker—A boat on port tack.

Port-Tack Lay Line—The line along which a port-tack boat can just lay the weather mark.

Progressive Persistent Shift—A persistent shift that continues to advance in the same direction after the commencement of the leg.

Race Plan—A scheme developed by the skipper before the start for the management of the race.

Reach—The course between the windward mark and the jibe mark, or between the jibe mark and the leeward mark, at a sailing angle lower than that of a beat and higher than that of a run.

Rhumb Line—The straight-line course between one mark and the next.

Right-of-Way—The right of one boat to continue her desired course in the presence of another.

Rounding Tack—The tack (following an approach tack) that takes a boat around the mark.

Run—The course between the windward mark and the leeward mark at a near dead-downwind sailing angle.

Sailing Angle—The angle between the heading of a boat and the wind; progressively larger in beating, reaching, and running.

Scoring System—The system by which the winner is selected in a series of races.

Sea Breeze—A small-scale air circulation caused by the heating of the land in the presence of cold water. The cold surface flow is on-shore from the water toward the land.

Separation—The eddying and deviation of the air aft of a segment of flow attached to a sail surface.

Sheeting Angle—The angle made by a chord of a sail with the center line of a boat; usually the angle of the boom to the center line.

Shift—A change in wind direction.

Speed—The rate at which a boat moves forward.

Stability—A condition characterized by warm air over a cold surface, associated with an absence of upper air flow, turbulence, or oscillating shifts at the surface.

Starboard End—The end of the starting line that is to starboard (and to windward of a starboard-tack boat) as the line is crossed; also "weather end," "windward end."

Starboard Tacker—A boat on starboard tack.

Starboard-Tack Lay Line—The line along which a starboard-tack boat can just lay the weather mark.

Starboard-Tack Parade—The series of boats in line approaching the weather mark on the starboard-tack lay line.

Starting Tack—The tack utilized to cross the starting line.

Strategic Advantage—A position or course that provides benefit by virtue of a difference in wind, current, or waves.

Strategy—The application of considerations of wind strength and direction, current strength and direction, and wave formation to the planning and management of a race.

Surfing—The utilization by a boat of the inclination and buoyant lift of a wave face, resulting in increased speed.

Tack Away—The tack that takes a boat away from her nearest competitors.

Tactical Advantage—A position or course that provides benefit in relation to nearby competitors.

Tactics—The application of considerations of the position of competitors to the management of a race.

Throw-out—The poorest position in a series of races, which a competitor may discard in determining his placement.

True Wind—The wind that would be present in the absence of a boat.

Twist—The variation with height in the angle of a chord of the sail to the apparent wind.

Up—See *High* (2).

Up-current—In the direction from which the current is flowing.

Up-current Tack—The tack more directly opposed to the direction of the current.

Upper Air Flow—The air flow above that at the surface; if from the same generating source, stronger than and veered to the air flow at the surface.

Upwind—To windward.

Upwind End—The end of the starting or finish line farther to windward.

Vector—A line employed to represent the effect of a force acting upon an object, which by its direction indicates the direction of the force and by its length indicates the strength of that force.

Veer—A clockwise shift in wind direction.

Vmg—Speed made good, determined to windward (or to leeward) by the combined effects of pointing, speed, and leeway.

Weather End—See *Starboard End.*

Weather-Quarter Position—The position of a boat parallel to, to windward of, and astern of, another boat.

Weather-System Wind—The wind that flows in response to the pressure gradient induced by large-scale pressure differences.

Wide—At a greater distance than usual from a mark or other object being passed.

Windward End—See *Starboard End.*

Windward—On the side toward the wind.

Windward (or Weather) Mark—The mark that terminates a windward leg.

Yaw, to—To turn, in the horizontal plane, about a vertical axis.

Index